All-Star Quilts of Valor

2nd Edition

37 Patriotic Patterns from Star Designers

QUILTS OF VALOR® FOUNDATION

CONTRIBUTING AUTHORS
Ann Parsons Holte
Tony L. Jacobson
Mary W. Kerr
Sue Reich

FOREWORD BY
Kimberly Einmo

Other Schiffer Books by the Author:

Quilts of Valor: A 50-State Salute, Quilts of Valor Foundation, contributing authors Ann Parsons Holte, Renelda Peldunas-Harter, Ann Rehbein, Sue Reich, foreword by Marianne Fons, ISBN 978-0-7643-5630-8

Other Schiffer Books on Related Subjects:

Quilts Presidential and Patriotic, Sue Reich, ISBN 978-0-7643-5041-2

Inspired by the Nation's Capital: A Fiber Art Souvenir of Washington, DC, Donna Marcinkowski DeSoto, foreword by John Kelly, ISBN 978-0-7643-6324-5

Flags across America, Dale Baskin and Karen S. Robbins, ISBN 978-0-7643-5489-2

Library of Congress Control Number: 2025939815

About the back cover image: Veterans of recent wars received Quilts of Valor at the State Capitol in Columbia, South Carolina, in April 2021.

Cover design by Lindsay Hess
Cover photography by Ashley Seitz
Interior design by Ashley Millhouse and Lori Malkin Ehrlich
Type set in Desire Basic / Tinos / News Gothic BT

ISBN: 978-0-7643-7135-6

Printed in India

Published by Schiffer Craft
An imprint of Schiffer Publishing, Ltd.
4880 Lower Valley Road
Atglen, PA 19310
Phone: (610) 593-1777; Fax: (610) 593-2002
Email: Info@schifferbooks.com
Web: www.schifferbooks.com

Dedicated to those who support our Quilts of Valor Foundation mission "to cover our veterans and service members with comforting and healing Quilts of Valor." Your hours of tireless service have not gone unnoticed.

CONTENTS

Foreword

The vision for this book was to invite leading quilt industry professionals to design a special Quilt of Valor complete with the pattern to inspire and encourage quilters to create patriotic quilts for the special service members in their own lives or to donate them to honor a worthy QOV recipient. I can think of no greater way to honor these modern-day heroes who have faithfully served our country than with the gift of a Quilt of Valor to show them their service was—and is—appreciated by a grateful nation and will be remembered in a tangible way. Isn't that what quilts do? They wrap a person in comfort and love. Each quilt is stitched together with the thoughts and prayers of the maker. A Quilt of Valor wraps each veteran in those prayers, thoughts, and appreciation for their dedication and service.

Being asked to write the foreword for a book would be a privilege for anyone. But being asked to write the foreword for this book is sincerely one of the highest honors I have ever received. I feel immensely privileged to participate in a small way in the collaboration of this book, both in writing the foreword and in contributing a Quilt of Valor design. But the spotlight must shine brightly on the talented group of individuals (three are Quilts of Valor Foundation past or present board members) who not only had the combined vision but put "boots on the ground" to make this book materialize:

Ann Parsons Holte was a coauthor of the first book published by QOV, *Quilts of Valor: A 50-State Salute,* and is a talented designer and pattern writer. Ann was part of the select team who traveled with the *50-State Salute* exhibit. She writes and lectures about quilts from Pennsylvania and generously donates her time and talents to many QOV projects, an organization and cause near and dear to her heart.

Tony L. Jacobson is a former board member and longtime supporter of QOV. A quilt designer, teacher, and shop manager, Tony also worked as the art director for *Fons & Porter Love of Quilting* magazine. Today, he continues to share his design talents by laying out the QOVF newsletter and designing QOVF-appropriate quilt patterns.

Mary W. Kerr is a talented, hardworking dynamo in the quilting industry with a huge heart for veterans. She served on the QOVF Board of Directors for six years. Her tireless efforts to recognize and help military personnel through a wide variety of projects and fundraising efforts are, quite simply, amazing. Mary lectures and exhibits widely, sharing her unique quilt collections and the books she has authored incorporating vintage and antique textiles of past generations.

Sue Reich, QOVF Board Emeritus, served on the QOVF Board of Directors for nine years and also has a long, outstanding history of dedicated service to men and women in uniform. A coauthor of *Quilts of Valor: A 50-State Salute,* she is also a supremely knowledgeable historian who has written numerous quilt books that focus on the relationship between textiles and our military (for example, *World War I Quilts, World War II Quilts*, and *Quilts Presidential and Patriotic*).

What QOVF volunteers understand and recognize is that a life of service in the armed forces is never easy. It takes determination and sometimes sheer grit to make it through long separations, extreme conditions, frequent household moves, and difficult decisions. But a life spent in military service can also be extremely rewarding. The strong sense of purpose, camaraderie, and close friendships formed during years spent in the military can—and frequently do—last a lifetime. And for those veterans returning from active duty with either (or both) physical or emotional scars, the gift of a QOV quilt shows them their sacrifice and hardships were not in vain.

I offer gratitude to the authors of this book for their vision and to QOVF volunteers who work tirelessly making quilts. There will be untold positive ripple effects on the veterans who will benefit in the years and decades to come.

Kimberly Einmo is proud to be the National Spokesperson for Janome-America. She is an international author, award-winning quilter, fabric designer, and quilt judge. A proud and active military wife, Kimberly and her husband of thirty-three years, Kent, moved their household twenty times in the past thirty-four years, including three tours overseas, and she is passionate about serving and supporting the QOVF community.

ABOVE, LEFT: Ginger Fondren, former QOVF Assistant Executive Director, awarded a Quilt of Valor to Pamela Douglas of New Hope, Alabama, on June 25, 2021, in Memphis, Tennessee, at the American Gold Star Mothers Convention. Pamela served our nation in the military and now volunteers for Working Dogs for Vets. *Photo by Patrick Hughes*

ABOVE, RIGHT: Michelle Nelson, USAF 2006–2007, former QOVF Board Member, awarded a QOV to Craig McKee, the National Honorary 300,000th veteran, on April 21, 2022, in Cincinnati, Ohio. McKee served in the US Air Force, earning the rank of Staff Sergeant, from 1992 to 2000. He became a combat journalist covering Kosovo, Albania, Poland, and missions across Europe and is an anchor and reporter at WCPO in Cincinnati.

ACKNOWLEDGMENTS

This book could not have come together without the generosity of our entire Army of Quilts of Valor volunteers and supporters. Thank you to the designers who chose to take time out of their busy schedules to support our mission with their creativity. These Stars donated their time, talents, and quilts in honoring our nation's veterans and service members.

Thank you to our QOV members who continue the mission to wrap every veteran in the love of a grateful nation. Quilts of Valor is a community of over 10,000 dedicated volunteers who have awarded more than 300,000 quilts and promote the Quilts of Valor Foundation.

Thank you to Patrick Hughes, Vietnam veteran and official photographer for American Gold Star Mothers, and Michelle Sexton of Mirroj Studio, Columbia, South Carolina, for sharing their photographic images.

Thank you to our editors, Sandra Korinchak and Karla Rosenbusch, and the staff at Schiffer Publishing, Ltd., for their unending encouragement and guidance. God bless each and every one of you!

ABOVE, LEFT: Vietnam veteran Dale Holte, US Air Force, was awarded a QOV in Grand Rapids, Michigan, in August 2019 by Maggie Klenke and Suzanne DiCarlo.

ABOVE, RIGHT: Quilts of Valor's Kimberly Einmo and her husband, Kent, a veteran of the US Air Force, assisted in awarding a quilt to Daniel Burgess, retired Staff Sergeant, US Army, during a 2020 episode of *Military MakeOvers*.

Quilts of Valor Foundation– It All Began with a Dream

Quilts of Valor Foundation began in 2003 with a dream. Delaware resident and founder Catherine Roberts' son Nat was deployed in Iraq. According to Catherine:

> The dream was as vivid as real life. I saw a young man sitting on the side of his bed in the middle of the night, hunched over. The permeating feeling was one of utter despair. I could see his war demons clustered around, dragging him down into an emotional gutter. Then, as if viewing a movie, I saw him in the next scene wrapped in a quilt. His whole demeanor changed from one of despair to one of hope and wellbeing. The quilt had made this dramatic change. The message of my dream was Quilts = Healing.
>
> The model appeared simple: create a volunteer team who would donate their time and materials to make a quilt. One person would piece the top and the other would quilt it. I saw the name for this special quilt. It was a Quilt of Valor, a QOV.

Catherine Roberts, founder of Quilts of Valor, and Chaplain John Kallerson, US Army, at Walter Reed Army Medical Center in April 2014 for the 100,000th Veteran award of a Quilt of Valor.

What Quilts of Valor Are

From the beginning, Catherine Roberts had definite ideas about standards of excellence for Quilts of Valor:

> I knew a Quilt of Valor had to be a quality-made quilt, not a "charity" quilt. A Quilt of Valor had to be quilted, not tied, which meant hand or machine quilting. Quilts of Valor would be "awarded," not just passed out like magazines or videos. A Quilt of Valor would say unequivocally, "Thank you for your service, sacrifice, and valor in serving our nation in combat."

Those standards appear on the QOVF website and are included in the Policy and Procedure Manual for the QOVF membership.

TOP: World War II veteran Marine Hershel "Woody" Williams was awarded a Quilt of Valor at the American Gold Star Mothers Convention in Memphis, Tennessee, in June 2021 by QOVF members Ginger Fondren and Nancy Cann. Awarded a Medal of Honor in 1948 by President Truman, Woody Williams is the last remaining World War II Medal awardee.

ABOVE: World War II Medal of Honor Recipient Hershel "Woody" Wilson signed a QOV block at the American Gold Star Mothers Convention in Memphis, Tennessee, in June 2021.

How the Foundation Grew

The first QOV was awarded in November 2003 at Walter Reed Army Medical Center (WRAMC) to a young soldier from Minnesota who had lost his leg in Iraq. That first award was the springboard for the Quilts of Valor movement, which spread across the nation as the daughters of World War II and Korean War soldiers, the sisters and wives of Vietnam veterans, and the mothers of the War on Terror soldiers expressed their gratitude to our service members and veterans sewing Quilts of Valor. According to Catherine:

> The team consisted of a quilt-topper, a person who pieces the top from various fabrics, and a quilter who uses a "longarm" quilting machine to create beautiful machine quilting. Our longarmers immediately played a crucial role in making our quilt tops go from ho-hum to "wow." Our "points of contact" throughout the world identified recipients and often facilitated the actual awards ceremonies.

Our Mission Statement

The organization's original mission statement said its purpose was "to cover all those service members and veterans wounded physically or psychologically with comforting and healing Quilts of Valor." Catherine Roberts recalls:

> No one really liked the word "psychologically." Brilliantly, Chaplain Kallerson (Walter Reed Army Medical Center) suggested using the phrase "touched by war" as a replacement for the words "wounded physically or psychologically." This simple phrase was perfect. The group's mission statement was revised to read, "The mission of the Quilts of Valor Foundation is to cover all combat service members and veterans touched by war with comforting and healing Quilts of Valor." Later, the words "all" and "combat" were removed, further reflecting our understanding of the true meaning "touched by war."

The Light of Inclusion

In the early days of the organization, the primary focus was on awarding quilts to service members wounded in the Iraq (Operation Iraqi Freedom, or OIF) and Afghanistan (Operation Enduring Freedom, or OEF) conflicts. Catherine Roberts remembers:

> I affectionately referred to these young men as "babies" to distinguish them from veterans of other conflicts. Among us civilians, there were no complaints, as we were in the throes of an ongoing war. However, there were faint rumblings from those who worked at Veterans Administration Medical Centers (VAMCs). They politely pointed out it wasn't fair to award a QOV to one group of wounded and exclude others. The light of inclusiveness began to glimmer.
>
> At an awards ceremony at a VAMC in White River Junction, Vermont, in 2006, we saw wounded veterans from all conflicts being awarded quilts, not our policy at the time. My husband, Chris, "got it" right away, but it took several years for me to really understand. That happened in 2009 in Bellingham, Washington. A group of us had gotten together for a quilting retreat. One of our activities for the weekend was to award quilts at an event called "American Veterans Tribute and Traveling Wall Exhibit" in Bellingham. I could not find a group of OIF/OEF veterans for the QOVs we brought that day. A group of Vietnam veterans were there to perform a "Patriot Guard" ride past the Vietnam traveling memorial wall on their motorcycles. This event changed my whole outlook on who should receive a Quilt of Valor. As we were awarding quilts, the Vietnam vets said over and over again, "Ma'am, this is the first time in forty years anyone has ever thanked me for my service." All of us were thunderstruck. From then on, any warrior who had been touched by war, no matter when his or her service, could receive a Quilt of Valor. No questions asked.

Candy Martin, US Army veteran and Gold Star Mother, was awarded a Quilt of Valor at the Gold Star Mothers Convention on June 25, 2021, by QOVF members Nancy Cann and Sue Reich. Candy served as American Gold Star Mothers president in 2016. *Photograph by Patrick Hughes*

Shane Kimbrough (Col., US Army, Ret.), veteran of Operation Desert Storm, NASA Astronaut, Commander of NASA/Space X Crew Mission 2, and honorary 200,000th QOV awardee in November 2018 in Houston, Texas, is featured with the Honor Guard attending his award ceremony.

Civilian Awardees

The philosophy of inclusion widened when Catherine became aware of the work that goes on at Air Force Mortuary Affairs Operations (AFMAO), located at Dover Air Force Base, Delaware. She recalls:

> I read an essay by Marine Lt. Col. Michael Strobl called "Taking Chance Home." In the essay, Strobl recounts how he escorted the body of Marine Private Chance Phillips to his home in Wyoming for burial. Strobl took the reader through AFMAO, describing who the staff was and what they did to prepare the remains of the fallen for burial. I realized that workers at Dover, though they were stateside, were as touched by war as anyone downrange or "in theater."
>
> We established a relationship with the AFMAO and set a date for an awards ceremony. The day of the ceremony I received a call from the chaplain saying we had a big problem—some of the staff at Dover were civilians. As they all worked as a team, a family, awarding Quilts of Valor only to military service members would not work. The decision was made to award quilts to all working at the Port Mortuary, and this policy has continued ever since.

The Evolution of the Foundation's Name

In the beginning years, the name of the organization was Quilts for Soldiers. Catherine Roberts explains:

> Because my son was in the Army, I thought all military service members were "soldiers." I didn't understand that different branches have different names for their members. Fortunately, a Marine straightened me out, and Quilts for Soldiers became Quilts of Valor.

The Foundation's Early Days

Catherine Roberts reminisces:

> In the beginning, a few of us handled everything. After we became a national nonprofit in 2005, we created a volunteer board of directors to govern, determining policies and direction.
>
> Without the selflessness of the individuals who have volunteered over the years and who work tirelessly for the Foundation now, we would not be the viable group we are today. It's difficult for me to convey to those who may be reading this history the debt I owe these individuals. They have devoted their time, their hearts, and their financial resources to the Foundation to keep it afloat, growing, and thriving. I know that many times, many volunteers have felt it was a thankless job, but they have given their service, their sacrifice, and sometimes their valor in service to our mission.

The Quilts of Valor Foundation Today

The Foundation consists of mostly unpaid volunteers: a board of directors, state and area coordinators, group leaders, and its most essential 10,000-plus dedicated sewing members. A small, salaried executive staff keeps the organization focused and functioning, and in adherence to the mission statement, core values, and policies.

Over the years, standards of excellence have been established that outline size, fabric, and workmanship. A Quilt of Valor must be at least twin size, typically made of 100% cotton. QOVs can be made with any pattern and by individuals or groups. Often the same QOV is pieced, quilted, bound, and awarded by different individuals.

Awards ceremonies of Quilts of Valor may be made individually or in a group. Frequently, family members and friends are in attendance to witness their loved one being honored. After providing a synopsis of the Quilts of Valor mission and a brief history of the veterans' or service members' military background, the following citation is read:

> The Quilts of Valor Foundation wishes to recognize you for your service to our nation. We consider it a privilege to honor you though we may never know the extent of your sacrifice and service to protect and defend the United States of America. As an expression of gratitude from a grateful nation, we award you this Quilt of Valor.

The quilt is unfolded so the awardee can view it. Then the quilt is wrapped around the shoulders of the veteran or service member as these words are uttered: "Welcome home and thank you for your service."

Since 2003, Quilts of Valor were awarded to thousands of active-duty military and veterans. Finally, in 2010, the Foundation began to keep count of the quilts and the veterans who received them. Over 300,000 of our nation's finest have been recognized with a Quilt of Valor. Even throughout the recent pandemic, our members spent hours at their sewing machines focused on the mission, creating and awarding Quilts of Valor when our nation returned to normal living.

Quilts of Valor Foundation is a service organization created to honor military service for their patriotism and gratitude. Over the past twenty years, many levels of QOVF deserve recognition and thanks: the QOVF's grassroots, volunteer membership continues to be the unsung heroes of the Foundation as they cut bits of cloth yardage and reassemble it into patriotic quilts to wrap the military awardees. The membership is spearheaded by group leaders and state coordinators who inspire beautiful quiltmaking, coordinate award ceremonies, manage donations and fundraising, and meet the record-keeping requirements of the Foundation. The very few paid executive and office staff are essential to ensure QOVF meets our financial and legal responsibilities, to act as the voice of QOVF, and to keep our records in order and manage our outreach to the world. Last, QOVF has a Board of Directors who meet monthly and continually work to support the Foundation as we aim for the goal of 400,000 Quilts of Valor awarded to veterans and military service members.

Anthony Fucini was awarded a QOV made by his aunt, Susan Fiondella, in April 2021 in Vero Beach, Florida. Anthony served with the Second Infantry Division, Fort Lewis, Washington, 2012–2015. He was deployed to Afghanistan in 2012.

Quilts of Valor Is Marching On

INTRODUCTION TO THE 2ND EDITION

Thanks to the generous support of the members and supporters of the Quilts of Valor Foundation, *All-Star Quilts of Valor* is being revised with the addition of more quilts in this new format, a soft cover, spiral-bound edition. The original *All-Star* book, published in 2022, was a huge success. A request for revisions and a second printing from one's publisher is always a great honor, and *All-Star* qualified on both counts.

These past four years, the Quilts of Valor Foundation has been marching on to fulfill our mission "to cover Service Members and Veterans touched by war with comforting and healing Quilts of Valor." Our recognition as an outstanding foundation within the Quilting and Military Industrial communities has grown. QOVF individual and group memberships have flourished. One can find QOVF booths at local and nationally known quilt shows each year. Exhibits featuring Quilts of Valor traveled with the American Quilters Society and were shown and awarded at the National Quilt Museum in Paducah, Kentucky. Paducah was also the host city for a QOVF Conference in 2023 to celebrate of the 20th Anniversary Year of QOVF. Army Chaplain John Kallerson, who worked with Catherine Roberts in 2003, was the Conference's Keynote Speaker and was finally awarded a Quilt of Valor. Two national news networks—MSNBC and Fox News—invited the Foundation to award two of their employees with Quilts of Valor. Retired Army Colonel Jack Jacobs received a QOV on September 1, 2023 on MSNBC.

On September 17, 2023, Marine Veteran, Johnny "Joey" Jones received a QOV on Fox News. Tables were turned in October, 2024, when AUSA—Association of the United States Army—presented the Quilts of Valor Foundation with its Distinguished Service Award at its annual meeting in front of nearly 40,000 attendees. Board President Lauri Leirdahl and Executive Director Lexie Millikan accepted the honors in Washington, D.C.

LEFT: Chaplain John Kallerson welcomed QOVF to Walter Reed Army Medical Center in 2003 to award the very first Quilts of Valor. Chaplain Kallerson was finally awarded with a QOV at the 20th Anniversary celebration of the Foundation at the 20th Anniversary Conference in Paducah, Kentucky.

TOP RIGHT: Quilt of Valor members, the best volunteers anywhere, prep patriotic swag bags in celebration of twenty years of Quilts of Valor.

BOTTOM RIGHT: The 20th Anniversary QOVF Planning Team celebrate with the cast of *Letters from Home* after their red, white, and blue performance.

As our Foundation marches on, the mission of Quilts of Valor continues to be our driving force. Hopefully, this revised *All-Star* book will inspire your quiltmaking skills to honor Service Members and Veterans and your creations will cover their shoulders with patriotic symbols of our nation's gratitude for their dedication and sacrifice.

TOP: Original QOVF members and Board traveled from far and wide to join in the 20th Anniversary celebration.

ABOVE: The National Quilt Museum in Paducah, Kentucky, exhibited the All Star quilts during the 20th Anniversary Celebration. This exhibit marked the third time our nation's veterans were honored by the museum.

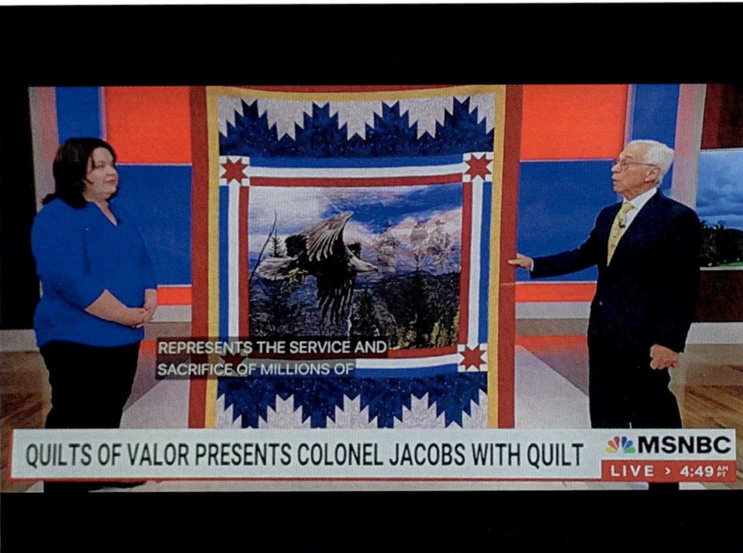

TOP: Twenty-six veterans and active-duty service members were awarded Quilts of Valor on November 11, 2023, at the National Quilt Museum in Paducah, Kentucky.

ABOVE, LEFT: Quilts of Valor Foundation made its debut on national television on September 1, 2023, on MSNBC. QOVF Executive Director Lori Thompson awarded retired Army Colonel Jack Jacobs with a QOV in New York City.

ABOVE, RIGHT: On September 17, 2023, Marine veteran Johnny "Joey" Jones received a QOV on Fox News in New York City from the QOVF Board President, Sue Reich.

TOP: American Gold Star Mothers is just one of the valued QOVF partnerships. The Connecticut Gold Star Moms honored Marine Corps veteran Harry, who served during the Vietnam War.

ABOVE: The Association of the United States Army honored Quilts of Valor Foundation in October 2024 with its Distinguished Service Award at its annual conference in Washington, DC. Executive Director Lexie Milliken, QOVF Board President Laurie Leirdahl, and QOVF IT Coordinator Les Wallace proudly accepted the award in honor of the extraordinary efforts of the 11,000+ members of Quilts of Valor.

The Honorary National 400,000th Quilt of Valor was awarded in Connecticut to Army veteran Drew Bartkiewicz who flew helicopters in the First Gulf War. The quilt was signed by hundreds of people with expressions of gratitude for his service. Upon receiving his Quilt of Valor, Drew wrote, "I just wanted to thank you again for the beautiful quilt you blessed me with. It is a treasure and will be so for the rest of my life."

“The mission of the Quilts of Valor Foundation is to cover all service members and veterans touched by war with comforting and healing Quilts of Valor.”

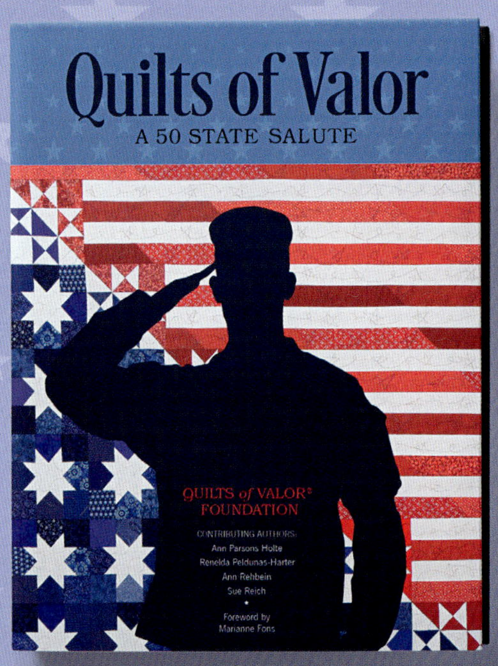

Quilts of Valor Foundation is an organization with the best volunteers! It's our grassroots members who continually design, create, and sew these civilian textile awards to honor the service and dedication of our service members and veterans. Kelly Harvey designed a quilt representing the state of Illinois named *Stars and Stripes*. It was chosen as the cover for the first QOV book, *Quilts of Valor: A 50-State Salute*. We are proud to include the pattern for her quilt here.

Stars and Stripes

Quilt designed and made by Kelly Harvey and Patty Gallmeyer

Quilt Size: 71" × 71" with 4" border

I started quilting because my mom wanted me to have a T-shirt quilt. She saved T-shirts ever since I was in kindergarten, and that quilt is my most prized possession. Fifteen years after that quilt, I have a longarm quilting business and teach quilting classes at our local quilt shop. The idea for this Quilt of Valor came when a friend donated the eight Ohio Star blocks. I sketched on the back of an envelope, "Let's put stars on one side and stripes on the other." Patty Gallmeyer created the design in the Electric Quilt design program. We've made and awarded six of these quilts. —*Kelly*

MATERIALS

TIP: This quilt uses assorted prints to create an interesting, scrappy look. Note that these instructions are for 100% cotton, first-quality, quilting-weight fabric that is at least 40" wide.

¾ yard blue for border

¾ yard red for border

Cut red and blue border fabric into: 4½" × WOF strips and set aside

4½ yards for backing

¾ yard for binding

CUTTING AND ORGANIZING

There are three elements to this quilt:

- Red and white stripes
- 9" finished-size blue and white Morning Star Blocks
- 9" finished-size red, white, and blue Split Star Blocks

Stripe Section

From assorted white fabrics, cut:

- (11) 2¾" × WOF strips

From assorted red fabrics, cut:

- (11) 2¾" × WOF strips

Morning Star Blocks

From assorted blue fabrics, cut:

- (84) 3½" squares for Star Background
- (84) 3½" squares for corner squares

From assorted white fabrics, cut:

- (21) 3½" squares for block center
- (168) 2" squares for star points

Split Star Blocks

From assorted white fabrics, cut:

- (7) 3½" squares for block corners (set aside)
- (25) 5" squares for HSTs and QSTs

From assorted blue fabrics, cut:

- (11) 5" squares for HST center square

From assorted red fabrics, cut:

- (7) 3½" squares for corners (set aside)
- (14) 5" squares for HSTs and QSTs

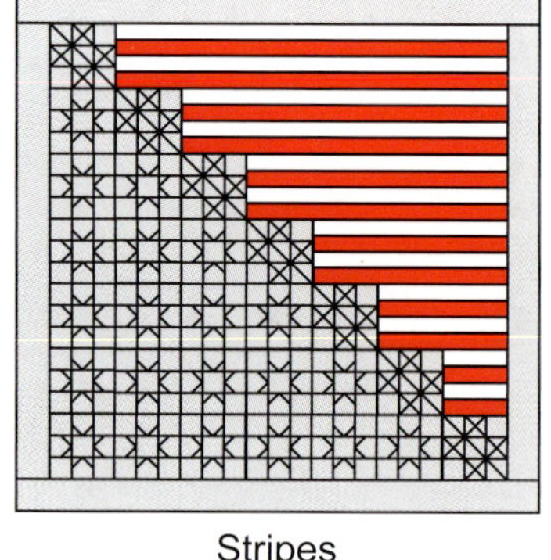

Stripes

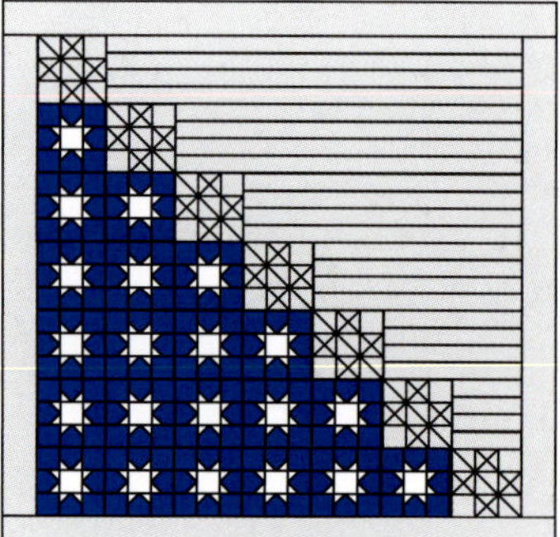

Morning Star Blocks

Split Star Blocks

ASSEMBLING THE ELEMENTS

Stripes

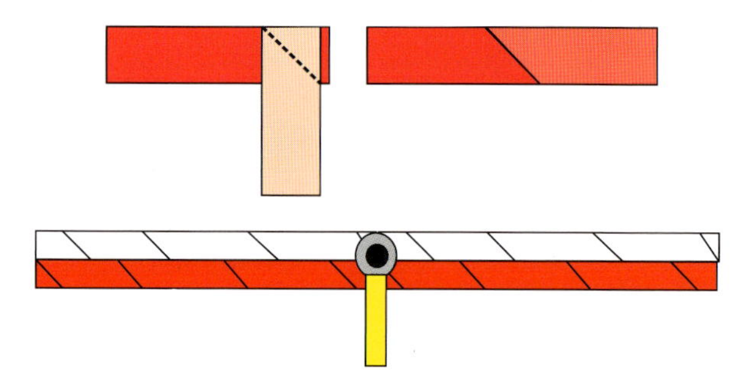

1. Use the previously cut assorted 2¾" × WOF red and white strips.
2. Cut these strips into various lengths from 9" to 12" long.
3. Attach the sections with diagonal seams to make a strip approximately 400" long.

4. Repeat for white strips.
5. Trim seam allowances to ¼".
6. Press diagonal seams open.
7. Attach the long red and white strips on a long edge to make a two-strip set approx. 400" long.
8. Cut this strip in half and sew the strips together to make a four-strip set that is approx. 200" long.
9. Cut the four-strip set into segments and attach labels as shown in illustration *Strip Segments*.
10. Set the segments aside until time to assemble the quilt.

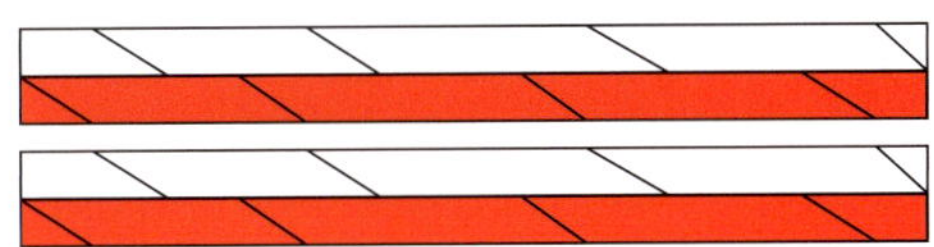

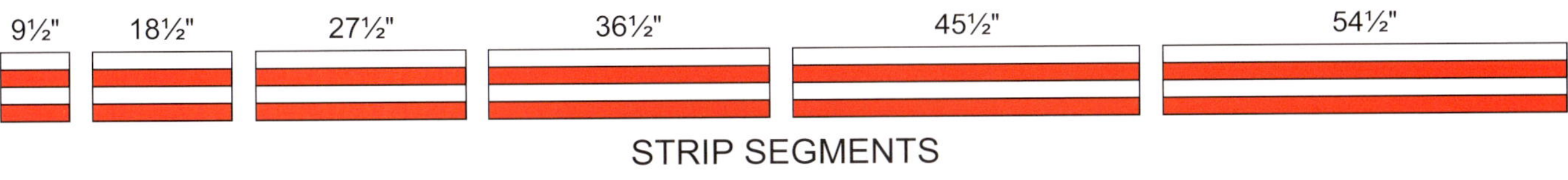

STRIP SEGMENTS

Morning Star Blocks

For each of the (21) 9" finished-size Morning Star Blocks, you will need:

White:

- 3½" square for center
- (8) 2" squares for star points

Blue:

- (4) 3½" squares for corner squares
- (4) 3½" squares for star background

Make Star Point Squares

1. Draw a diagonal line across the wrong side of each 2" white Star Point square.
2. Place 2" white Star Point square right sides together in a corner of a 3½" blue Star Background square, as shown.
3. Sew just next to the drawn line in order to place the seamline just a bit closer to the corner (this allows for the "foldover" on the corner).
4. Trim excess fabric and press seam allowance open.
5. Repeat at adjoining corner of 3½" blue Star Background square.
6. Press and trim to 3½", if necessary.
7. Make (4) for each block.

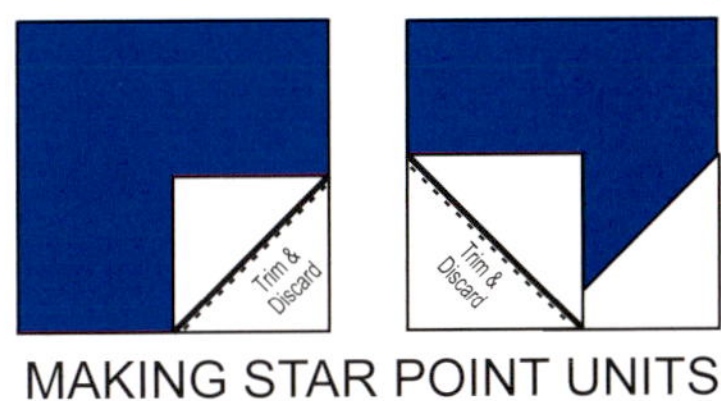

MAKING STAR POINT UNITS

Assemble Morning Star Blocks

1. Attach squares and star point units as shown.
2. Make (21) blocks.

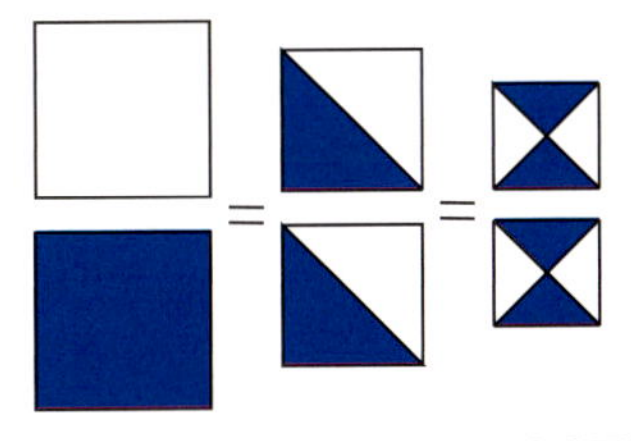
MAKING HSTS AND QSTS

Split Star Blocks

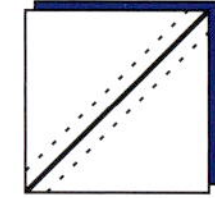

TIP: The squares for the Half-Square Triangles (HSTs) and the Quarter-Square Triangles (QSTs) were cut larger than needed and then will be trimmed to the correct size after the units are sewn. Some HSTs will be trimmed to 3½" square. Some HSTs will be used to make QSTs and trimmed afterward.

Make Half-Square and Quarter-Square Triangle Units from Oversized 5" Squares

1. Draw diagonal line on back of all (25) white 5" squares.
2. Place white squares right sides together with all red and blue 5" squares.
3. Sew ¼" on each side of the drawn line.
4. Cut apart on the drawn line.
5. Press seam allowance toward darker fabric.
6. You will now have (22) Blue+White HSTs and (28) Red+White HSTs.

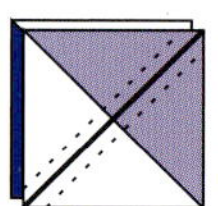

- TRIM ONLY (7) of the Blue+White HSTs to 3½" and set aside for Centers
- TRIM ONLY (14) of the Red+White HSTs to 3½" and set aside for Corners

Make QSTs from the remaining (15) Blue+White HSTs and (14) Red+White HSTs

1. Draw diagonal line perpendicular to the seamline.
2. Place two, same-color HSTs right sides together, nesting the seamline, with light and dark fabrics opposite each other.
3. Sew ¼" on each side of the drawn line.
4. Cut apart on the drawn line.
5. Press seam allowance open or "spin" the seam allowances so they all go in the same direction and then press.
6. Trim to 3½" square, being sure to line up the center of the QST at 1¾" in both directions.

Assemble the Split Star Blocks

MAKING THE SPLIT STAR BLOCK

- After all units are trimmed to 3½", for each block, you will need:

(1) White Corner Square
(1) Red Corner Square
(1) Blue+White HST for center
(2) Red+White HSTs for corners
(2) Blue+White QSTs for center sides
(2) Red+White QSTs for center sides

- Be sure to turn the HSTs and QSTs in the proper direction. Refer to the illustration *Making the Split Star Block* to assemble (7) blocks.

ASSEMBLING THE QUILT

Rows

1. Attach the rows of blocks as shown in the illustration.
2. Add the strip sets to complete the rows.
3. After the rows are attached to each other, the top should measure 63½" square.

Borders

1. Cut (4) 4½" × WOF strips each from red and blue fabric.
2. Attach strips end to end or by using diagonal seam method to make long strips.
3. Cut (1) red and (1) blue 63½" for Left and Right Borders.
4. Cut (1) red and (1) blue 71½" for Top and Bottom Borders.
5. Add the Left and Right Borders first. Then add the Top and Bottom Borders.

Finishing

- Layer top with backing and batting.
- Quilt as desired.
- Add binding.
- Remember to label your quilt.

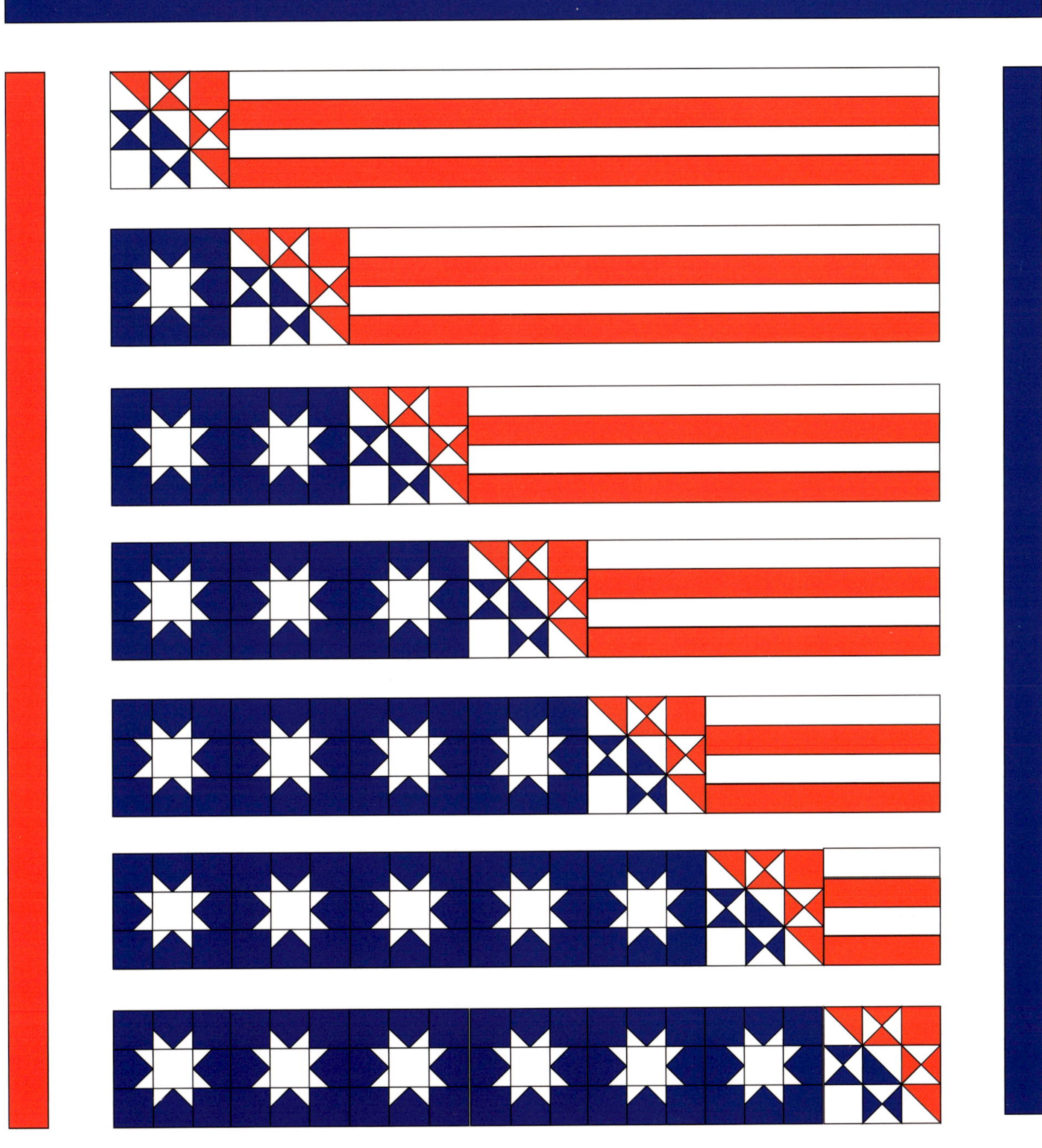

ASSEMBLING THE QUILT AND ADDING BORDERS

V Is for Victory

Quilt designed by Georgia J. Bonesteel • Machine-quilted by Maryanne Gilbert

Quilt Size: 62¼" × 79"

Celebrate the red, white, and blue with oversized equilateral triangles. Combine "V" blue-and-white triangles with red-and-white striped triangles made with scraps from your stash. Patriotic fabrics accent and frame this quilt.—*Georgia*

MATERIALS

2 yards navy print (includes binding)

3 yards white print

1⅓ yards of red print scraps

5 yards for backing

TIP: Georgia recommends prewashing all fabrics, especially the reds, with ¼ cup of white vinegar.

CUTTING

Measurements include ¼" seam allowances.

TIP: You will need to piece together the templates as indicated on pages 9–10

From navy print, cut:

- (16) 2½" strips. From strips, cut (27) D trapezoids (template on page 9) and (27) C trapezoids (template on page 10).
- (3) 3½" strips. Piece strips together to make (2) 3½" × 63" top and bottom borders.
- (8) 2¼" strips for binding

From white print, cut:

- (4) 11" strips. From strips, cut (12) A Full Triangles and (12) A Half Triangles (template on page 10).
- (4) 7" strips. From strips, cut (27) B Triangles (template on page 9).
- (12) 2½" strips for strip sets

From red prints, cut:

- (12) 3½" strips for strip sets
- (6) 2½" strips for strip sets

MAKING STRIPED TRIANGLE BLOCKS

1. Lay out (2) 3½" red strips, a 2½" red strip, and (2) 2½" white strips as shown in the *Strip Set Diagrams*.
2. Sew the five strips together to create one strip set. Make six strip sets.
3. Place full A triangle template on top of the strip set aligning the gray lines with the seam lines of the strip set. Trim strip set as shown in the *Strip Set Diagrams*.
4. Rotate the template 180 degrees to cut the next full A triangle. You should be able to get five full A triangles out of each strip set.
5. Cut a total of 27 full A triangles from the strip sets.

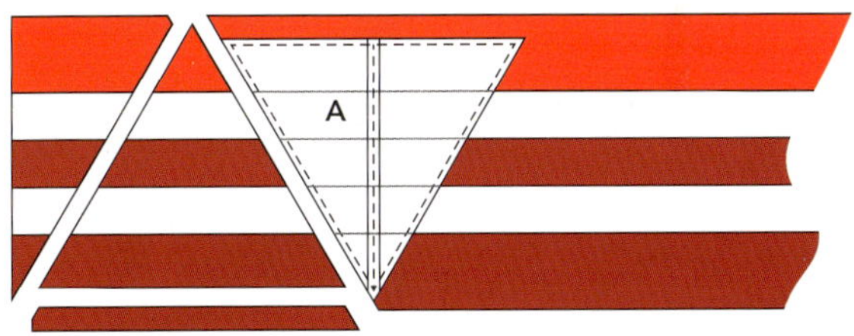

Strip Set Diagrams

"V" TRIANGLE BLOCKS

1. For each "V" triangle block you will need a white print B triangle, a navy print C trapezoid, and a navy print D trapezoid.
2. Attach the navy print C trapezoid to the white print B triangle as shown in *V-Block Assembly Diagrams*. Press toward the navy blue print.
3. Attach the navy blue D trapezoid to the rest of the "V" triangle block as shown. Press to the navy blue print to complete one "V" triangle block. Make 27 "V" triangle blocks.

V-Block Assembly Diagrams

QUILT TOP ASSEMBLY

1. Lay out red-and-white striped triangles, navy blue-and-white "V" triangles blocks, and white full- and half- triangle blocks as shown in *Quilt Top Assembly Diagrams*.
2. Sew blocks together to create diagonal rows.
3. Sew rows together to complete the quilt top center.
4. Add top and bottom navy borders to complete the quilt top.

TIP: Georgia found it very helpful to place the completed triangles on a flannel design wall. It enabled her to balance the striped triangles.

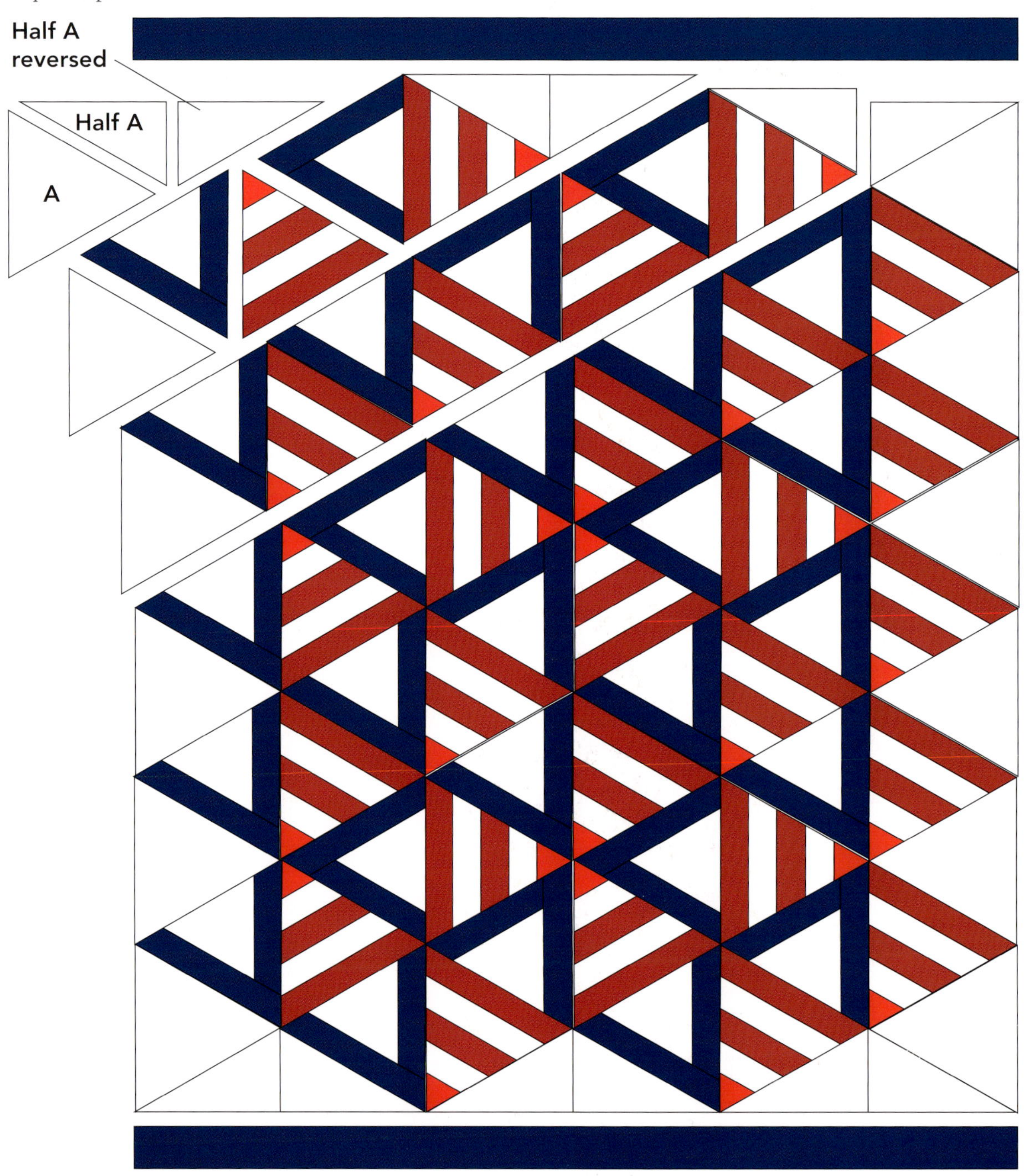

Quilt Top Assembly Diagrams

FINISHING

1. Divide backing into (2) 90" length panels. Join panels vertically.
2. Layer backing, batting, and quilt top; baste. Quilt as desired.
3. Join 2¼" wide binding strips into one continuous piece for double-fold binding. Add binding to quilt.

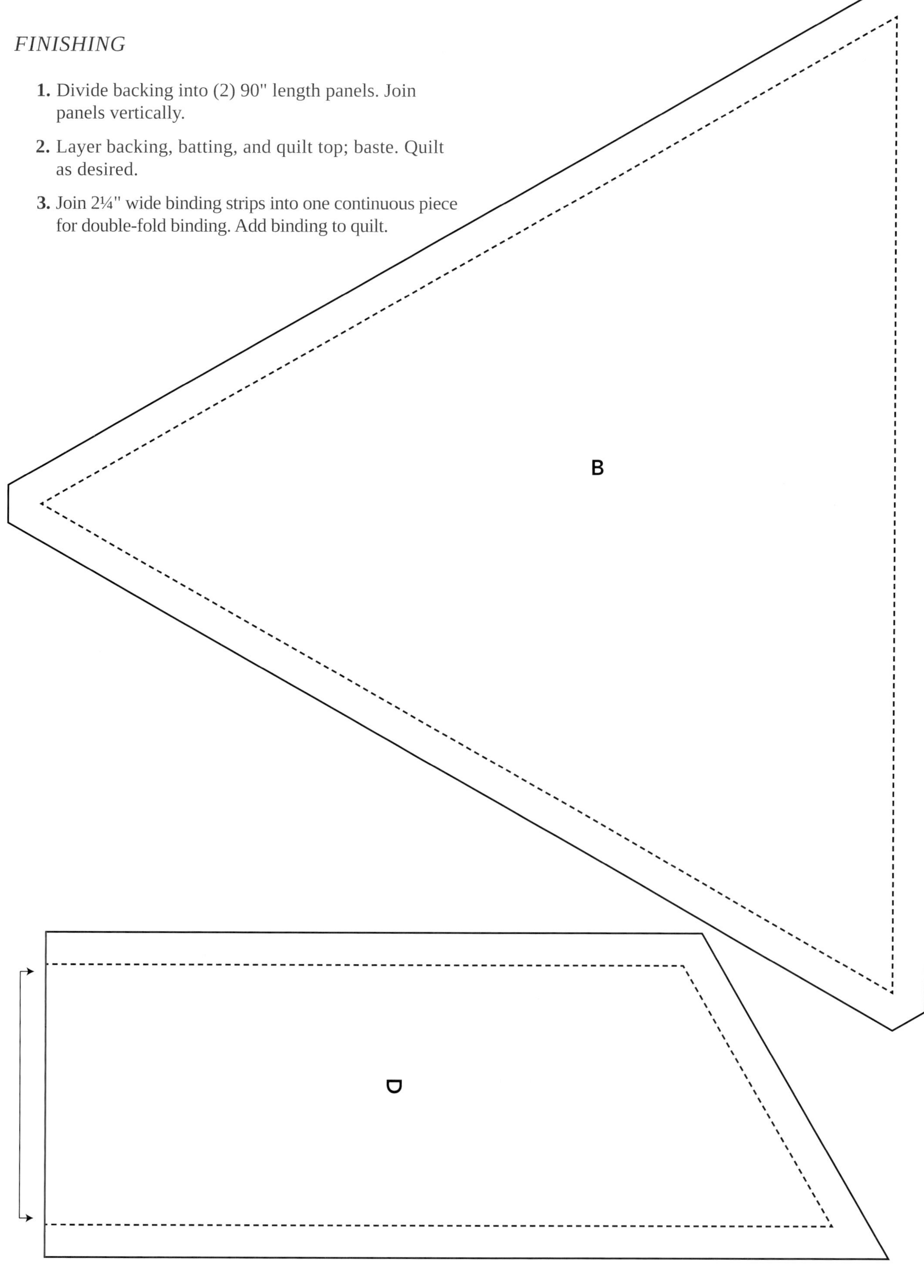

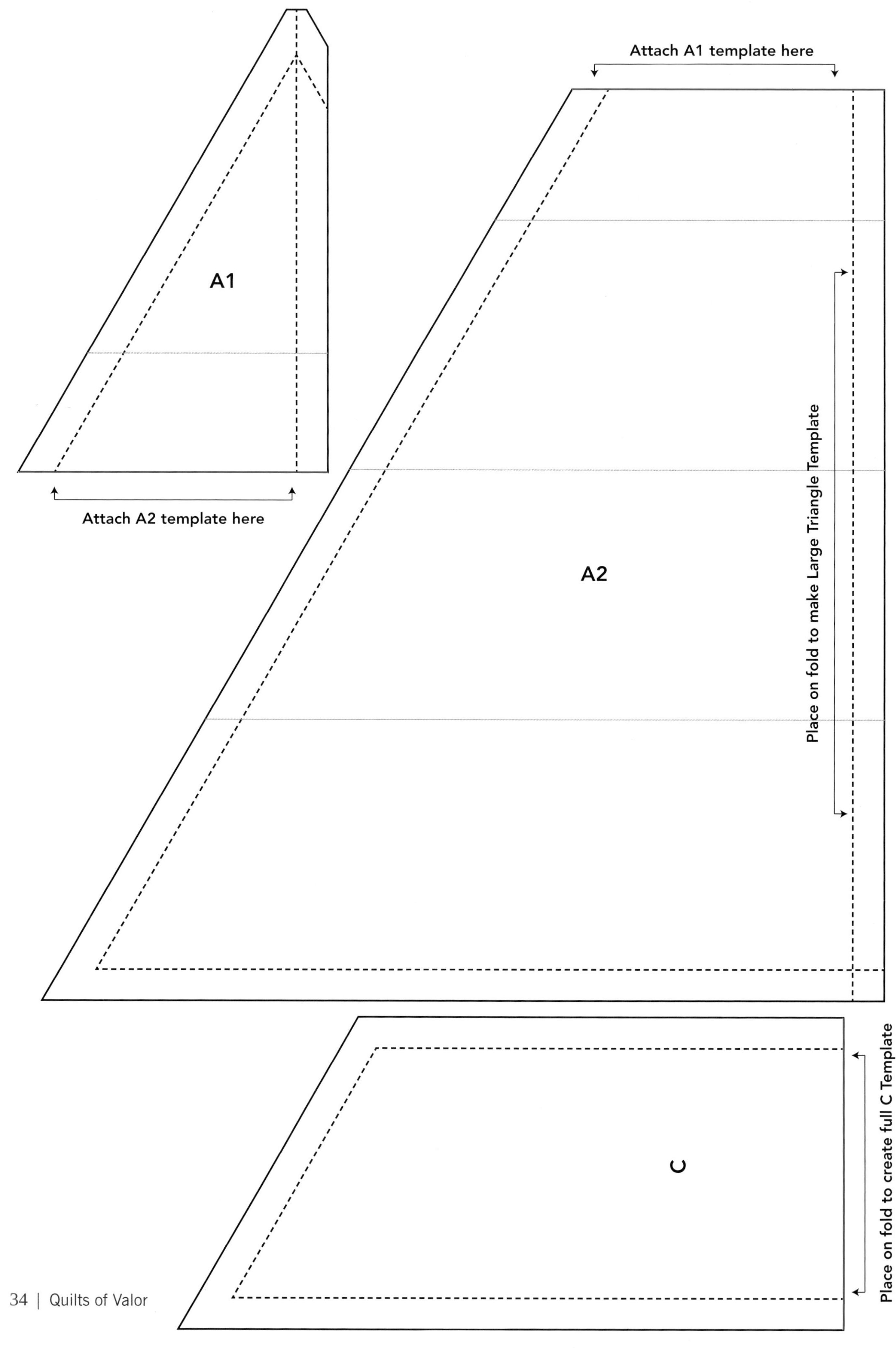

Attach A1 template here
A1
Attach A2 template here
A2
Place on fold to make Large Triangle Template
C
Place on fold to create full C Template

Stars All Around

Quilt designed by Bonnie K. Browning • Quilted by Julie Quiltoff

Quilt Size: 63" × 80" | Block Size: 8½" Finished (9" Unfinished)

Borders: 1", 2", and 3" with cornerstones

My husband, Wayne Browning, served in the US Army during the Vietnam Conflict—it was never declared a war. He was proud to serve his country and respected the American flag. This quilt is made up of stars and stripes to pay homage to our flag. Wayne received a Quilt of Valor at our AQS QuiltWeek in Des Moines and asked that it be displayed at his Celebration of Life. I made this quilt to thank another veteran for their service to our country. *—Bonnie*

MATERIALS

Yardage is for pieced borders cut from 40+" width of fabric (WOF) strips.

- 2¾ yards blue
- 2¼ yards white
- 1¾ yards red
- 5 yards 42"–44" wide fabric for backing OR 2 yards of 103" wide backing
- ¾ yard for binding

CUTTING

Measurements include ¼" seam allowance.
For units used in blocks, refer to the *Blocks Used in "Stars All Around"* illustration.

From blue fabric, cut:

- (10) 9⅜" E squares for Sawtooth Blocks #1 and #2 (Half-Square Triangle)—cut these in half on the diagonal
- (16) 5½" A squares for Star Block #1 Flying Goose Background
- (28) 4¾" C squares for Star Blocks #1 and #2 Block Center
- (48) 3" B squares for Star Block #2 Star Points
- (64) 2⅝" D squares for Star Block #1 Block Corners
- (4) 1½" squares for Border #1 Corner Blocks
- (4) 2½" squares for Border #2 Corner Blocks
- (4) 3½" squares for Border #3 Corner Blocks

From white fabric, cut:

- (12) 5½" A squares for Star Block #2 Flying Goose Background
- (64) 3" B squares for Star Block #1 Star Points
- (48) 2⅝" D squares for Star Block #2 Block Corners
- (15) 1½" × WOF F strips for Sawtooth Blocks #1 and #2 (strip sets)
- (6) 2½" × WOF for Border #2

  Attach these strips end to end.

  *Cut into (2) 2½" × 53½" for Top/Bottom

  *Cut into (2) 2½" × 70½" for Left/Right

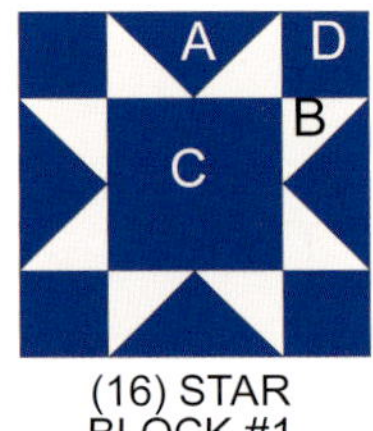

(16) STAR BLOCK #1

(12) STAR BLOCK #2

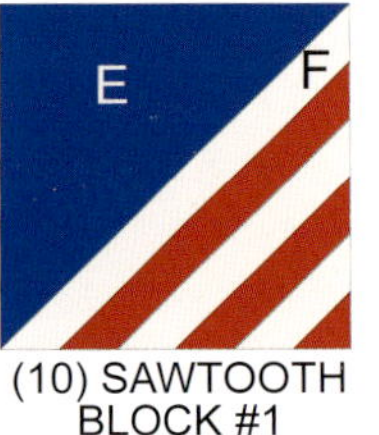

(10) SAWTOOTH BLOCK #1

(10) SAWTOOTH BLOCK #2

BLOCKS USED IN "STARS ALL AROUND" QUILT

From red fabric, cut:

- (15) 1½" × WOF F strips for Sawtooth Blocks #1 and #2 (strip sets)
- (7) 1½" × WOF strips for Border #1

  Attach these strips end to end.

  *Cut into (2) 1½" × 51½" for Top/Bottom.

  *Cut into (2) 1½" × 68½" for Left/Right.
- (7) 3½" × WOF strips for Border #3

  Attach these strips end to end.

  *Cut into (2) 3½" × 57½" for Top/Bottom.

  *Cut into (2) 3½" × 74½" for Left/Right.

*After assembling the quilt top, double-check the measurement to verify these border lengths.

ASSEMBLING THE BLOCKS

Four-at-a-Time Flying Goose Units / Star Points

For Star Block #1 and Star Block #2, refer to *Four-at-a-Time Flying Goose Diagram.*

1. Draw a diagonal line on the wrong side of the 3" B squares (both blue and white).
2. Right sides together, lay (2) 3" marked white B squares on opposite corners of a 5½" blue A square. Sew ¼" on each side of the drawn line.
3. Cut on the drawn line and press the seam allowances open.

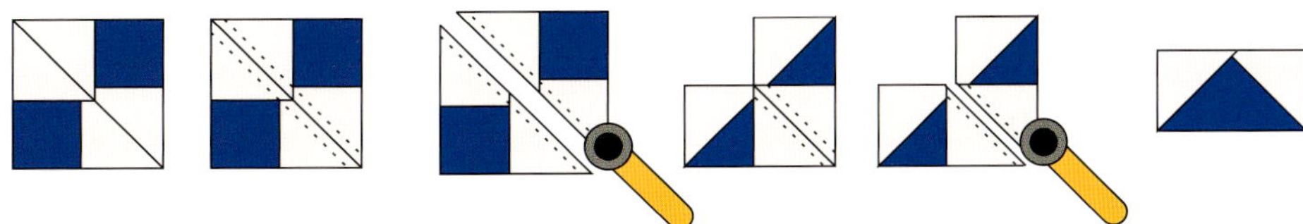

FOUR-AT-A-TIME FLYING GOOSE DIAGRAM

4. Place another marked white B square, right sides together, at the corner of the unit and sew ¼" on each side of the drawn line.
5. Cut on the drawn line; press the seam allowances open.
6. Trim off the ears.

- Repeat with other half of original unit to make (4) Flying Goose units.
- Use the remaining 5½" blue A squares and 3" white B squares to make a total of (64) units for Block #1.
- Use the 5½" white A squares and 3" blue B squares to make a total of (48) Flying Goose units for Block #2.

Assemble the Star Blocks

- Refer to the illustration *Star Block Assembly* to assemble the (16) Star Blocks #1 and (12) Star Blocks #2.

1. Use the Star Block 4¾" C blue center squares, the 2⅝" D blue block corner squares, and the Block #1 Flying Goose units to attach three rows.
2. Note the arrows indicating the direction to press the seams.
3. Join the rows, nesting the seam allowances, to complete the blocks.
4. After joining the rows, press the seam allowances open.

- Use the same method to assemble the Star Block #2, using the C blue center squares, the white D corner squares, and the Block #2 Flying Goose units.

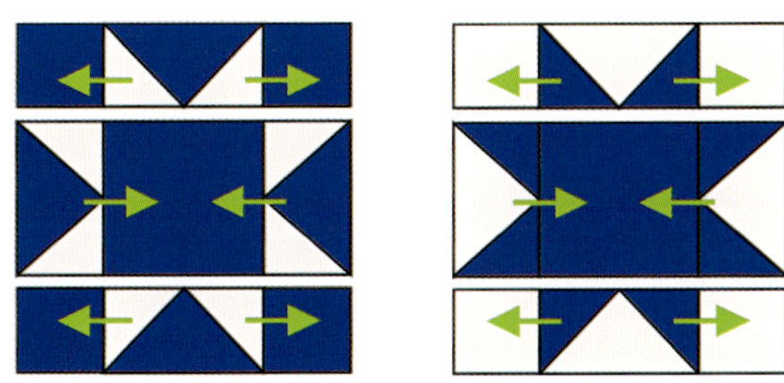

STAR BLOCK ASSEMBLY

Assembling the Sawtooth Blocks

Sewing the Strip Sets

- Sew five strip sets of (3) red and (3) white F strips with a very accurate ¼" seam allowance. Press seam allowances open. The strip set should measure 6½" × 40+".

Cutting the Strip Sets

- Start by cutting a 45-degree angle on one end of the strip set.

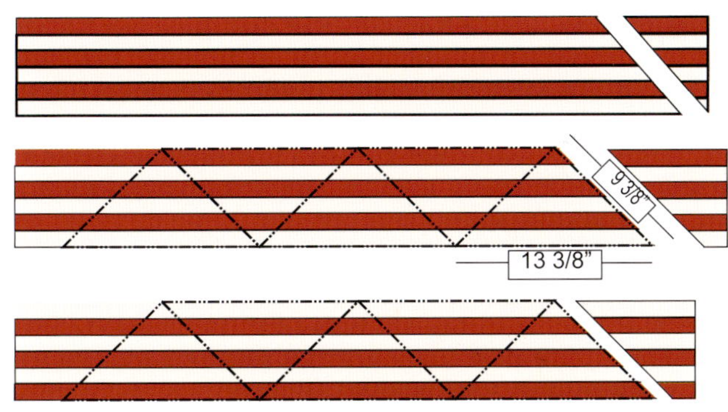

CUTTING THE STRIP SETS

- Use a 6" × 24" ruler or a large square ruler to measure and cut triangles from the strips sets as illustrated in *Cutting the Strip Sets.*
- Cut (5) triangle units from each strata set.
- In order to have (10) Strata Blocks with Red at the center seam and (10) Strata Blocks with White at the center seam, you will turn the sets (or the ruler) so that the base of the triangle is on the red or white side.
- Cut the strata triangles by placing your ruler on the 45-degree cut side of the strip set.
- The length of the cut should measure 9⅜" from base to point.
- Rotate the ruler to make a right angle that extends back to the base.
- Before cutting, double-check by measuring the distance from the first cut along the base: it should be 13⅜".

Please notice that:

- the base of the triangle is 13⅜" and the sides measure 9⅜".
- the top of the triangle is 90 degrees and the other two angles are 45 degrees.

Attaching the Sawtooth Blocks

1. After cutting the strip set triangles, attach them to the blue E half-square triangles.
2. Press seam allowance open or toward blue corner.

- Make (10) Sawtooth Blocks from each color arrangement.

MAKING THE SAWTOOTH BLOCKS

ASSEMBLING THE QUILT TOP

- Refer to *Assembling the Quilt Top and Adding Borders* illustration as you assemble the blocks into rows.

Notice that there are (8) rows in this quilt.

Rows 1 and 8 are the same.

Rows 2 and 7 are the same.

Rows 3–6 are the same.

Remember to rotate the rows as necessary to complete the top design.

ADDING THE BORDERS

1. Press the finished quilt top to determine actual border measurements.
2. Measure the Left/Right and Top/Bottom edges.
3. Cut 1½" red strips to these lengths.
4. Add side strips first.
5. Attach a small, blue square to each end of the Top/Bottom strips and attach.
6. Repeat with the 2½" white strips and the 3½" red strips.

FINISHING

1. Divide 42"–44" wide backing into (2) 78" length panels. Join panels vertically. Cut down wide backing fabric to 71" × 88".
2. Layer backing, batting, and quilt top. Baste and quilt as desired.
3. Join (8) 2¼" × WOF strips into one continuous piece for double-fold binding. Add binding to quilt.

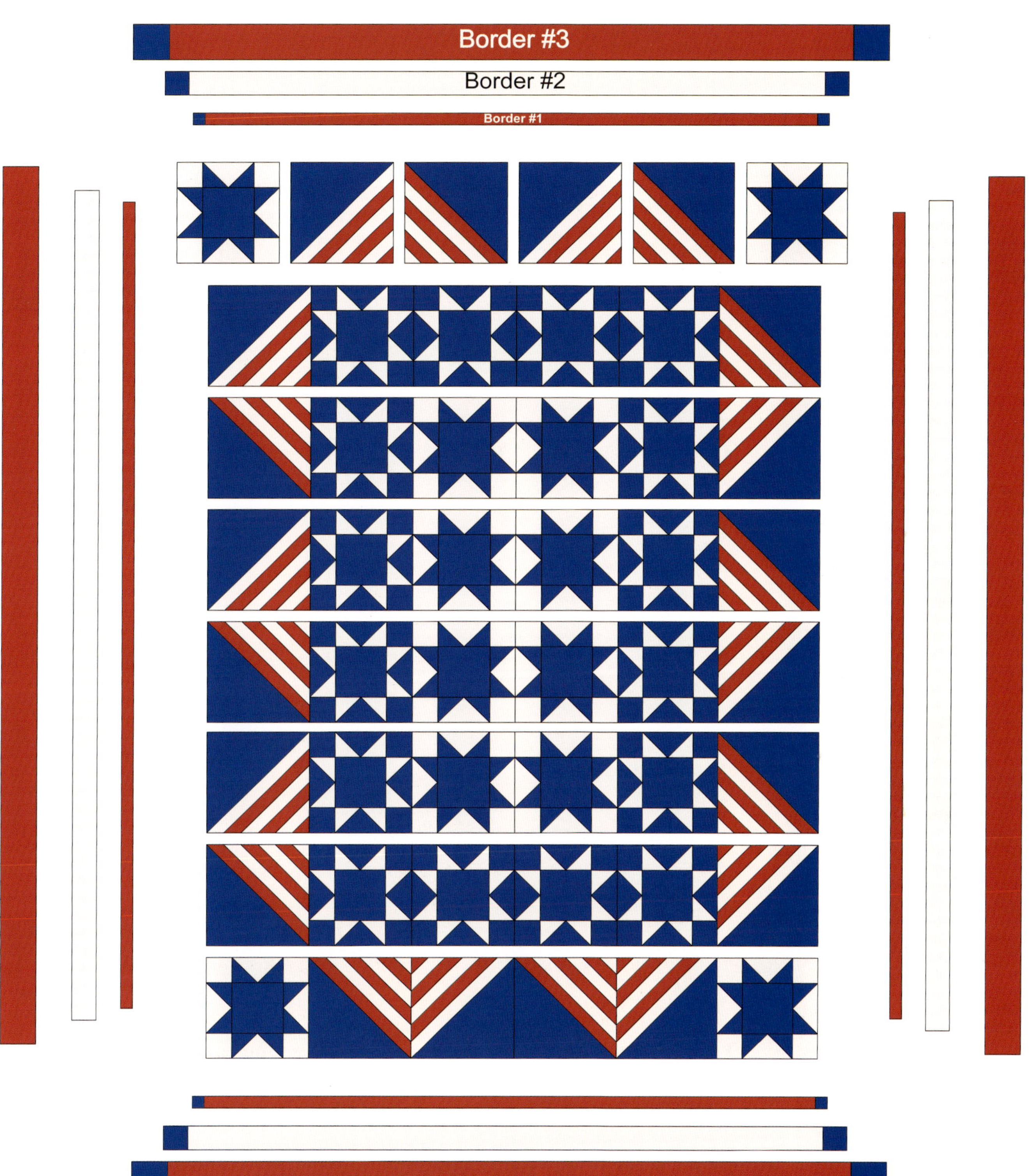

ASSEMBLING THE QUILT TOP AND ADDING BORDERS

The Road Home

Quilt designed by Pepper Cory • Pieced by Mary Frankle, Mary Henris, and Jan Spickett
Quilted by Lori House

Quilt Size: 82" × 82" | Block Size: 6" | Border: 5"

An Air Force brat herself, Pepper Cory is only too aware of the challenges faced by military families. She chose prints in shades of red, navy blue, and the colors of sand to make a quilt that would honor our servicemen and servicewomen and the people who love them.—*Pepper*

MATERIALS

3 yards tan/cream prints

1½ yards red prints

2½ yards navy prints

4½ yards medium blue print for border

7½ yards 42"–44"-wide backing OR 2½ yards 108"-wide backing

¾ yard binding

90" × 90" batting

ALSO NEEDED

Template material

Printable fabric sheets or fabric photo no larger than 12½" × 12½"

Note that many resources provide instruction for printing photos on fabric, and there are services that will do it for you. Consult your local quilt shop or the internet.

PREPARATION AND CUTTING

1. Wash and press fabrics.
2. Refer to *Full Size Templates for 6" Drunkard's Path Blocks*. Make templates for patches B and C, transferring the dots on the patterns to your templates with a hole punch or an awl.
3. All measurements include ¼" seam allowance. Align squares with crosswise or lengthwise grain of fabric.
4. Refer to the materials and cutting information; mark around the B and C templates on the back of fabric.
5. Mark through the holes to transfer the dots to the patches.

From tan/cream prints, cut:

- (16) 6½" A squares
- (76) B units for Block Y

From red prints, cut:

- (32) 6½" A squares
- (16) B units for Block Z

A A B C B C

Block Y Block Z

QUILT BLOCK UNITS

From navy prints, cut:

- (92) C units for Blocks Y and Z
- (9) 2¼" × 40" for binding

From medium blue print, cut:

- (2) 5½" × 84½" borders
- (2) 5½" × 74½" borders
- (4) strips for photo frame to make 12½" square

From backing fabric, cut:

- (3) panels 29" × 90"

From binding fabric, cut:

- (9) 2½" × WOF strips

ASSEMBLING BLOCKS

Piece Blocks Y and Z:

1. With right sides facing and matching the dots, pin the curved edges of a B and a C together.
2. Sew on the stitching line.
3. Press the seam allowance toward the C unit.
4. Referring to the *Quilt Block Units Diagrams*, make (76) Block Ys and (16) Block Zs.

Piece the Fabric Photo:

1. Add a strip of medium blue print to each side of the fabric photo.
2. Press the strips away from the photo, using a pressing cloth to protect the photo's surface.
3. Similarly, sew strips to the top and bottom of the photo. Trim the photo block to 12½" × 12½".

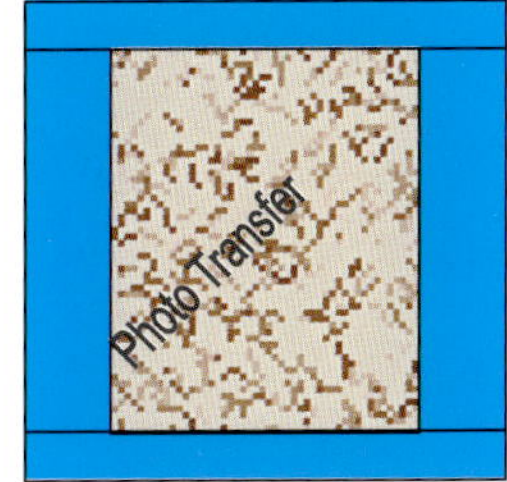

ASSEMBLING THE QUILT TOP

1. Referring to the *Quilt Top Assembly Diagram,* assemble four, identical corner units from A squares and from Y and Z blocks.
2. Also, refer to the diagram to assemble four, identical side units from A Squares and from Y Blocks.
3. When you are ready to assemble the quilt top, turn each unit ¼ turn as you lay out the (4) corners and (4) side units. Place the 12½" framed photo block in the center as shown.
4. When you're satisfied with the arrangement, join the block units into rows. Then join the rows. Press the quilt top.

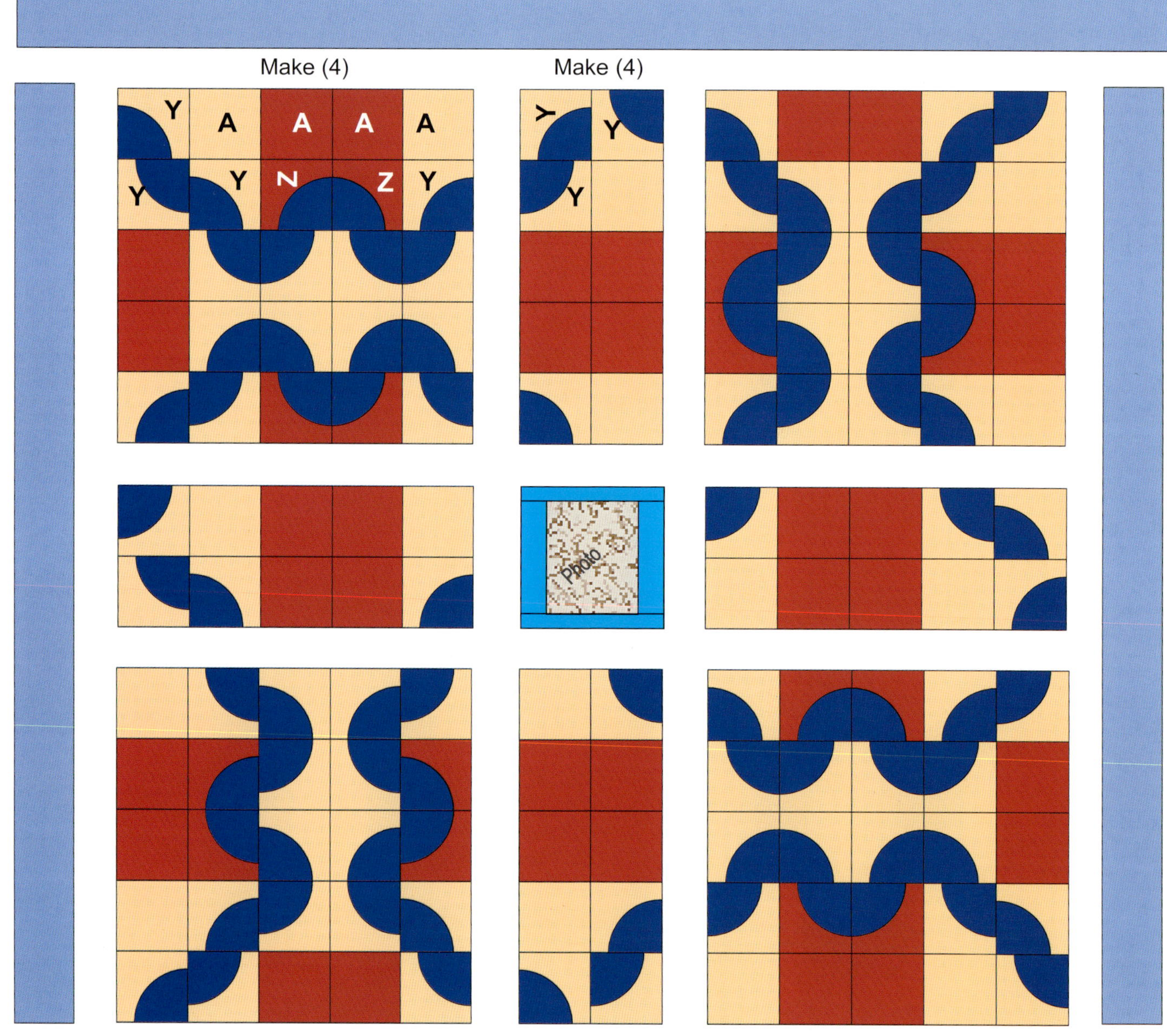

QUILT TOP ASSEMBLY DIAGRAM

ADDING BORDERS

Left/Right Borders

1. Measure through the center of the quilt from top to bottom.
2. Trim the shorter blue print borders to this length.
3. Matching centers and ends, sew the borders to the left and right sides of the quilt.

Top/Bottom Borders

1. Measure through the center of the quilt from left to right, including the borders you just added.
2. Trim the remaining borders to this length.
3. Matching centers and ends, sew them to the sides of the quilt top.

QUILTING

1. Refer to the *Liberty Eagle* and *Star* quilting designs.
2. Mark Star motifs along the borders. Mark the Liberty Eagle motif in several blocks, as desired. Layer the quilt batting, backing, and top. Baste.
3. Quilt on the marked lines. Quilt wavy lines around the Drunkard's Path patches to fill in remaining areas. Bind the quilt to finish.

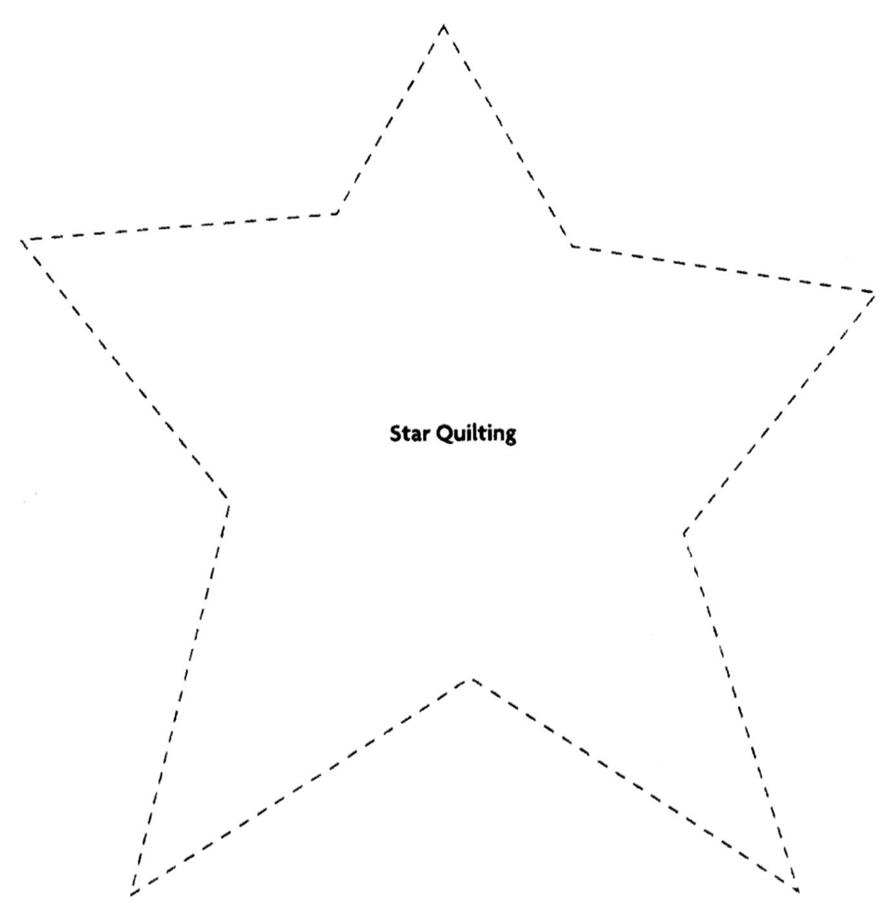

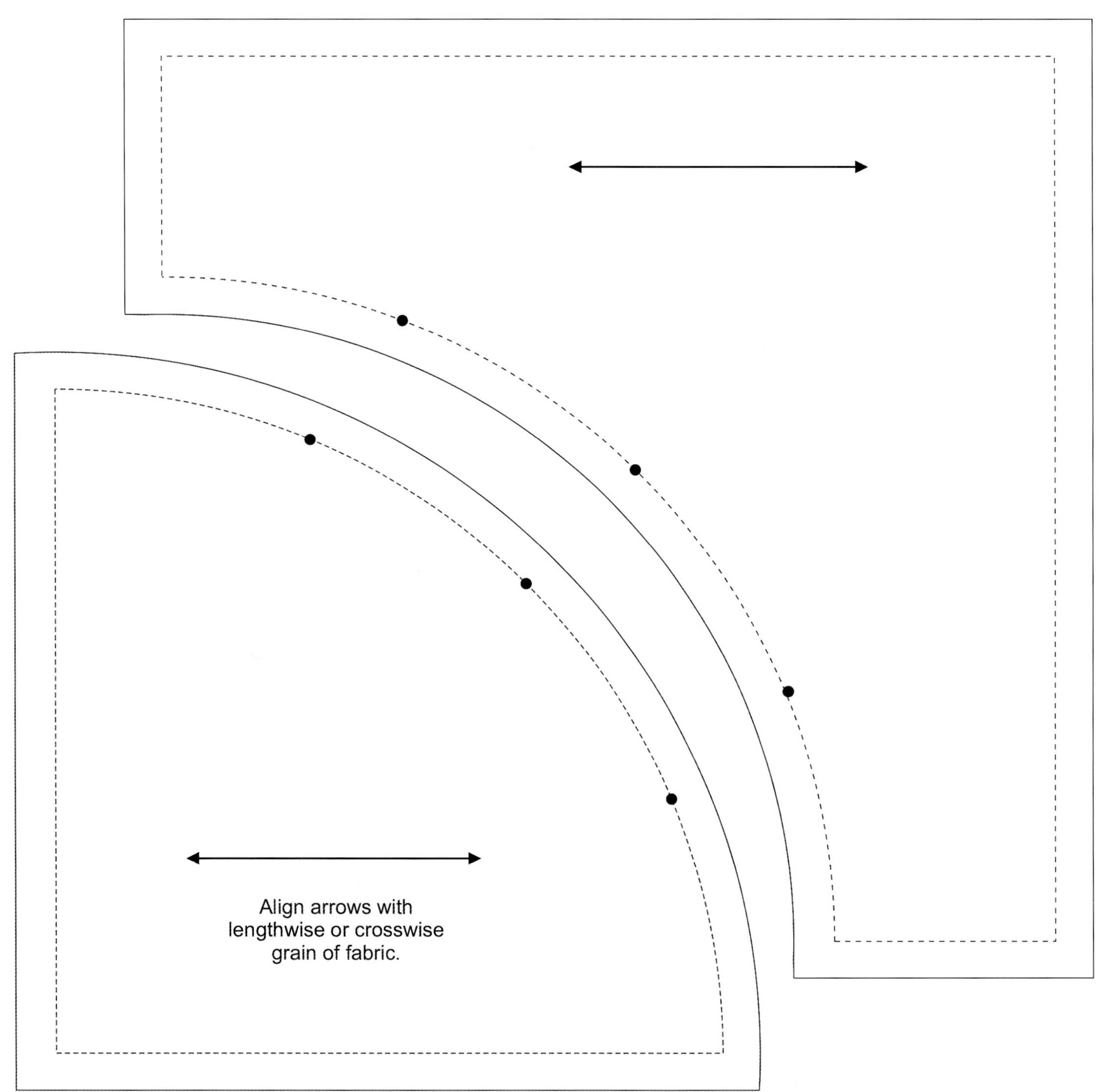

FULL SIZE TEMPLATES FOR 6" DRUNKARD'S PATH BLOCKS

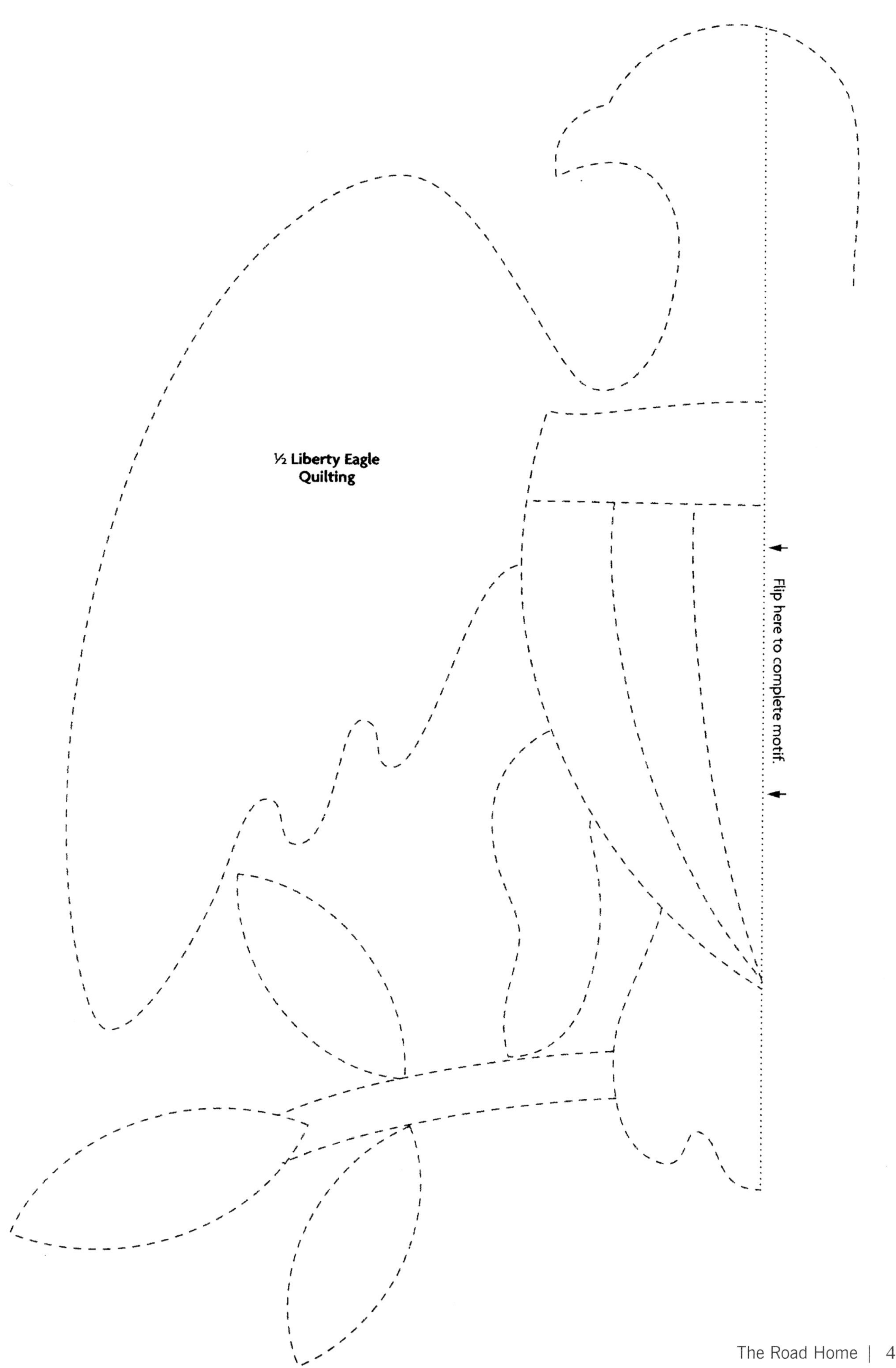
½ Liberty Eagle
Quilting
Flip here to complete motif.

Four Stars

Quilt designed, pieced, and quilted by Jenny Doan

Quilt Size: 69" × 69" | Finished Block Size: 16" × 16"

It is a wonderful experience to be involved with Quilts of Valor. To have even the smallest sense of what these veterans have given for our country is humbling. Creating a quilt to honor their service is the very least I can do. The red, white, and blue fabrics speak to me as I stitch them together, and I feel gratitude for freedom and for the land that I love. My greatest hope is that this feeling comes through in the quilts I create. They are truly made with love. —*Jenny*

TIP: Notice that Jenny's quilt uses an assortment of red and blue prints for the stars and that the colors and different prints are more randomly placed. Feel free to arrange the red and blue print strips in an arrangement that pleases you. For this pattern, the red and blue colors alternate.

MATERIALS

(16) 2½" × 40+" strips red print

(16) 2½" × 40+" strips blue print

2¼ yards for background

¾ yard for border

4¼ yards 40+" wide, seamed vertically OR 2¼ yards 108" wide backing

¾ yard binding

TOOL

The Binding Tool by TQM Products, available from Missouri Star Quilt Co.

CUTTING

Strips for Blocks

- Keep each 2½" print strip folded in half.
- Use the Binding Tool to cut (2) Binding Tool shapes from each of the folded strips, as shown in *Binding Tool Cutting* illustration.
- Each folded strip will yield (2) pairs of Binding Tool shapes: one left-angled shape and one right-angled shape per pair.
- You will have a total of (128) Binding Tool shapes: (32) Left Angle Red, (32) Right Angle Red, (32) Left Angle Blue, and (32) Right Angle Blue. Keep these organized in two stacks: left-angled shapes and right-angled shapes.

Background

From the background fabric, cut:

- (4) 8½" strips across the width of the fabric

  Subcut each strip into 8½" squares.

  Each strip will yield (4) squares.

  (16) squares are needed.

- (4) 2½" × WOF strips

  Subcut each strip into 2½" squares.

  Each strip will yield (16) squares.

  (64) squares are needed.

- (4) 8⅞" × WOF strips

  Subcut each strip into 8⅞" squares.

  Each strip will yield (4) squares.

  Subcut each of the (16) 8⅞" squares once on the diagonal to create triangles.

  (32) triangles are needed.

Borders

Cut (7) 3" × WOF strips.
Attach these strips end to end to make one long strip. You will trim the borders from this strip.

Binding

Cut (8) 2½" strips across width of binding fabric.
Join strips with diagonal seam; press seams open. Press in half lengthwise to prepare binding.

ASSEMBLING THE BLOCKS

STEP 1 WITH LEFT ANGLE STRIP

1. Working with the pile of left-angled shapes, sew a 2½" background square to the blunt end of each of the (32) red and (32) blue shapes as shown in *Step 1* illustration.
2. Press the seam allowance toward the square.
3. Each of the (16) blocks will need (4) of these units:

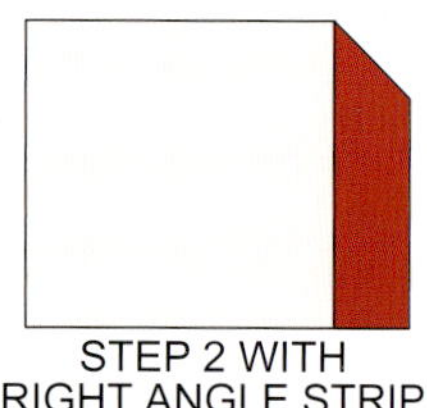
STEP 2 WITH RIGHT ANGLE STRIP

(2) red and (2) blue.

4. Working with the (16) 8½" background squares, sew a right-angled red shape to one side, as shown in *Step 2* illustration.

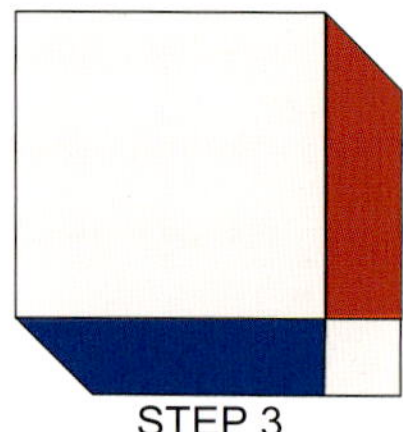
STEP 3

5. Press the seam allowance toward the square.
6. Nest the seams and sew a blue left-angled unit to the bottom of the larger square and right-angled unit as shown in the *Step 3* illustration.

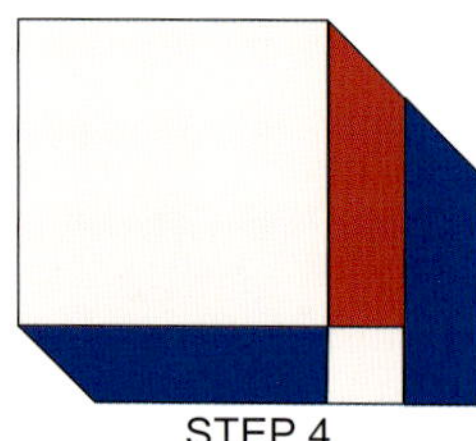
STEP 4

STEP 5

7. Sew a right-angled blue shape to the side of the unit as shown in the *Step 4* illustration.
8. Repeat to add (4) left-angled units to the bottom and (4) right angled shapes to the side, as shown in the *Step 5* illustration, alternating red and blue.

STEP 6

9. Sew an 8⅞" background triangle to both angled edges of the block as shown in the *Step 6* illustration. Line up the triangle to hang ¼" off block.
10. Press toward the outside to complete the block.

Make (16) blocks.
Blocks should measure 16½" unfinished.

ASSEMBLING THE QUILT TOP

1. Arrange the blocks into four rows of four blocks, as shown in the *Assembling the Quilt Diagram*.
2. Sew the blocks together to form the rows, rotating the blocks to the correct orientation.
3. Press the seams of the odd-numbered rows to the right. Press the seams of the even-numbered rows to the left.
4. Sew the rows together to complete the center of the quilt. Press top.

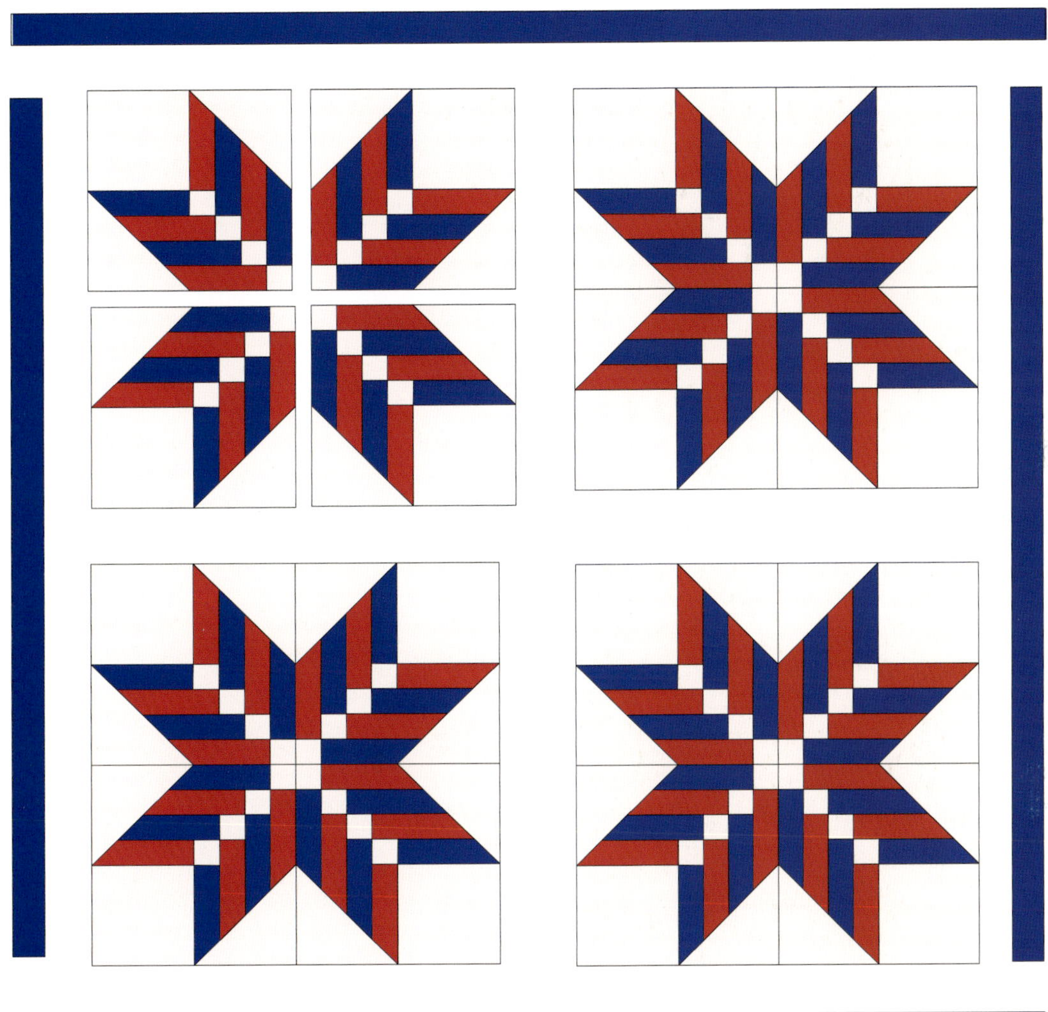

ASSEMBLING THE QUILT

ADDING THE BORDER

1. From the long strip of 3" wide border fabric, measure, cut, and attach the borders.
2. Measure through the center of the quilt from top to bottom. Cut the left/right borders to this measurement (approximately 64½"). Add left/right borders first.
3. Measure through the center of the quilt from side to side, including the borders you just added. Cut the top/bottom borders to this measurement (approximately 69½") and attach.

FINISHING

1. Divide 42"–44" wide backing into (2) 77" panels and join vertically. Cut down wide backing to 77" square.
2. Layer backing, batting, and quilt top. Baste and quilt as desired.
3. Add binding to complete the quilt.

Stars and Bars

Quilt designed by Kimberly Einmo • Pieced by Nancy Fiedler
Machine quilted by Carolyn Archer, Ohio Star Quilting

Quilt Size: 62" × 78" | Finished Block Size: 8"

My husband served as an officer in the US Air Force for 23 years before retiring in 2006. We loved every moment of our time in the military and during those years we moved 18 times! We viewed each move as an opportunity to experience everything good our great country has to offer. Stars and Bars is a clever combination of blocks which, when set side by side, form a beautiful secondary design. The stars and bars are inspired by the ranks worn on epaulets of men and women in the armed forces. The blocks are easy to piece and a great way to showcase your favorite patriotic prints. Have fun with this design; you could even make it scrappy. Most of all, I hope you will enjoy making this quilt for your favorite active duty or retired military service member or donate it to your local QOV chapter to be awarded to a very deserving veteran. *—Kimberly*

MATERIALS

2½ yards light background #1

½ yard medium patriotic print #2

1 yard medium light blue #3

⅞ yard medium light red #4

⅞ yard medium dark red #5

1½ yards dark blue #6 (includes binding)

5 yards 42"–44" wide backing OR 2½ yards 108"-wide backing

CUTTING

Only these three blocks are used to make this quilt! Note: "WOF" means "width of fabric"—usually 40+ inches. A good idea is to label the shapes as you cut. For example, "#1A" means "Fabric #1, Shape A."

BAR BLOCK

STAR BLOCK

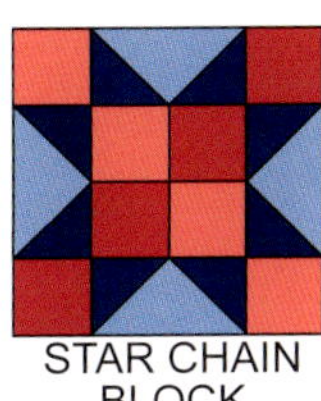

STAR CHAIN BLOCK

From #1 light background fabric, cut:

- (4) 8½" × WOF strips

  Subcut into (60) 8½" × 2½" rectangles.

  Label #1A for Bar Blocks.

- (2) 2½" × WOF strips

  Subcut into (32) 2½" squares.

  Label #1B for Star Blocks.

- (2) 5¼" × WOF strips

  Subcut into (8) 5¼" squares.

  Cut these squares twice diagonally to yield (32) triangles.

  Label #1C for Star Blocks.

- (8) 3½" × WOF strips

  Piece these end to end.

  Label #1D for Outer Borders.

From #2 medium patriotic print, cut:

- (4) 2½" × WOF strips

  Label #2E Strip Sets for Bar Blocks.

- (1) 4½" × WOF strip

  Subcut into (8) 4½" squares.

  Label #2F for Star Blocks.

From #3 medium light blue, cut:

- (4) 2½" × WOF strips

  Label for #3E Strip Sets for Bar Blocks.

- (4) 5¼" × WOF strips

  Subcut into (25) 5¼" squares.

  Cut these squares twice diagonally to yield (100) triangles.

  Label #3C for Star Chain Blocks.

From #4 medium light red, cut:

- (4) 2½" × WOF strips

  Label #4E Strip Sets for Bar Blocks.

- (8) 2½" × WOF strips

  Set aside (4) strips and label #4G Four-Patch Units for Star Chain Blocks.

  Subcut remaining (4) strips into (50) 2½" squares.

  Label #4B for Star Chain Blocks.

From #5 medium dark red, cut:

- (4) 2½" WOF strips

  Label #5E Strip Sets for Bar Blocks.

- (8) 2½" × WOF strips

  Set aside (4) strips and label #5G Four-Patch Units for Chain Star Blocks.

  Subcut remaining (4) strips into (50) 2½" squares.

  Label #5B Squares for Chain Star Blocks.

From #6 dark blue, cut:

- (10) 2⅞" × WOF strips

  Subcut (132) 2⅞" squares.

  Cut these once diagonally for (264) triangles.

  Label #6H for Star Blocks and Chain Star Blocks.

- (8) 2¼" × WOF strips

  Piece together with diagonal seam for binding.

ASSEMBLING THE BLOCKS

Bar Blocks

1. Sew 2½" × WOF strips #2E, #3E, #4E, and #5E together in the order as shown to form a strip set as shown in *Strip Set for Bar Blocks.*
2. Press seam allowances in direction of arrow.
3. Make (4) Strip Sets.
4. Cut (30) 4½" segments from sets.
5. Sew 2½" × 8½" #1A strips on either side of the strip unit, as shown in *Bar Block Assembly*.
6. Press seams toward the strip unit (away from the background fabric).
7. Blocks should measure 8½" square unfinished. Square up, if necessary.
8. Make (30) Bar Blocks.

#5E
#4E
#2E
#3E
4 1/2"

STRIP SET FOR BAR BLOCKS

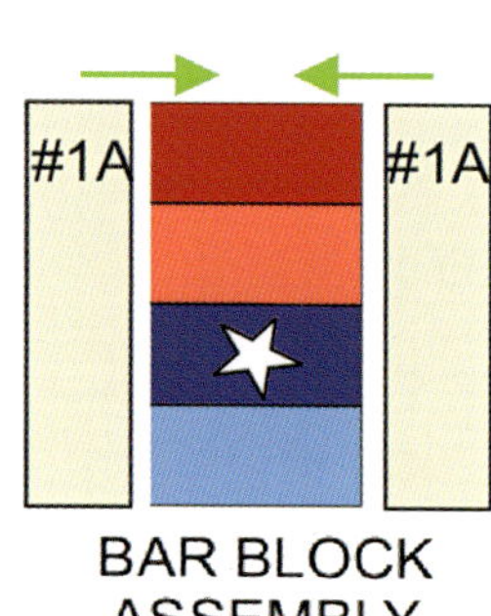

BAR BLOCK ASSEMBLY

Star Blocks

STAR BLOCK ASSEMBLY

FLYING GOOSE UNIT

1. Sew #6H Triangles (cut from ⅞" squares) to the short sides of a #1C Triangle to create a Flying Goose unit as shown in *Flying Goose Unit* illustration.
2. Press seams toward small triangles. Units should measure 2½" × 4½" unfinished.
3. Trim dog ears and square up, if necessary.
4. Make (32).
5. Refer to *Star Block Assembly* to assemble Star Blocks by using:

- (4) Flying Goose units
- (4) #1B 2½" corner squares, and
- (1) #2F 4½" square in the center

6. Press seams as shown. Square up if necessary to 8½" × 8½" unfinished size.
7. Make (8) Star Blocks.

Star Chain Block

1. Sew #6H triangles (cut from 2⅞" squares) to the short sides of a #3C triangle to create a Flying Goose unit.
2. Press seams toward small triangles.
3. Units should measure 2½" × 4½". Trim dog ears and square up, if necessary.
4. Make (100) Flying Goose units.
5. Create four-patch units by sewing 2½" strips #4G and #5G into strip sets as illustrated in *Making Four-Patch Units.*
6. Strip set should measure 4½" wide. Make (4) strip sets.
7. Press seam allowance toward darker fabric.
8. Cut (50) 2½" wide segments.
9. Rotate one segment and place right sides together on top of another unit and stitch.
10. Press seam allowance open.
11. Make (25) four-patch units.

Four-patch units should measure 4½" × 4½". Square up, if necessary.

Flying Goose Unit

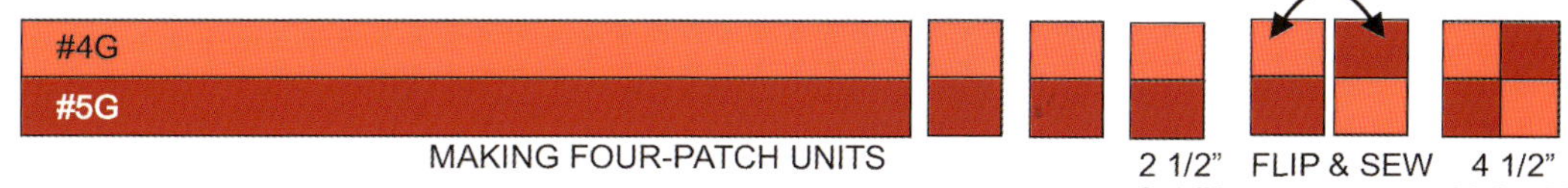

MAKING FOUR-PATCH UNITS

12. Refer to *Star Chain Block Assembly* to assemble the block by using

- (4) Flying Goose units,
- (2) #4B 2½" squares, and
- (2) #5B 2½" squares.
- (1) four-patch unit in the center.

Star Chain Block should measure 8½" × 8½". Square up if necessary.

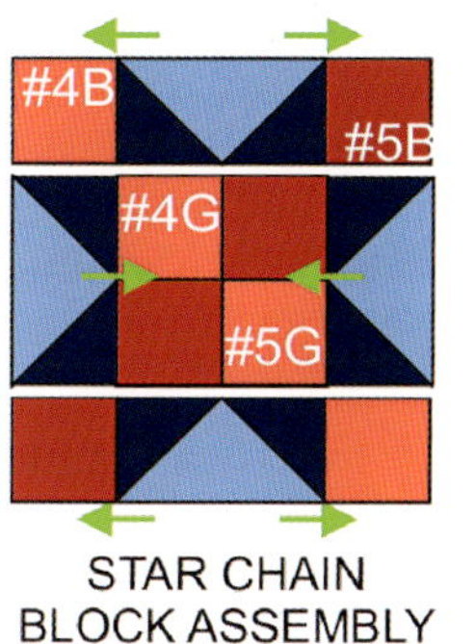

STAR CHAIN BLOCK ASSEMBLY

ASSEMBLING AND FINISHING THE QUILT

1. Assemble the quilt blocks into rows, being careful to rotate the blocks to create the secondary design, as shown in *Stars and Bars Quilt Top Assembly*.
2. Measure through the center of the top from top to bottom. Use this measurement to cut the left and right borders. Attach to sides.
3. Measure through the center from left to right, including the borders just added. Use this measurement to cut the top and bottom borders. Attach to top/bottom of quilt top.
4. Divide 42"–44" wide fabric into (2) 70" lengths and join vertically. Cut wide backing to 70" × 86".
5. Quilt as desired. Enjoy!

STARS AND BARS QUILT TOP ASSEMBLY

From Sea to Shining Sea

Quilt designed by Marianne Fons • Machine-quilted by LuAnn Downs

Quilt Size: 66" × 80" | Finished Block Size: 14" × 8"

Making Quilts of Valor has given me a way to express my patriotism. This design was inspired by a nineteenth-century quilt in the collection of the International Quilt Museum in Lincoln, Nebraska. —*Marianne*

MATERIALS

15 fat quarters* in assorted medium and dark blue prints and stripes

15 fat quarters* in assorted cream prints and stripes

⅝ yard gold print

5 yards for backing

*fat quarter = 18" × 20"

CUTTING

Measurements include ¼" seam allowances.

From blue print fat quarters, cut:

- (82) 2½" wide strips. From strips, cut (40) 2½" × 6½" C rectangles, (160) 2½" × 4½" B rectangles, and (220) 2½" A squares.

From cream print fat quarters, cut:

- (82) 2½" wide strips. From strips, cut (40) 2½" × 6½" C rectangles, (160) 2½" × 4½" B rectangles, and (220) 2½" A squares.

From gold print, cut:

- (8) 2¼" strips for binding

BLOCK ASSEMBLY

1. Lay out three blue print A squares, four cream print B rectangles, one blue print C rectangle, three cream print A squares, four blue print B rectangles, and one cream print C rectangle as shown in *Block Diagrams*.
2. Join into rows; join rows to complete one block. Make a total of 40 blocks.

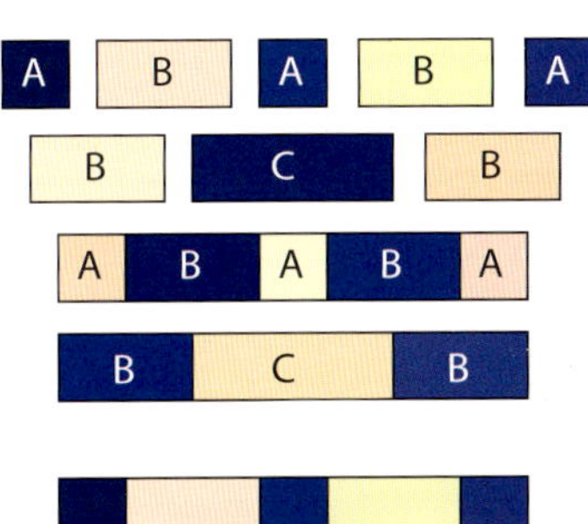

Block Diagrams

PIECED SASHING-STRIPS ASSEMBLY

1. Join two blue print A squares and two cream print A squares as shown in *Sashing Unit Diagrams*. Make 50 sashing units.
2. Add one sashing unit to the left side of each block as shown in *Sashed Block Diagrams*.

A

A

Sashing Unit Diagrams

Sashed Block Diagrams

QUILT TOP ASSEMBLY

1. Lay out sashed blocks and remaining sashing units as shown in the *Quilt Top Assembly Diagram*.
2. Sew blocks and sashing strips together to create rows.
3. Sew rows together to complete the quilt top.

FINISHING

1. Divide backing into (2) 90" length panels. Join panels vertically.
2. Layer backing, batting, and quilt top; baste. Quilt as desired.
3. Join 2¼" wide binding strips into one continuous piece for double-fold binding. Add binding to quilt.

Quilt Top Assembly Diagram

Cascade of Stars

Quilt designed and quilted by Ann Parsons Holte

Pieced by Ann Parsons Holte, Cindy Shultz, and Kathryn Otto

Quilt Size: 62" × 80" | Finished Column Width: 10" Star Columns, 12" Stripe Columns | Finished Sashing Width: 2"

This quilt features my version of the quilt-as-you-go method. The goal of this method is for you to be able to make the whole quilt on your home machine. The columns are pieced, layered with batting and backing, and quilted individually. The columns are then joined and the joint is covered by a sashing tube that is topstitched in place. —*Ann*

MATERIALS

5½ yards for backing

Select a busy backing print that is at least 42" usable width.

¾ yard for binding

TIP: Choose a quilting thread that matches the backing fabric as closely as possible. Use this thread in the bobbin throughout the quilting and topstitching process, regardless of what color of thread you use on the top of the quilt.

The question is: How scrappy do you want the quilt to be? If the answer is "Not at all!," you will only need three fabrics for the front (red, white, and blue). Choose 100% cotton, first-quality, quilting-weight fabric. Prewash and iron all fabric.

Non-Scrappy: One Red, One White, One Blue

2¼ yards blue for Star Block background

1 yard red for Stripe Strips

3¼ yards white for Star Blocks, Stripe Strips, and Sashing

On the other hand, if your answer is "Coordinated Scrappy," you will need lots more fabric because of all those extra seams and all the variety needed. The sample in the photograph shows my version of "Coordinated Scrappy." For this look, I assembled:

Coordinated Scrappy, Using Fat Quarters

19 blue fat quarters

8 red fat quarters

21 white fat quarters

Scrappy Scrappy

You might also want to use actual scraps that you find in boxes and bags around your sewing area. The cutting directions tell you how many pieces of each size and color patch you will need.

BATTING

Thin or mid-loft, 100% cotton or a blend of 80% cotton and 20% polyester

Fusible 80/20 cotton/polyester batting is good for strip quilts. Press the adhesive side to the wrong side of the backing strips, which prevents slipping while quilting the column. You can also spray temporary adhesive onto nonfusible batting to achieve the same effect. You will need:

11½ yards of 24" wide fusible, mid-loft, 80% cotton/ 20% poly blend.

There will be leftover strips for borders or for narrow strips on another quilt.

OR

A piece of batting that is about 85" square—a queen size will be plenty.

CUTTING FROM FAT QUARTERS

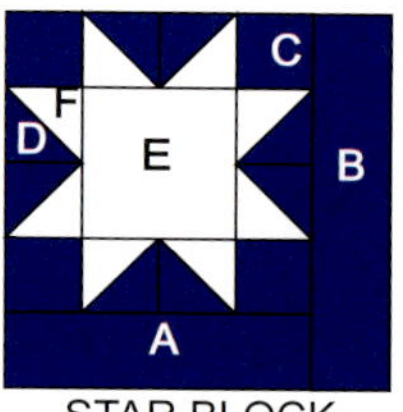

STAR BLOCK

From blue fat quarters, cut:

- (24) 5¾" for D HST squares
- (24) 2½" × 8½" for A rectangles
- (24) 2½" × 10½" B rectangles
- (96) 2½" C squares

From red fat quarters, cut:

- (40) 2½" × 12½" H rectangles

From white fat quarters, cut:

- (24) 5¾" F HST squares
- (24) 4½" E squares
- (40) 2½" × 12½" G rectangles

TIP: You will also need white for the sashing tubes later on. You can either use 1¼ yards of a single fabric or you can piece together the scraps from cutting the white shapes. I cut the scraps into 5½" wide × whatever length is available from the scraps. They will be pieced together to form a long strip that is 5" wide × 320+" long.

CUTTING FROM YARDAGE

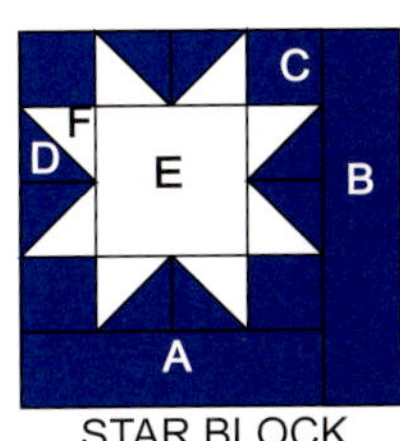

STAR BLOCK

From blue yardage, for (24) Star Blocks, cut and label:

- (4) 5¾" × WOF strips

  Subcut (24) 5¾" squares for D half-square triangle units (HSTs).

- (20) 2½" × WOF strips

  Subcut (6) strips into (24) 2½" × 8½" A rectangles.

  Subcut (8) strips into (24) 2½" × 10½" B rectangles.

  Subcut (6) strips into (96) 2½" × 2½" C squares.

From white yardage, for (24) Star Blocks, cut and label:

- (6) 5¾" × WOF strips

  Subcut (24) 5¾" squares for F HSTs.

- (3) 4½" × WOF strips

  Subcut (24) 4½" E squares.

From white yardage for Stripe Strips, cut and label:

- (14) 2½" × WOF strips

  Subcut (40) 2½" × 12½" rectangles G.

From white yardage for Sashing Tubes (set aside 1¼ yards)

TIP: Wait to cut these strips until after the panels are quilted and joined. The width of the strips may need to be adjusted.

From red yardage for Stripe Strips, cut and label:

- (14) 2½" × WOF strips

  Subcut (40) 2½" × 12½" rectangles H.

FROM BACKING FABRIC, CUT AND LABEL:

For Star Block Columns

- (7) 14½" × WOF strips

  Join end to end, then cut (3) 14½" × 82½" strips.

For Strip Stripe Columns

- (5) 16½" × WOF strips

  Join end to end, then cut (2) 16½" × 82½" strips.

For Back joining strips

- (9) 1" × WOF strips

  Join end to end, then cut (4) 1" × 82½" strips.

Binding

- Cut (8) 2½" × WOF strips.

  Join end to end and press in half lengthwise.

Batting

TIP: Scraps of batting can be attached with a large zigzag seam or with light, fusible interfacing strips.

- For Star Block Columns, cut (3) 14½" × 82½" strips.
- For Stripe Strip Columns, cut (2) 16½" × 82½" strips.

ASSEMBLING THE BLOCKS

Star Blocks

- Use the Blue and White 5¾" squares D and F to make (96) HSTs, as shown in the *Eight-at-a-Time HSTs* illustration. Each Star Block will use

(1) 4½" white center square E.

(8) Blue+White half-square triangles D/F.

(4) 2½" blue squares for corners C.

(1) 2½" × 8½" blue rectangle A.

(1) 2½" × 10½" blue rectangle A.

1. Assemble (4) pairs of Blue+White HSTs for each block as shown in *Attach HSTs in Pairs*.
2. Sew the three rows together to form the star.
3. Add the A and B rectangles, as shown in illustration *Assembling the Star Block*.

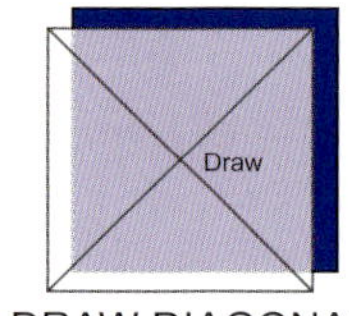

DRAW DIAGONAL LINES

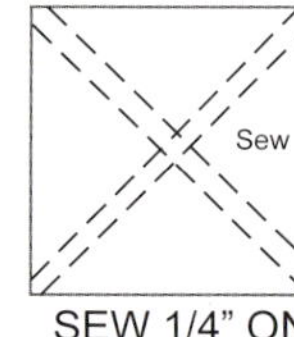

SEW 1/4" ON EACH SIDE

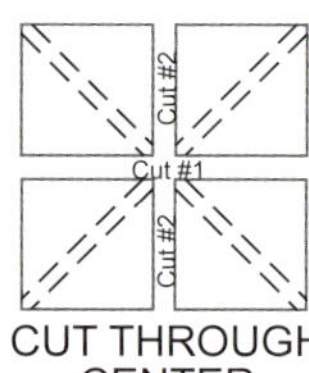

CUT THROUGH CENTER

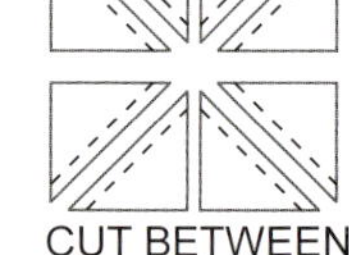
CUT BETWEEN SEWN LINES

MAKING EIGHT-AT-A-TIME HALF SQUARE TRIANGLES

PRESS SEAM TO DARK SIDE

ATTACH HSTs IN PAIRS

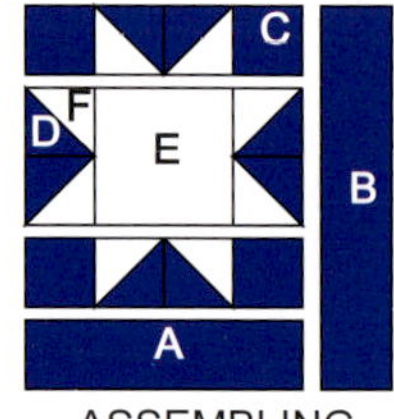

ASSEMBLING THE STAR BLOCK

ASSEMBLING THE COLUMNS

Star Block Columns

Attach (8) Star Blocks for each column, being sure to rotate the blocks to achieve the "cascade" effect. As you construct the three columns, refer to *Assembling the Columns* illustration and notice that:

- Star Block columns 1 and 3 begin with left-side star blocks, with the B rectangle on the right.
- The center Star Block column begins with a right-side star block, with the B rectangle on the top.

Stripe Strip Columns

Alternate (20) red and (20) white 2½" × 12½" rectangles for each column.

TIP: At this point, you could cut 2½" strips of sashing fabric, attach the columns together, and send it out for quilting as a regular quilt top. However, if you want to do it all yourself on your home sewing machine and learn a new quilting technique, proceed to the next step.

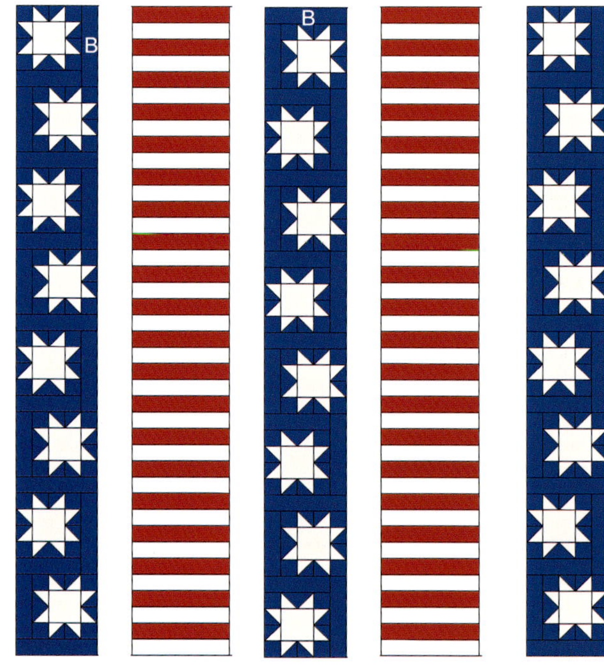

ASSEMBLING THE COLUMNS

QUILTING THE COLUMNS

Star Block Columns

1. Use the (3) strips of 14½" × 82½" backing and fusible batting or regular batting.
2. Press backing to adhesive side of batting (follow package instructions) or pin regular batting in place.
3. Center the Star Block column on the Backing+Batting strip, as shown in *Quilting the Columns* illustration.
4. Quilt as desired, carrying out the quilting to the raw edges.

Stripe Strip Columns

1. Use (2) strips of 16½" × 82½" backing and fusible batting or regular batting.
2. Press backing to adhesive side of batting or pin regular batting in place.
3. Center the Red+White Stripe Strip column on the Backing+Batting, as shown in *Quilting the Columns* illustration.
4. Quilt as desired, carrying out the quilting to the raw edges (see Tip, above).

TIP: If your quilting stops before the raw edge (because of a particular motif, for example, such as a wreath that you don't want to carry out to the edge), take the time to stay-stitch all around the edges, just a thread or two from the raw edge.

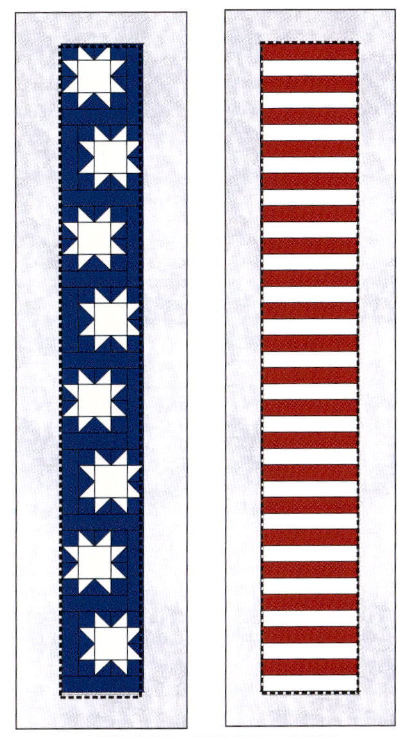

QUILTING THE COLUMNS

ASSEMBLING THE QUILT

Trim Batting and Backing

TIP: Because the sashing width for this quilt is 2" finished, you will trim off the excess batting and backing in order to leave enough space between the panels for the sashing to cover once the columns are joined.

1. Trim around the panels, measuring from the raw edge, so that ¾" of batting and backing extends all around as shown in *Trimming the Backing and Batting* illustration.
2. Why ¾"? In the next step, the columns will be attached so that the two batting edges butt against each other. There will be ¾" + ¾" = 1½" of batting visible on the front side of the column. So, the sashing strip must cover the batting AND must overlap each column by ¼" to completely cover the edges and the seam allowance.

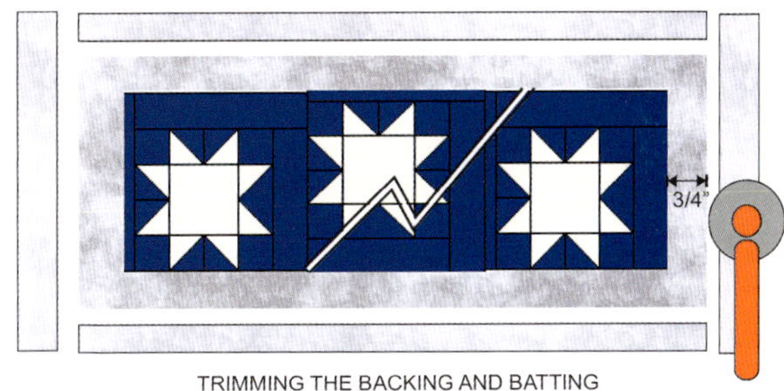

TRIMMING THE BACKING AND BATTING

Attach the First and Second Columns

TIP: In the illustration *Joining Columns (Back)*, the backing is yellow and the joining strip is green. You will actually use a busy backing fabric and the joining strip will be cut from the same fabric.

1. Working from the back, sew a 1" × 82½" Back Joining Strip to the back of the first Star Block column, right sides together, on the long edge of the side to be joined.
2. Press the strip away from the column.
3. Attach the next column (Red & White Stripe column) to the other edge of the Back Joining Strip. Pay attention to aligning elements from each column, such as the bottom of a block in the Star Block column aligning with a seam in the Stripe Strip column.
4. Press the strip again.
5. Looking at the front, you will see that the batting edges butt against each other.
6. Measure the distance from one raw edge to the other. It should be 1½".
7. Adding ½" for overlapping ¼" on each of the raw edges, the sashing width should be 2" finished.
8. However, if the distance from raw edge to raw edge is more or less than 1½", adjust that amount before the next step.

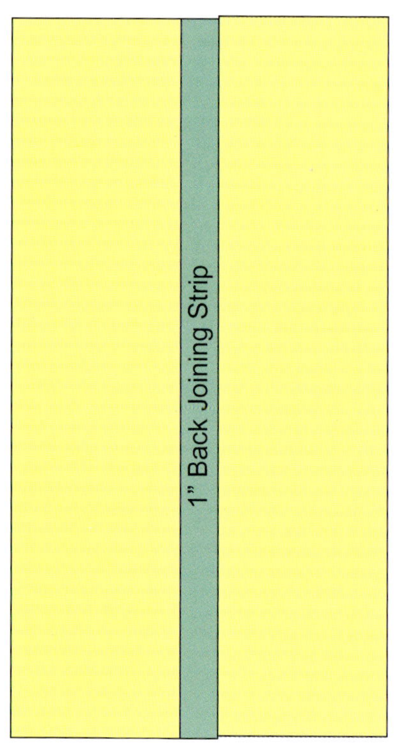

JOINING COLUMNS (BACK)

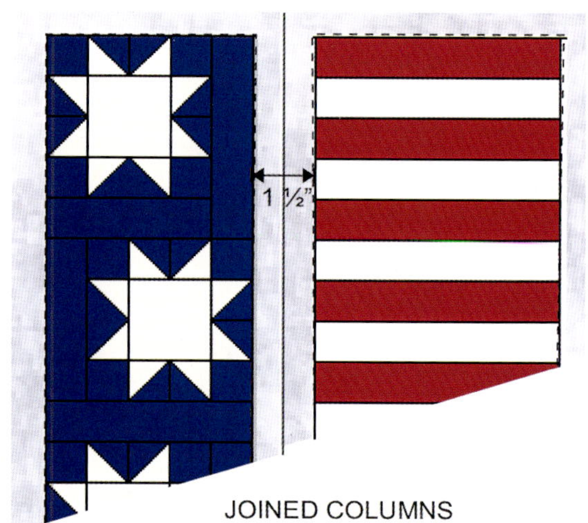

JOINED COLUMNS

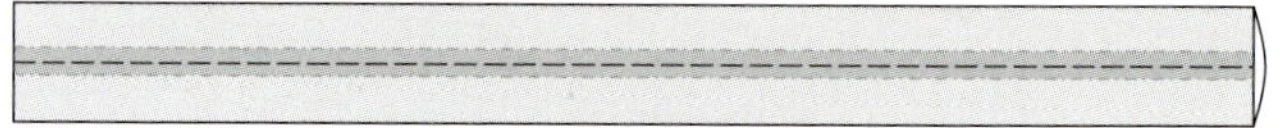
SASHING TUBE

MAKING SASHING TUBES

Cutting

If the distance between the raw edges is 1½":

Cut (9) 4¾" × WOF strips from the reserved white fabric.

- Piece strips end to end, then cut.
- (4) 4¾" × 82½" strips

Why 4¾"?

- (1½" gap + ½" seam allowance overlap) = 2" finished sashing width
- (2" finished sashing × 2 for a tube) + ¾" for seam allowance + folds = 4¾" strips

But what if the distance is more or less than 1½"? Here's the formula:

- Gap between raw edges + ½" overlap = finished sashing width
- (2 × finished sashing width) + ¾ = width of strip to cut for tube

TIP: If you used scraps of white fabric to construct the sashing strips, trim them to the correct width. A good idea is to press the seam allowances open for a smoother sashing.

1. Sew these strips WRONG sides together.
2. Press the tube, roughly centering the seam on one side, with the seam allowance pressed open.

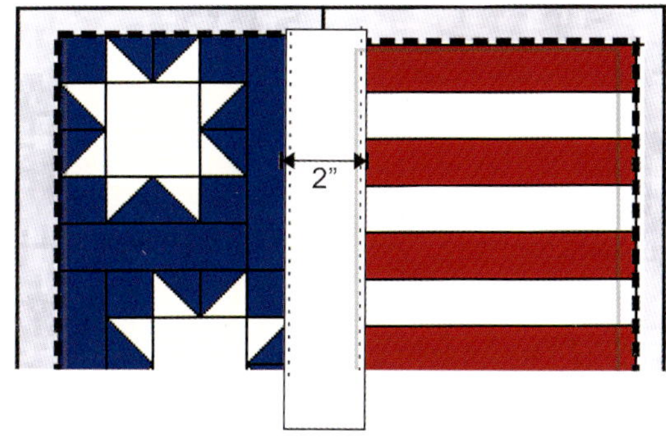

COVERING THE JOINT

ATTACHING THE SASHING TUBES TO THE JOINED COLUMNS

1. Working from the front, press the joint between the first two columns so that it lies flat.
2. Pin the first Sashing Tube as shown in the *Covering the Joint* illustration, centered between the first and second columns. Be sure that the tube covers each column by ¼".
3. Match the top thread in your sewing machine with the sashing.

- Match the bobbin thread with the backing.
- A good idea is to increase the stitch length to about 2.5–3.
- Topstitch very close to the folded edge of the tube for the entire length.

4. Repeat on the other edge of the tube. Quilt the tube, if necessary, generally keeping the amount/density of quilting in the tube the same as in the columns.

CONTINUE ADDING COLUMNS

1. Working from the back, attach another Back Joining Strip to the right edge of the Stripe Column.
2. Add the next Star Column in the same manner.
3. Turn to the front to add the next Sashing Tube.
4. Continue across the quilt, working from the back to join columns and then the front to add the sashing tube.

TIP: Adding columns in this manner keeps the least bulk under the arm of the machine. The quilt "grows" to the left of the needle.

FINISHING THE OUTER EDGE

Trim off the excess batting and backing from the outer edges, flush with the raw edges of the column.

- By machine: Attach folded binding strip to the back edge of the quilt. Fold to the front, press, and topstitch binding in place.
- By hand: attach folded binding strip to the front, fold to the back, and hand-stitch in place.

21-Star Salute

Quilt designed by Tony L. Jacobson • Machine-quilted by Penny Barnes

Quilt Size: 63" × 84" | Finished Block Size: 12"

Salute by cannon or artillery is a military tradition that originated in the fourteenth century. The 21-gun salute is the highest honor rendered. Salute your favorite service person with this 21-star salute quilt. —*Tony*

MATERIALS

- ⅔ yard white print #1
- ½ yard white print #2
- 1⅛ yards blue print #1
- 1⅛ yards red print #1
- ⅞ yard blue print #2
- ⅞ yard red print #2
- 2½ yards background print
- ⅝ yard stripe for binding
- 5⅓ yards for backing

CUTTING

Measurements include ¼" seam allowances.

From white print #1, cut:

- (5) 3⅞" strips. From strips, cut (48) 3⅞" B squares.

From white print #2, cut:

- (4) 3⅞" strips. From strips, cut (36) 3⅞" B squares.

From blue print #1, cut:

- (1) 7¾" strip. From strips, cut (4) 7¾" C squares.
- (2) 7¼" strips. From strips, cut (6) 7¼" A squares.
- (1) 6⅞" strip. From strips, cut (6) 6⅞" D squares.
- (2) 3½" strips. From strips, cut (12) 3½" E squares.

From red print #1, cut:

- (1) 7¾" strip. From strips, cut (4) 7¾" C squares.
- (2) 7¼" strips. From strips, cut (6) 7¼" A squares.
- (1) 6⅞" strip. From strips, cut (6) 6⅞" D squares.
- (2) 3½" strips. From strips, cut (12) 3½" E squares.

From blue print #2, cut:

- (1) 7¾" strip. From strips, cut (3) 7¾" C squares.
- (1) 7¼" strip. From strips, cut (5) 7¼" A squares.
- (1) 6⅞" strip. From strips, cut (5) 6⅞" D squares.
- (1) 3½" strip. From strips, cut (9) 3½" E squares.

From red print #2, cut:

- (1) 7¾" strip. From strips, cut (3) 7¾" C squares.
- (1) 7¼" strip. From strips, cut (5) 7¼" A squares.
- (1) 6⅞" strip. From strips, cut (5) 6⅞" D squares.
- (1) 3½" strip. From strips, cut (9) 3½" E squares.

From background print, cut:

- Cut the following background pieces lengthwise from the background print: (1) 12½" × 84½" F rectangle, (2) 6½" × 84½" G rectangles, and (1) 3½" × 84½" H rectangle.

From binding fabric, cut:

- (8) 2¼" strips

MAKING STAR POINT UNITS

1. On the wrong side of white print #1 B squares, draw a diagonal line from corner to corner. Draw lines ¼" away from each side of the previously drawn line as shown in *Star Point Unit Assembly Diagrams.*

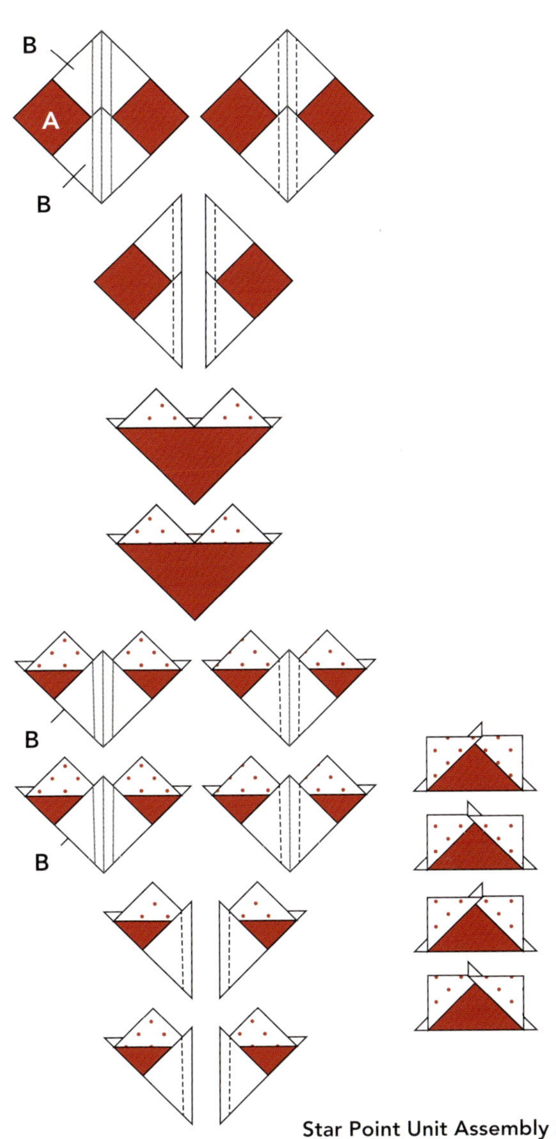

Star Point Unit Assembly Diagrams

2. Place (2) marked B squares on red print #1 A square, right sides together. Stitch on the outer marked lines. Cut on the centerline and press the seams toward the white print #1 triangles as shown.

3. Place (2) marked B squares on the triangle units in step 2 as shown in *Star Point Unit Assembly Diagrams*. Stitch on the outer marked lines.

4. Cut on the centerline and press seams toward white print #1 triangles, as shown, to make four star point units.

5. Repeat steps 1 through 4 to make a total of (24) white print #1 / red print #1 star point units as shown in *Star Point Unit Diagrams*.

6. In the same manner, make (24) white print #1 / blue print #1 star point units, (18) white print #2 / red print #2 star point units, and (18) white print #2 / blue print #2 star point units. You will end up with two extra of each of the #2 star point units.

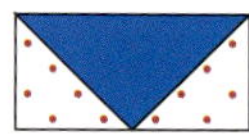

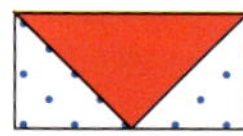

Star Point Unit Diagrams

HALF-SQUARE TRIANGLE UNITS

1. Draw a diagonal line from the upper left corner to the lower right corner and another line from the upper right corner to the lower left corner on the wrong side of the red print #1 C squares, as shown in *Half-Square Triangle Diagrams*.

2. Draw lines ¼" away from each side of the previously drawn lines, as shown in *Half-Square Triangle Diagrams*.

3. Layer a marked red print #1 C square on top of a blue print #1 C square, right sides together; stitch on outer marked lines as shown.

4. Cut stitched squares into four equal sections as shown.

NOTE: The vertical and horizontal center of your square should be 3⅞".

5. Cut on the centerlines to make eight half-square triangle units.

6. Press seam allowances toward the darker fabric. Make a total of (24) red print #1 / blue print #1 half-square triangle units.

7. In the same manner, make (18) red print #2 / blue print #2 half-square triangle units.

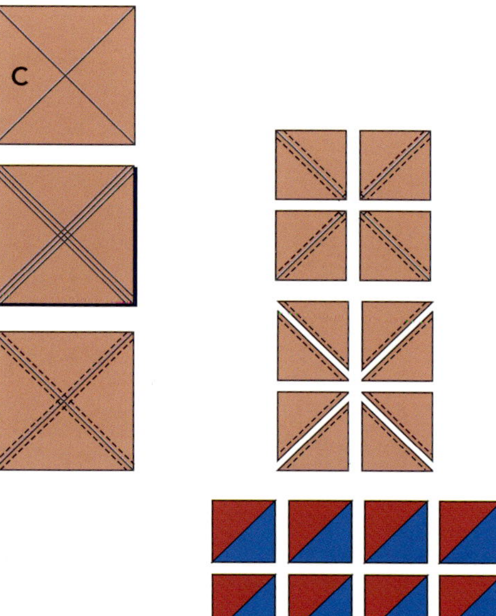

8-at-a-Time Half-Square Triangle Diagrams

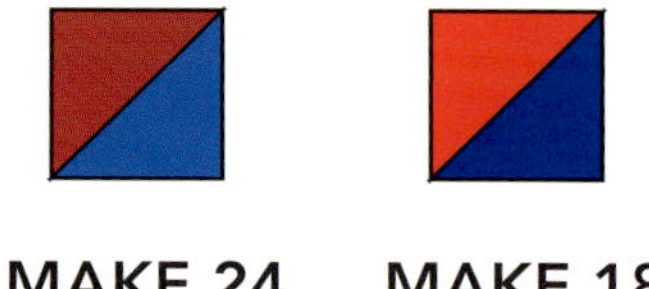

Half-Square Triangle Diagrams

MAKING CENTER HALF-SQUARE TRIANGLE UNITS

1. Draw a diagonal line from the upper left corner to the lower right corner on the wrong side of the red print #1 D squares, as shown in *Center Half-Square Triangle Diagrams*.
2. Draw lines ¼" away from each side of the previously drawn lines, as shown in *Center Half-Square Triangle Diagrams*.
3. Layer a marked red print #1 D square on top of a blue print #1 D square, right sides together; stitch on outer marked lines as shown.
4. Cut on the centerlines to make two center half-square triangle units.
5. Press seam allowances toward the darker fabric. Make a total of (12) red print #1 / blue print #1 center half-square triangle units.
6. In the same manner, make (9) red print #2 / blue print #2 center half-square triangle units.

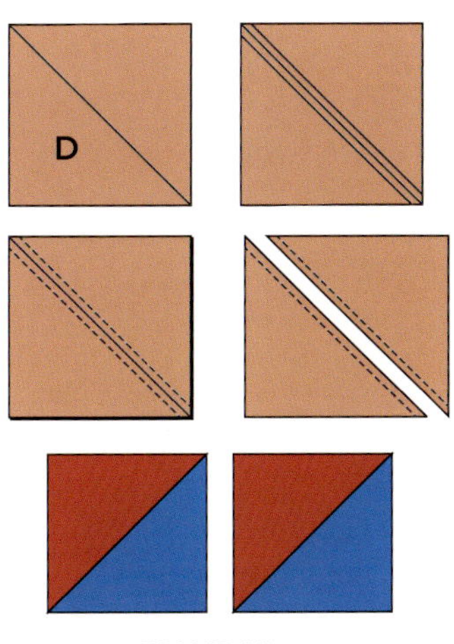

MAKE 12

MAKE 9

Center Half-Square Triangle Unit Diagrams

STAR BLOCK ASSEMBLY

1. Lay out one red print #1 E square, two white print #1 / red print #1 star point units, two white print #1 / blue #1 print star point units, one red print #1 / blue print #1 center half-square triangle, and one blue print #1 E square as shown in *Star Block Diagrams*.
2. Sew units together to create rows. Sew rows together to make star blocks. Make (12) star blocks.
3. In the same manner, make nine red print #2 / blue print #2 star blocks.

MAKE 12

MAKE 9

Star Block Diagrams

QUILT TOP ASSEMBLY

1. Lay out blocks into vertical rows as shown in *Quilt Top Assembly Diagram*.
2. Sew blocks together to create rows.
3. Lay out pieced rows and background strips F, G, and H as shown in *Quilt Top Assembly Diagram*. Sew rows and strips together vertically to complete the quilt top.

FINISHING

1. Divide backing into (2) 96" length panels. Join panels vertically.
2. Layer backing, batting, and quilt top; baste. Quilt as desired.
3. Join 2¼" wide binding strips into one continuous piece for double-fold binding. Add binding to quilt.

Quilt Top Assembly Diagram

Wrapped in a Quilt

Quilt designed by Heidi Kaisand • Machine-quilted by Emily Keller

Quilt Size: 67" × 84½" | Finished Block Size: 12"

Use a favorite patriotic fabric as the focal point of this quilt adapted from Heidi's Pigs in a Blanket Quilt design.—*Heidi*

MATERIALS

- 3¾ yards of patriotic print
- ⅔ yard of red print
- 1½ yards of navy print
- 1⅛ yards of white solid
- 76" × 95" of quilt batting
- 5⅓ yards of backing fabric

CUTTING

Measurements include ¼" seam allowances.

From patriotic print, cut:

- (2) 18¼" strips. From strips, cut (4) 18½" B squares. Cut each square diagonally twice with an "X" to create a total of 14 setting triangles.
- (1) 9⅜" strip. From strip, cut (2) 9⅜" C squares. Cut each square diagonally to create a total of 4 corner triangles.
- (4) 12½" strips. From strips, cut:
  (12) 12½" A squares
- (7) 4½" strips. Use strips for strip sets.

From red print, cut:

- (7) 2½" strips for strip sets.

From navy print, cut:

- (7) 2½" strips for strip sets.

From white solid, cut:

- (14) 2½" strips for strip sets.

STRIPS SET BLOCKS

1. Assemble a 4½" patriotic print strip, (1) 2½" red print strip, (1) 2½" navy print strip, and (2) 2½" white solid strips as shown in *Strip Set Diagram*. Sew strips together to create strip set. Create (7) strip sets.
2. Cut strip sets into (20) 12½" segments.

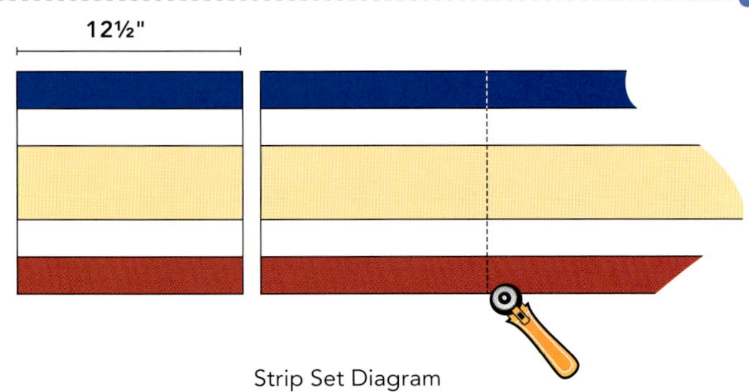

Strip Set Diagram

QUILT TOP ASSEMBLY

1. Lay out patriotic print A squares, strip set blocks, patriotic print setting triangles, and patriotic print corner triangles as shown in *Quilt Top Assembly Diagram*.
2. Sew blocks together diagonally to create rows.
3. Sew rows together to complete the quilt top.

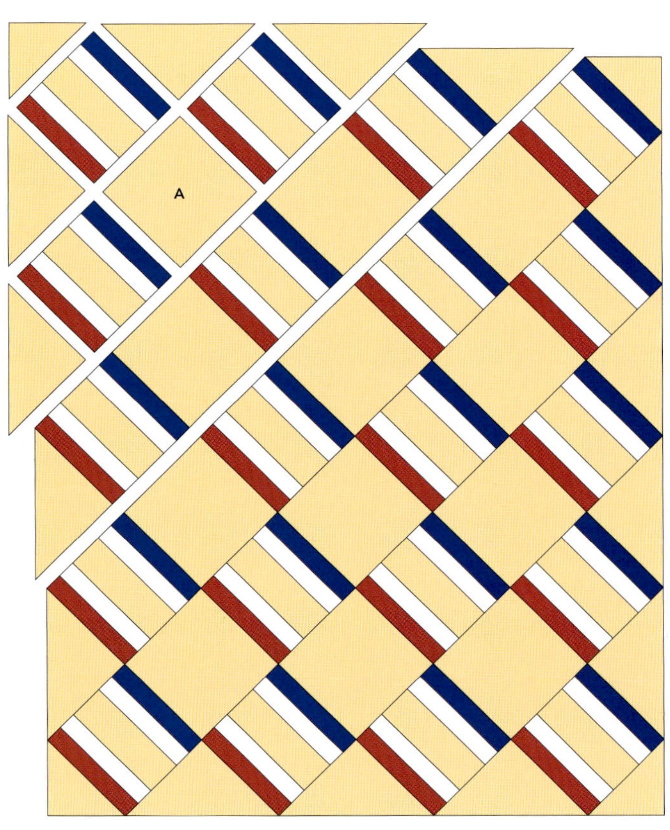

Quilt Top Assembly Diagram

FINISHING

1. Divide backing into two 96" length panels. Join panels vertically.
2. Layer backing, batting, and quilt top; baste. Quilt as desired.
3. Join 2½" wide binding strips into one continuous piece for double-fold binding. Add binding to quilt.

Stars in My Eyes

Quilt designed by Mary W. Kerr • Machine-quilted by Lynn Small O'Neal

Quilt Size: 65" × 65" | Finished Block Size: 13"

As a military wife, I have often been reduced to tears when the flag parades by and our service members honor the colors. There is something magical that happens when patriots come together to celebrate our country. Stars in My Eyes reflects my tears and our proud military traditions. Thank you to all who serve. *—Mary*

MATERIALS

2⅛ yards navy print

2⅛ yards red print

2 yards white print

⅝ yard binding print

4¼ yards for backing

CUTTING

Measurements include ¼" seam allowances.

From navy print, cut:

- (13) 4½" strips. From strips, cut:
  (50) 4½" × 5½" C rectangles and (45) 4½" E squares
- (1) 5⅞" strip. From strip, cut:
  (3) 5⅞" A squares
- (1) 4⅞" strip. From strip, cut:
  (5) 4⅞" B squares

From red print, cut:

- (13) 4½" strips. From strips, cut:
  (50) 4½" × 5½" C rectangles and (45) 4½" E squares
- (1) 5⅞" strip. From strip, cut:
  (3) 5⅞" A squares
- (1) 4⅞" strip. From strip, cut:
  (5) 4⅞" B squares

From white solid, cut:

- (3) 5½" strips. From strips, cut:
  (20) 5½" F squares
- (16) 3" strips. From strips, cut:
  (200) 3" E squares

From binding print, cut:

- (8) 2¼" strips for binding

MAKING TRIANGLE-SQUARE UNITS

1. Draw a diagonal line from the upper left corner to the lower right corner on the wrong side of the red print A squares, as shown in *Triangle-Square Unit Diagrams.*
2. Draw lines ¼" away from each side of the previously drawn line, as shown in *Triangle-Square Unit Diagrams.*
3. Layer a marked red print A square on top of a navy print A square, right sides together; stitch on outer marked lines as shown.
4. Cut on the centerlines to make two triangle-square units.
5. Press seam allowances toward the darker fabric. Make a total of five red print / navy print center triangle-square units.
6. In the same manner, use red print and navy print B squares to make corner triangle-square units. Make a total of 10 red print / navy print corner triangle-square units.

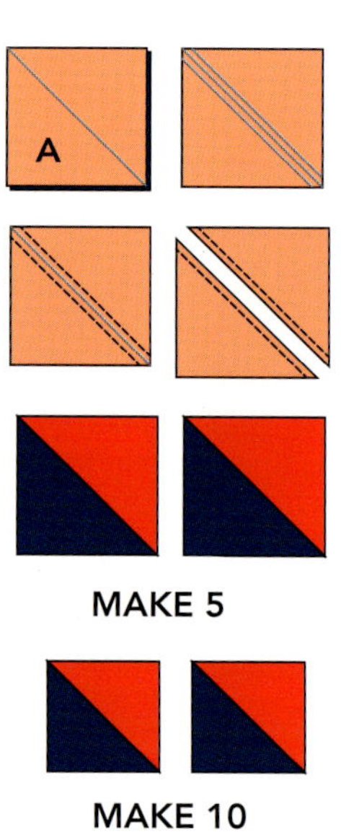

Half-Square Triangle Unit Diagrams

MAKING STAR POINT UNITS

1. Draw a diagonal line from the upper left corner to the lower right corner on the wrong side of the white print D squares, as shown in *Star Point Unit Diagrams*.
2. Lay 1 white print D square atop one red print C rectangle on the 5½" side, with right sides together, as shown in *Star Point Unit Diagrams*.
3. Stitch on drawn line. Trim ¼" from the stitched line as shown in *Star Point Unit Diagrams*.
4. Press corner triangle open as shown.
5. Repeat steps 1 through 4 on the adjacent corner of the star point unit to complete one star point unit. Make 50 red print star point units.
6. In the same manner using navy print C rectangles, make 50 navy print star point units.

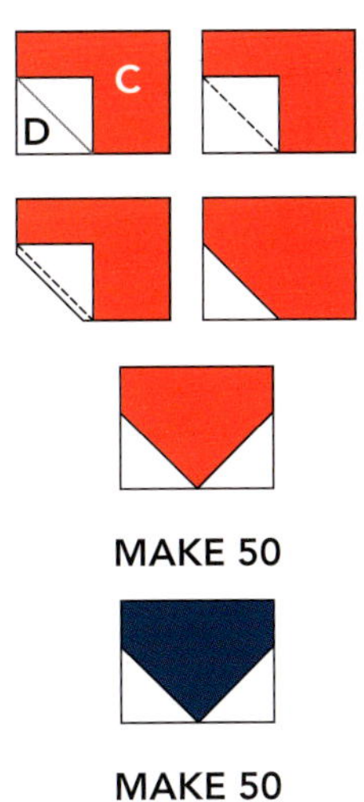

Star Point Unit Diagrams

STAR BLOCK #1 ASSEMBLY

1. Lay out four red print E squares, four red print star point units, and one white solid F square as shown in the *Star Block #1 Diagrams*.
2. Assemble the units into rows; sew rows together to complete one red print star block #1. Make 10 red print star blocks #1.
3. In the same manner, lay out four navy print E squares, four navy print star point units, and one white solid F square to make one navy print star block #1. Make 10 navy print star blocks #1.

STAR BLOCK #2 ASSEMBLY

1. Lay out two red print / navy print corner triangle units, two red print star point units, two navy print star point units, and one red print / navy print center triangle-square unit as shown in the *Star Block #2 Diagrams*.
2. Assemble the units into rows; sew rows together to complete one star block #2. Make five star blocks #2.

Star Block #1 Diagrams

Star Block #2 Diagrams

QUILT TOP ASSEMBLY

1. Lay out star blocks as shown in the *Quilt Top Assembly Diagram*.
2. Sew blocks together to create rows.
3. Sew rows together to complete the quilt top.

FINISHING

1. Divide backing into (2) 76½" length panels. Join panels vertically.
2. Layer backing, batting, and quilt top; baste. Quilt as desired.
3. Join 2¼" wide binding strips into (1) continuous piece for double-fold binding. Add binding to quilt.

Quilt Top Assembly Diagram

Compatriots

Quilt designed and made by Robin Koehler • Quilted by Barbara Manning

Quilt Size: 80½" Square | Finished Block Size: 20" Square

It has been my honor to be a part of this project to pay tribute to the men, women, and children who sacrifice more than we know to serve our country. My history is that of a military child, joining the Coast Guard myself out of high school, marrying, and becoming a military spouse who raised two lovely military children. There is risk and reward and adventure and hardship with this life, and I wouldn't change a moment because being a part of something bigger is what is needed of us all. —*Robin*

FABRIC

Note: All fabric requirements are based on 42" usable width
WOF means width of fabric
HSTs are half-square triangles
RST means right sides together

- 7/8 yard red #1
- 3/4 yard red #2 (for appliqué)
- 7/8 yard blue #1
- 1 1/4 yard blue #2 (for appliqué)
- 1 2/3 yards cream #1
- 1/2 yard cream #2 (for appliqué)
- 1 yard cream #3
- 2 1/2 yards for border
- 3/4 yard for binding
- 2 1/2 yards of 108" wide or 7 1/2 yards 42"–44" wide pieced for backing
- 90" × 90" batting

ADDITIONAL MATERIALS

- Fusible web: 4 yards (yardage based on 17" width)
- Basic sewing supplies, including rotary cutter and 6" × 24" ruler with 45-degree markings
- Scissors for fabric and paper cutting
- Threads to match fabrics
- Pencils for tracing appliqué shapes and marking vines to background
- Spray starch or substitute (Mary Ellen's Best Press™)
- Glue for basting (Roxanne Glue Baste-It™)
- Bias tape maker for 1/4" tape (Clover)
- Quilter's Rule™ Quick Quarter II 12" Ruler

CUTTING

From red #1, cut:

- (4) 6" × WOF strips

  Subcut these into (22) 6" squares.

  Subcut (16) of these 6" squares once on the diagonal for (32) triangles.

From blue #1, cut:

- (4) 6" × WOF strips

  Subcut these into (22) 6" squares.

  Subcut (16) of these 6" squares once on the diagonal for (32) triangles.

From blue #2, cut:

- (1) 18" square

From cream #1, cut:

- (2) 14 1/2" × WOF strips

  Subcut (4) 14 1/2" background squares.

  Set aside remainder of strips for star appliqué.

- (2) 6" × WOF strips

  Subcut (12) 6" squares.

- (2) 5 1/2" × WOF strips

  Subcut (8) 5 1/2" squares.

From cream #3, cut:

- (2) 14 1/2" × WOF strips

  Subcut (4) 14 1/2" background squares.

From border fabric, cut:

- (4) 20 1/2" × 40 1/2" rectangles

From binding, cut:

- (9) 2 1/2" × WOF strips for miter-sewn, continuous folded binding

Note: The rest of the fabrics are for appliqué and will be addressed in that section.

ASSEMBLING THE BLOCKS

TIP: All seams are sewn with a scant ¼" seam allowance.

Half-Square Triangles

1. Use spray starch or starch substitute at each pressing step to help keep bias edges sharp.
2. Referring to *Making Half-Square Triangles* illustration, draw a diagonal line on the wrong side of a 6" cream #1 square.
3. Draw another line ¼" to either side of the center line.
4. Place 6" red #1 square RST.
5. Sew on each dashed sew line.
6. Press, then cut apart on drawn cut line.
7. Press open and trim to 5½" square.
8. Sew remaining (5) 6" red #1 squares to (5) 6" cream #1 squares to make (12) Red+Cream HSTs, as shown in *Red+Cream HSTs* illustration.
9. Repeat with (6) cream #1 and (6) blue #1 6" squares to make (12) Blue+Cream HSTs, as shown in *Blue+Cream HSTs* illustration.

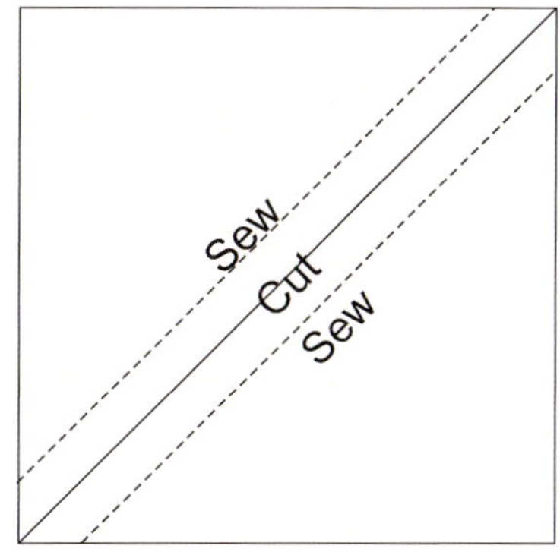

MAKING HALF-SQUARE TRIANGLES

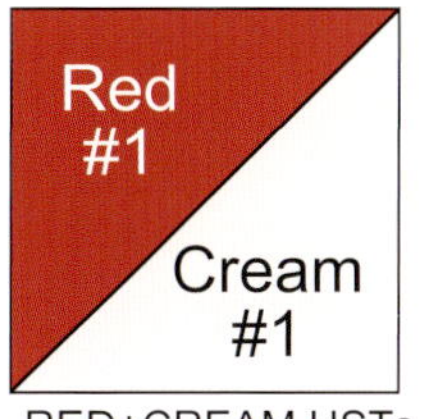

RED+CREAM HSTs

BLUE+CREAM HSTs

SETTING TRIANGLE UNITS

TIP: Trim all Setting Triangle Units A, B, C, and D so that there is a ¼" seam allowance as shown in the circled area of each diagram.

Unit A

1. Orient a Blue+Cream HST as shown in *Unit A* illustration.
2. Sew 6" red #1 triangles to the right of and beneath the HST by aligning outer edges and stitching toward the middle (note arrows).
3. Press seam allowance toward the red triangles.
4. Make (12) Unit A.

Unit B

1. Orient a Red+Cream HST as shown in *Unit B* illustration.
2. Sew 6" Blue #1 triangles to the right and beneath the HST by aligning outer edges and stitching toward the middle (note arrows).
3. Press seam allowance toward the blue triangles.
4. Make (12) Unit B.

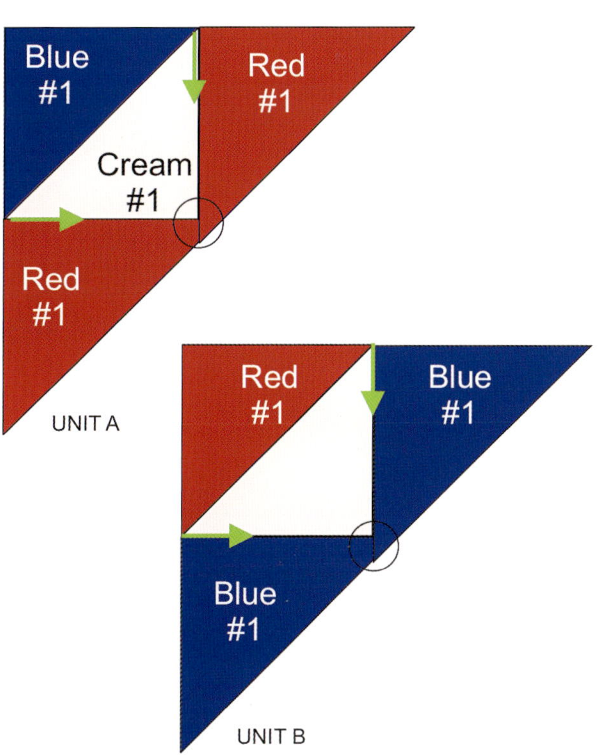

UNIT A

UNIT B

Unit C

1. Repeat Setting Triangle steps to sew remaining red #1 triangles to 5½" cream #1 squares, as shown in illustration *Unit C*.
2. Make (4)

Unit D

1. Repeat Setting Triangle steps to sew remaining blue #1 triangles to 5½" cream #1 squares, as shown in *Unit D* illustration.
2. Make (4)

Square-in-a-Square Assembly

TIP: Fold each 14½" center square right sides together in both directions, and gently finger-crease to find centers for setting triangle alignment.

Square 1

1. Center then sew (1) Unit A and (1) Unit C setting triangles to opposite sides of a 14½" cream #3 square as shown in *Square 1 – Step 1* illustration.
2. Press seam allowance toward the square.
3. Center then sew (2) Unit A to remaining sides of cream #3 square, as shown in *Square 1 – Step 2* illustration.
4. Press seam allowance toward the square.
5. Trim to 20½" square, being sure to leave ¼" seam allowance beyond cream square corners, as shown.
6. Make (4) Square 1 Units.

Square 2

1. Repeat process to sew (3) Unit B and (1) Unit D setting triangles to all four sides of a 14½" cream #1 Square.
2. Press seam allowance toward the square.
3. Trim to 20½" square, being sure to leave ¼" seam allowance beyond cream square corners.
4. Make (4) Square 2 Units.

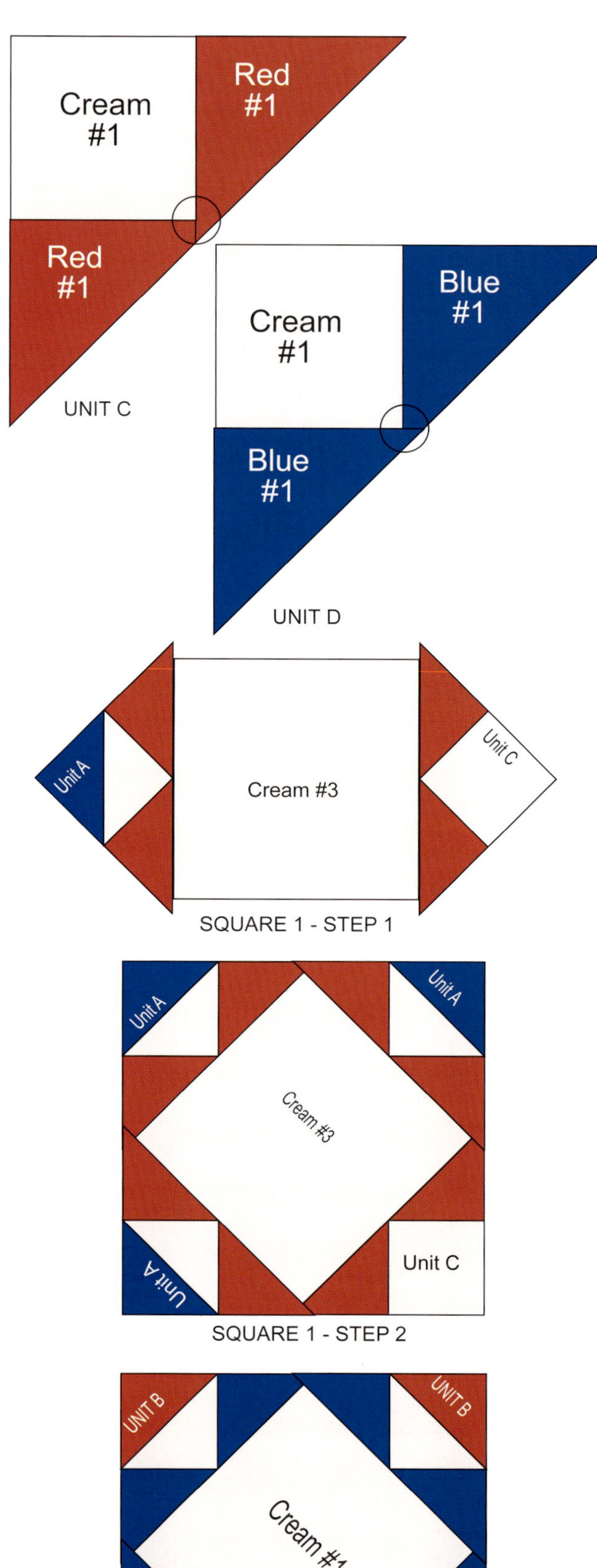

APPLIQUÉ

1. Trace appliqué templates onto the paper side of fusible web.
2. Cut templates out approximately ⅛" beyond the traced line of the designs.
3. Following manufacturer instructions, fuse templates to the wrong side of fabrics, and cut out ON THE TRACED LINES.

TIP: Sometimes, allowing the fusible web to cool for at least an hour really helps with the paper release.

Use a straight pin to score the paper backing in the center of the appliqué piece. Peel paper from this point to avoid fraying your edges.

Petals

Refer to *Petals Diagram*. Trace each petal separately. You will need:

- (16) red #2
- (16) blue #2

Stars

Refer to *Stars Diagram*. Trace each star separately. You will need:

- (4) Large Stars in blue #2
- (4) Medium Stars in red #2
- (8) Small Stars in cream #1
- (16) Small Stars in cream #2

Note: The *asterisks on the Large Star are for vine alignment.

CUTTING BIAS TAPE

Bias Tape

1. Referring to *Cutting Bias Tape* illustration, make a diagonal cut across 18" blue #2 square.
2. Layer triangles RST.
3. Make cuts ½" apart to make (16) strips approximately 25" long.
4. Follow instructions on bias tape maker to make ¼" bias tape vines.

TIP: Spray each strip well with starch or starch substitute. Put strip through the tape maker while still damp for crisp edges that won't open.

5. Trim each vine to 17" long, which allows for a bit extra when applying vines to the background.

Applying Vines

TIP: Fold border 20½" × 40½" rectangles in half in both directions and gently crease to find centers

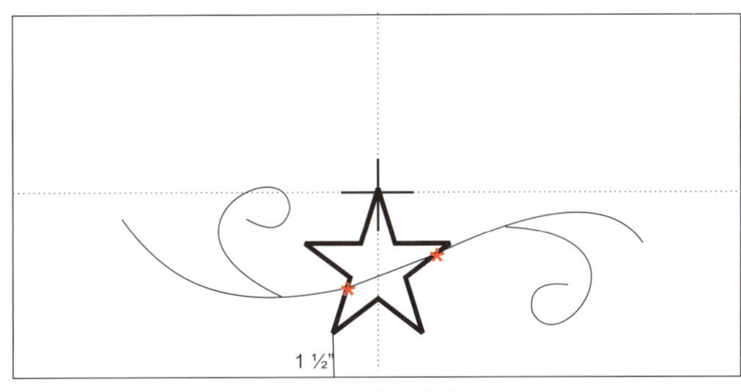

APPLYING VINES

Note: Small arrow on *Applying Vines* illustration marks the placement of Large blue #2 star 1½" in from bottom edge and centered on the border. Pin star to background to trace vine placement to all borders. Trace an extra set of vines for more exact placement to create the effect of vine going through the star.

1. Use *Vine Diagram* to Mark vine on all four borders.
2. Starting with a Curl Vine and working in 1"–2" increments, lay a fine (beaded) line of basting glue along traced line. Gently press bias vine along glue line.
3. When working tight curves, work in shorter increments so that the curve can be worked smoothly. Do not pull the vine too tightly as the bias will then draw up the background fabric once in place.
4. Glue all eight Curl Vines in place.
5. Repeat the process to glue all eight long vines in place, covering the end of the Curl Vine in the process.
6. Leave at least ½" excess vine at either end so you won't be short when placing stars.
7. Vines can now be stitched by hand or machine.
8. The exposed Curl Vine end can be machine-stitched over or tucked in if stitching by hand.

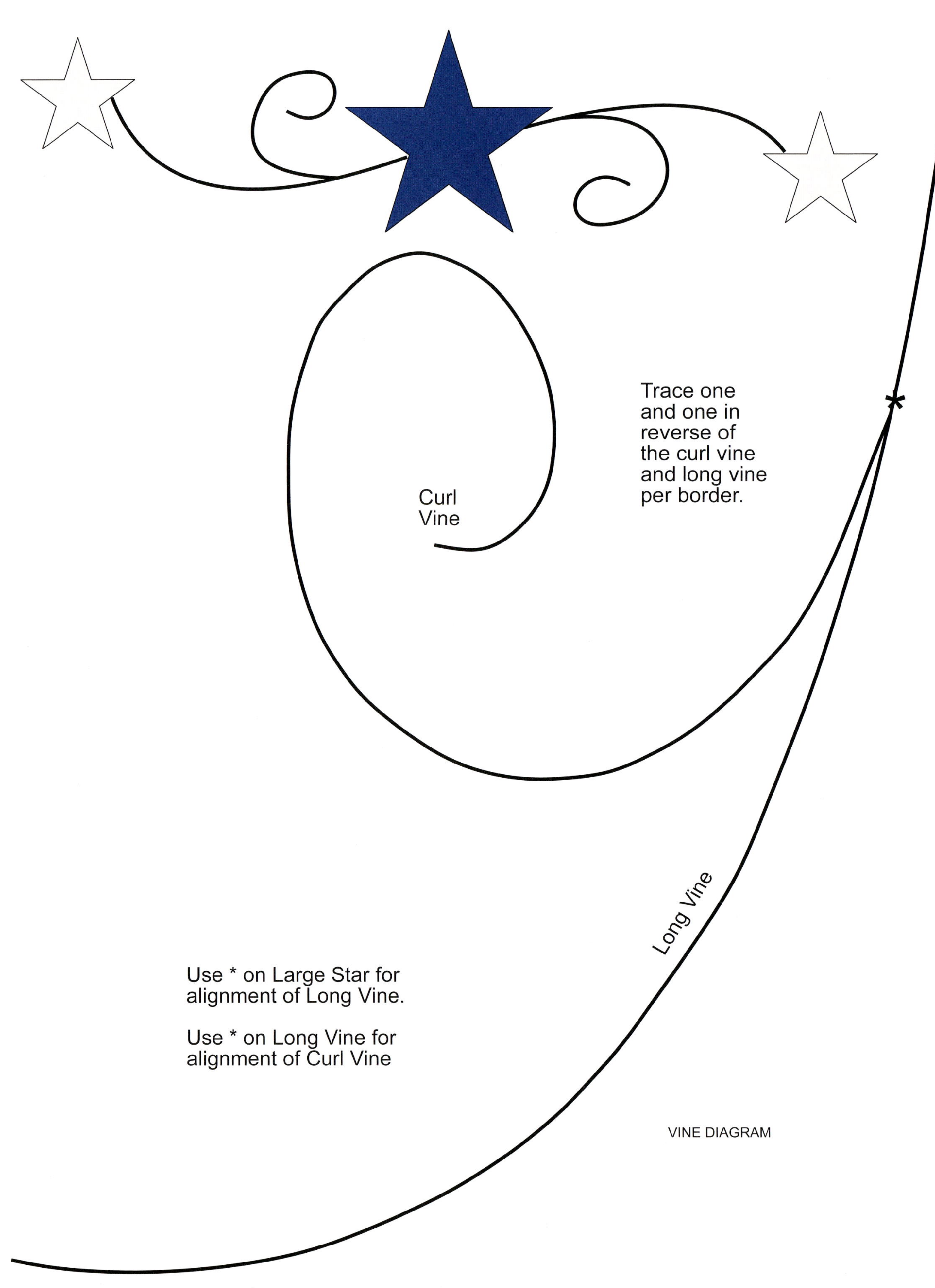
Trace one
and one in
reverse of
the curl vine
and long vine
per border.
Curl
Vine
Long Vine
Use * on Large Star for
alignment of Long Vine.
Use * on Long Vine for
alignment of Curl Vine
VINE DIAGRAM

Appliqué Finishing

Note: Once vines are stitched in place, fuse stars over vine ends as shown in illustration *Appliqué Border Star Placement.*

1. Center red #2 Star 1½" from upper border edge and fuse.
2. Cream #1 Stars are aligned with side and bottom red Star points.
3. Blue #2 Star is 1½" up from bottom edge.
4. Cream #2 Stars are fused to the end of the vines with right star placed ¾" from bottom edge.
5. Petals are centered and fused onto 20½" blocks as shown in *Petal and Star Placement* illustration. Then, a cream #2 Star is fused to centers.

Note: Fuse stars AFTER quilt assembly to keep all facing same direction, then stitch down.

6. Use the block placement of cream #1 squares for directionality of Star Blocks.
7. Red petals are set against the blue, Unit B/D, setting triangles of Square 2.
8. Blue petals are set against the red Unit A/C, setting triangles of Square 1.
9. Make four of each colorway.
10. Stitch fused edges down by using an adjusted blind hem or zigzag stitch in threads to match appliqué fabrics.

APPLIQUE BORDER STAR PLACEMENT

PETAL AND STAR PLACEMENT

TIP: Set zigzag stitches approximately ⅛" in width and length for fusible appliqué.

ASSEMBLING THE QUILT

1. Pin at all seam intersections during assembly.
2. Sew (2) red petal blocks and (2) blue petal blocks together, as shown in *Quilt Assembly* illustration, for center.
3. Note placement of the solid corner square to the outer corners.
4. Press top blocks to the right and bottom blocks to the left for nesting final seam.
5. Once the four-block center is sewn, sew a border to the right and left, noting direction of stars.
6. Press seam allowances toward the borders.
7. Sew a red petal block and a blue petal block to each end of a border rectangle, noting the placement of solid corner square.
8. Press seam allowances toward the border rectangle.
9. Make (2).
10. Sew one to the top of the quilt center, again paying attention to the solid corner placement.
11. Rotate the second border and sew to the bottom of the quilt center.
12. Press seam allowances toward the borders.

QUILT ASSEMBLY

FINISHING AND QUILTING

TIP: If you are quilting this yourself, here are some suggestions:

- Baste well.
- Stitch in the ditch all vertical and horizontal seams to stabilize the quilt well.
- Outline all appliqué. Use the stitching of appliqué edges as quilting.

BINDING

- Use the 2½" strips cut at the beginning to make continuous folded binding.

TIPS: Remember to label and date your work!
Create a wonderful, oversized accent pillow by making one large block with the leftover scraps.

STARS
1"

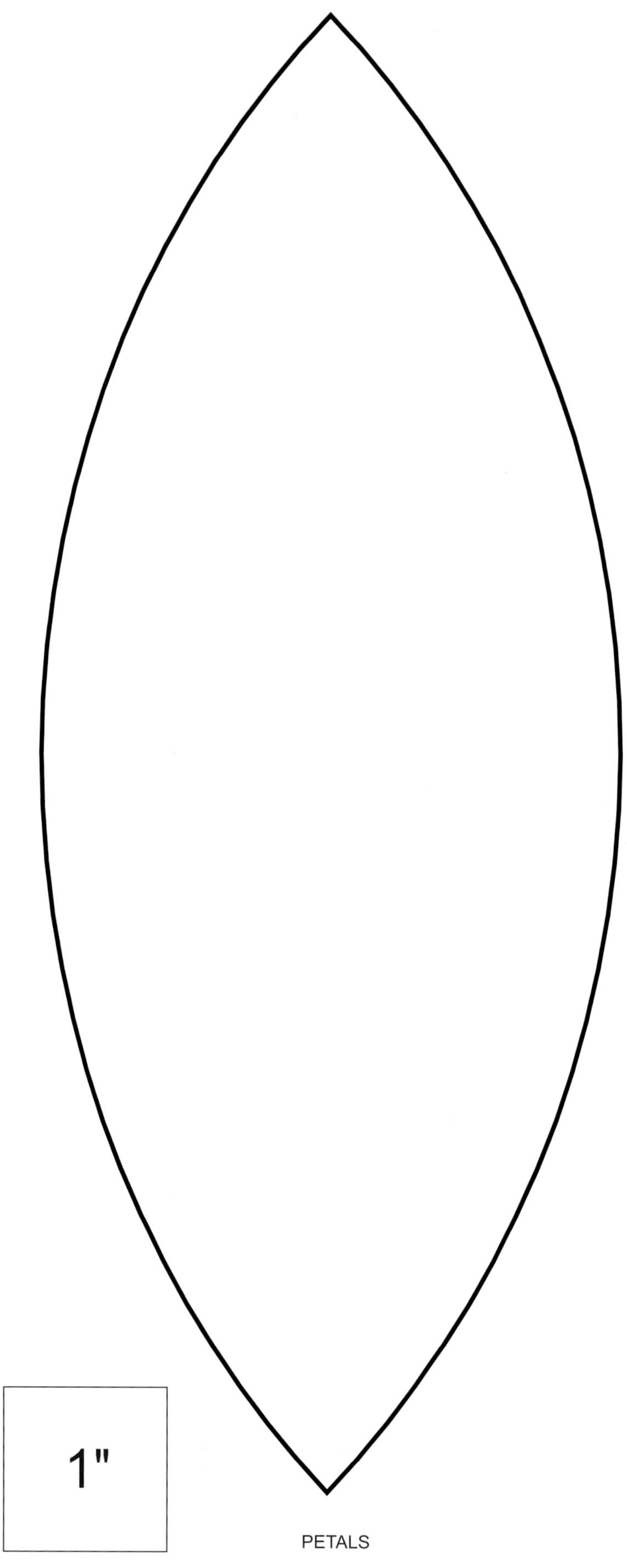
1"
PETALS

The Patriot

Designed, pieced, and quilted by Andrew Lee, the "Combat Quilter"

Finished Size: 70" × 86" with 3" border

Making this quilt is a great way to use up lots of scraps while creating a quilt that a veteran will love. As a veteran myself with twenty years in the military, including three combat deployments, I get to use my creativity to make something that also makes a difference to other veterans. —*Andrew*

MATERIALS

1 yard for border

¾ yard for binding

5½ yards backing

78" × 94" batting

USING SCRAPS

Various red, blue, and white/tan/cream/beige fabrics are all you need for this quilt. A good way to start is to go through all your fabrics that fall into these color ranges and begin to cut. "Red" might include brown, copper, rust, and dark gold. "Blue" might include light, medium, and dark shades. The light background creates the contrast with the darker colors. For the quilt, you will need:

Patch Size	Dark	Light
2½" × 2½"	200	580
4½" × 4½"	37	60
8½" × 8½"	2	5
2½" × 4½"	64	68
4½" × 8½"	4	8

USING FAT QUARTERS (APPROX. 18" × 20")

Select an assortment of red, blue, and white fat quarters. For the quilt, you will need approximately:

- 10 Dark (including reds and blues)
- 20 Light (white, tan, cream, beige)

After cutting the patches, begin making blocks. You will make a combination of Light Stars on a Dark background, and Dark Stars on a Light background. Notice that the (3) 16" Star Blocks feature large centers that are red, white, and blue.

SUMMARY OF STAR BLOCKS AND FILLER BLOCKS

Star Blocks

Choose Red+Light and Blue+Light for the Star Blocks. You will need:

- (33) 8" finished-size Star Blocks:
  - (17) Dark Star / Light Background
  - (16) Light Star / Dark Background
- (3) 16" finished-size Star Blocks:
  - (2) Dark Star / Light Background
  - (1) Light Star / Dark Background

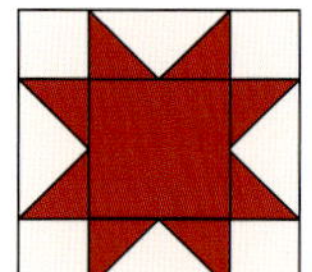

8" FINISHED SIZE STAR BLOCKS

Filler Blocks

Choose Light fabrics for the filler blocks. You will need:

- (35) 8" Filler Blocks:
  - (7) made from 2x2 array of 4½" squares
  - (24) made from 4x4 array of 2½" squares
  - (4) made from single 8½" squares

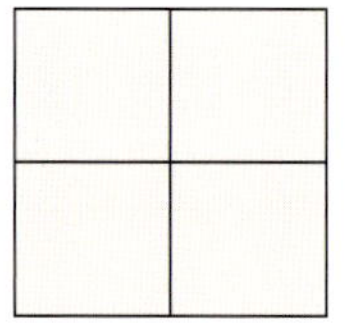

FILLER BLOCKS

CUTTING AND ORGANIZING

Border

1. From border fabric, cut (8) 3½" × WOF strips.
2. Attach end to end and set aside.

Binding

1. From binding fabric, cut (9) 2½" × WOF strips.
2. Attach end to end with diagonal seam.
3. Press in half lengthways and set aside.

8" finished-size Star Blocks

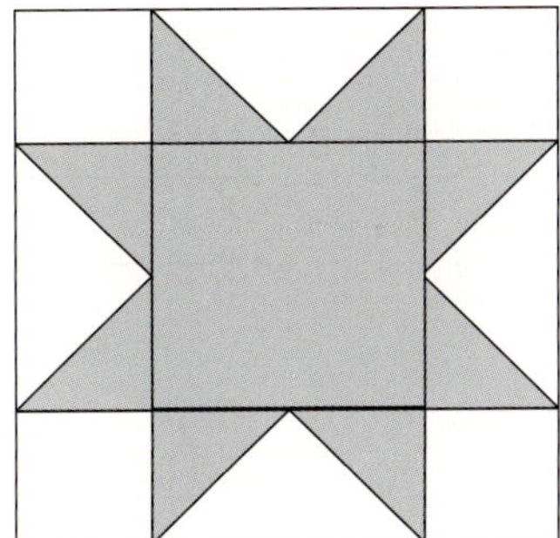
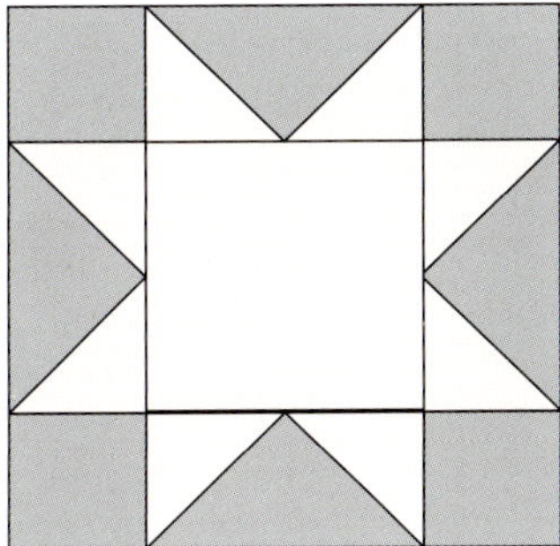

STAR BLOCKS

- For (17) Dark Star / Light Background Blocks, cut:
  - (17) 4½" squares Dark (for Star Center)
  - (136) 2½" × 2½" squares Dark (for Flying Goose / Star Points)
  - (68) 2½" × 4½" rectangles Light (for Flying Goose / Background)
  - (68) 2½" squares Light (for Corners)
- For (16) Light Star / Dark Background Blocks, cut:
  - (16) 4½" squares Light (for Star Center)
  - (128) 2½" × 2½" squares Light (for Flying Goose / Star Points)
  - (64) 2½" × 4½" rectangles Dark (for Flying Goose / Background)
  - (64) 2½" squares Dark (for Corners)

16" Star Blocks

- For (2) Dark Star / Light Background Blocks, cut:
  - (2) 8½" squares Dark (for Star Center)
  - (16) 4½" squares Dark (for Flying Goose / Star Points)
  - (8) 4½" × 8½" rectangles Light (for Flying Goose / Background)
  - (8) 4½" squares Light (for Corners)
- For (1) Light Star / Dark Background Blocks, cut:
  - (1) 8½" square Light (for Star Center)
  - (8) 4½" squares Light (for Flying Goose / Star Points)
  - (4) 4½" × 8½" rectangles Dark (for Flying Goose / Background)
  - (4) 4½" squares Dark (for Corners)

Filler Blocks

- For (24) 8" Filler Blocks, cut:
  - (384) 2½" squares
  - (28) 4½" squares
  - (4) 8½" squares

MAKING THE STAR BLOCKS

Flying Goose / Star Point Units

All the Star Blocks are made in the same manner, whether they are 8" finished size or 16" finished size. Refer to *Flying Goose / Star Points* illustration.

1. Place a square at the left end of the rectangle, right sides together.
2. Sew a diagonal seam from corner to corner.
3. Trim the outer corner, leaving ¼" seam allowance.
4. Press seam allowance open.
5. Add another square to the right end of rectangle.
6. Sew diagonal seam corner to corner, crossing the first seam.
7. Trim outer corner, leaving ¼" seam allowance.
8. Press seam allowance open.

- Make (68) 8" Dark Star Points / Light Background units.
- Make (64) 8" Light Star Points / Dark Background units.
- Make (8) 16" Dark Star Points / Light Background units.
- Make (4) 16" Light Star Points / Dark Background units.

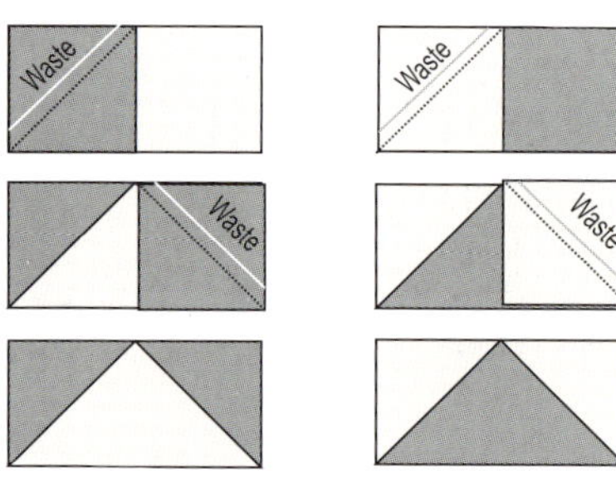

FLYING GOOSE / STAR POINTS

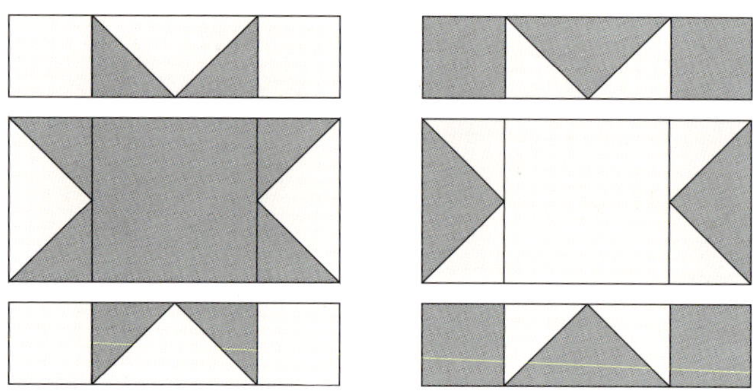

Assembling the Star Blocks

- Assemble the block as shown in *Assembling the Star Blocks* illustration.
- All of the Star Blocks are assembled in the same manner to produce the Dark Star / Light Background or Light Star / Dark Background Blocks.

 1. Attach corner squares to each side of Flying Goose unit.
 2. Press seam allowances toward corners.
 3. Attach Flying Goose units to each side of center square, making sure that the "points" are in the correct position.
 4. Press seam allowances toward center square.
 5. Attach the rows together to make the block, nesting the seams, and again making sure that the "points" are correct.

- The blocks should measure 8½" square unfinished or 16½" square unfinished.

ASSEMBLING THE QUILT

- After you have made all the 8" Star Blocks, the 16" Star Blocks, and the 8" Filler Blocks, you are ready to assemble the quilt. Refer to the *Quilt Assembly Diagram* for attaching the blocks into rows.
- Notice that the odd rows consist of 8" finished size blocks attached in rows.
- The even rows will have two partial rows of 8" blocks attached to a 16" block.

Adding the Borders

1. Measure through the center of the top from top to bottom to get the length for the side borders.
2. Cut (2) Left/Right border strips to this length and attach to the sides.
3. Measure through center from left to right, including the borders you just added.
4. Cut (2) Top/Bottom border strips to this length and attach.

Finishing

- Layer top, batting, and backing.
- Quilt as desired.
- Add binding.
- Remember to label your quilt.

QUILT ASSEMBLY DIAGRAM

Stars and Stripes

Quilt designed by Mark Lipinski • Machine-quilted by Kathleen Mitchell

Quilt Size: 67" × 81" | Finished Block Size: 7"

Mark rates this quilt as "challenging" because of the curved piecing. However, the blocks are pretty large and are doable by a quilter with some experience. Notice how he used a wonderful stripe fabric in the outer borders and a diagonal print for the binding. This makes the binding look like it was cut on the bias. Make a scrappy version by using red, white, and cream scraps from your stash.—*Mark*

MATERIALS

- 1⅜ yards navy print
- 1½ yards red print
- 2¼ yards cream print #1
- ⅝ yard brown print
- 1½ yards navy stripe print
- ¼ yard cream print #2
- ⅝ yard diagonal stripe for binding
- 5 yards for backing

CUTTING

Measurements include ¼" seam allowances.

From navy print, cut:

- (2) 7½" strips. From strips, cut (10) 7½" F squares.
- (12) 2¼" strip. From strip, cut (92) 2¼" B squares and (60) 2¼"× 4" A rectangles.

From red print, cut:

- (6) 5½" strips. From strips, cut (38) E quarter circles (use the template on page 68).
- (2) 4" strips. From strip, cut (19) 4" C squares.

From cream print #1, cut:

- (7) 7½" strips. From strips, cut (38) D backgrounds (use the template on page 68).
- (1) 4" strip. From strip, cut (16) 2¼" × 4" A rectangles.
- (7) 2¼" strip. From strip, cut (120) 2¼" B squares.

From brown print, cut:

- (6) 2½" strips. Piece strips together to make (2) 2½" × 63½" outer side borders and (2) 2½" × 53½" outer top and bottom borders.

From navy stripe print, cut:

- (7) 7½" strips. Piece strips together to make (2) 7½" × 67½" outer side borders and (2) 7½" × 53½" outer top and bottom borders.

From cream print #2, cut:

- (3) 2¼" strips. From strips, cut (16) 2¼" B squares and (16) 2¼"× 4" A rectangles.

From diagonal stripe, cut:

- (8) 2¼" strips for binding.

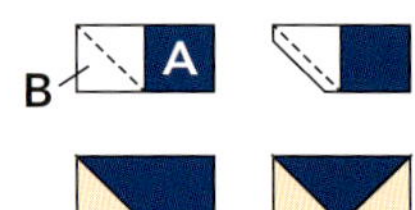

Star Point Assembly Diagrams

Star Point Diagrams

STAR POINT UNIT ASSEMBLY

1. Draw a diagonal line from the upper left corner to the lower right corner on the wrong side of the cream print #1 B squares as shown in *Star Point Assembly Diagrams*.
2. Layer a marked cream print #1 B square on top of a navy print A rectangle, right sides together; stitch on marked line as shown.
3. Trim ¼" away from stitched line. Press seam allowance toward cream print #1.
4. In the same manner follow steps 1 through 3 to make another star point on the adjacent corner to complete one star point unit. Make a total of 60 cream print #1 / navy print star point units (*Star Point Unit Diagrams*).
5. In the same manner, use cream print #2 B squares and navy print A rectangles to make star point units. Make a total of 16 cream print #2 / navy print star point units.

STAR BLOCK ASSEMBLY

1. Lay out four navy print B squares, four cream print #1 / navy print star point units, and one red print C square as shown in the *Star Block Diagrams*.
2. Assemble the units into rows; sew rows together to complete one cream print #1 / navy print star block. Make 15 cream print #1 / navy print star blocks.
3. In the same manner, lay out four cream print #2 B squares, four cream print #2 / navy print star point units, and one red print C square to make one cream print #2 / navy print star block. Make four cream print #2 / navy print star blocks.

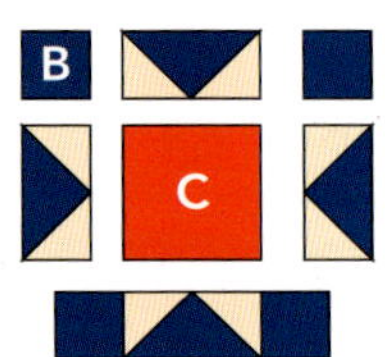

Star Block Diagrams

CURVED BLOCK DIAGRAMS

1. Lay out one red print E quarter circle and one cream print #1 D background as shown in the *Curved Block Diagrams*.
2. Match and pin the red print E quarter circle and the cream print #1 D background at the marks. Ease pieces to fit as you sew. Make 38 curved blocks.

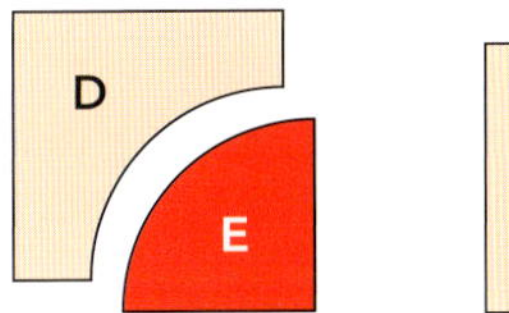

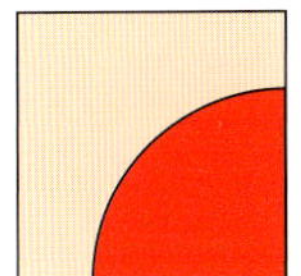

Curved Block Diagrams

QUILT TOP ASSEMBLY

1. Lay out star blocks, navy print F squares, and curved blocks as shown in the *Quilt Top Assembly Diagram*.
2. Sew blocks together to create rows.
3. Sew rows together to complete the quilt top center.
4. Attach brown print inner side borders to the quilt top center and then attach brown print inner top and bottom borders.
5. Attach navy stripe outer side borders.
6. Sew a cream print #2 / navy print star block to either end of the top and bottom navy stripe outer borders.
7. Sew outer top and bottom borders to the quilt top center to complete the quilt top.

Quilt Top Assembly Diagram

FINISHING

1. Divide backing into (2) 90" length panels. Join panels vertically.
2. Layer backing, batting, and quilt top; baste. Quilt as desired.
3. Join 2¼" wide binding strips into one continuous piece for double-fold binding. Add binding to quilt.

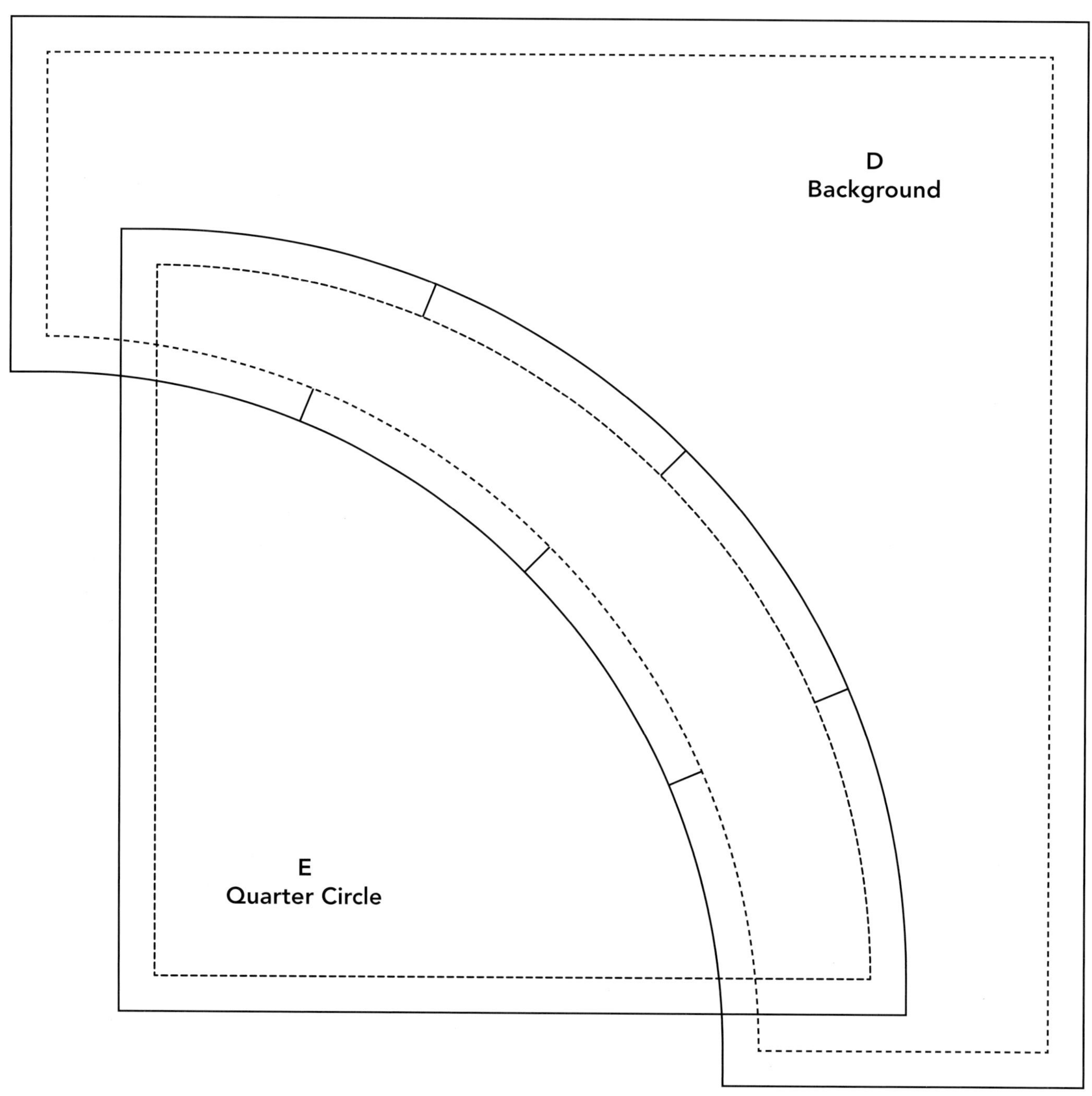

Guide Star

Quilt designed and quilted by Ebony Love

Quilt Size: 66" × 78½" | Finished Block Size: 12½"

MATERIALS

- 1½ yards of navy print (includes binding)
- ⅛ yard of gold print
- ⅝ yard of red
- 4½ yards white print
- Full-size quilt batting
- 5 yards of backing fabric

CUTTING

Measurements include ¼" seam allowances.

From navy print, cut:

- (1) 3½" strip. From strip, cut (9) 3½" C squares.
- (7) 3½" strips. With strips folded in half lengthwise, wrong sides together, cut 96 half rectangles through the double layer of each strip, using the Rec Tool or Template B on page 72, for a total of 96 left-facing and 96 right-facing half-rectangles.
- (7) 2½" strips for binding

From gold print, cut:

- (1) 3½" strip. From strip, cut (3) 3½" C squares.

From red print, cut:

- (5) 3½" strips. From strips, cut (48) 3½" C squares.

From white print, cut:

- (4) 2⅞" strips. From strips, cut (24) 2⅞" squares. Cut along the diagonal to make 48 half-square triangles.
- (4) 5⅜" strips. From strips, cut (24) 5⅜" squares. Cut along both diagonals to make 96 quarter-square triangles.
- (8) 3½" strips. From strips, cut 96 isosceles triangles using the Tri Tool or Template A on page 72.
- (3) 13" strips. From strips, cut (8) 13" F squares.
- (7) 8½" strips. Piece strips together to make (2) 8½" × 79" side borders and (2) 8½" × 50½" top and bottom borders.

TRI-REC UNIT ASSEMBLY

1. Lay out a white print A isosceles triangle, a navy print B half rectangle, and a navy print B half rectangle reversed as shown on the *Tri-Rec Unit Diagrams*.
2. Assemble (4) pairs of Blue+White HSTs for each block as shown in *Attach HSTs in Pairs*.
3. Sew navy print reversed B half rectangle to the left side of the triangle unit to complete 1 tri-rec unit. Make 96 tri-rec units.

Tri-Rec Unit Diagrams

CENTER BLOCK UNIT ASSEMBLY

1. Lay out four red print C squares, four tri-rec units, and one navy print C square, as shown in the *Center Block Unit Diagrams*.
2. Sew units into rows, sew rows together to complete one center block unit. Press seams open. Make nine center block units with navy print C square centers.
3. In the same manner make three center block units with gold print C square centers.

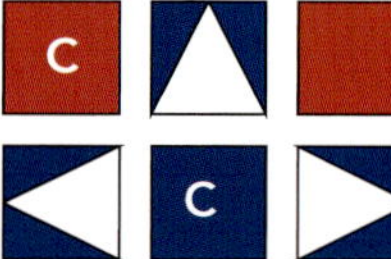

MAKE 9

MAKE 3

Center Block Unit Diagrams

CORNER BLOCK UNIT ASSEMBLY

1. Lay out two white print quarter-square D triangles and one tri-rec unit, as shown in *Corner Block Unit Diagrams*.
2. Sew units together. Press seams open.
3. Attach white print E half-square triangle as shown to complete one corner block unit. Make 48 corner block units.

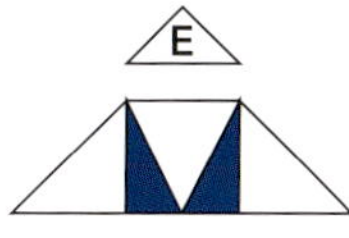

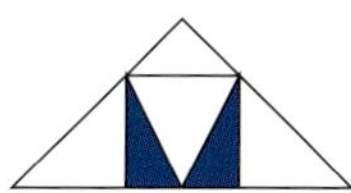

Corner Block Unit Diagrams

BLOCK ASSEMBLY

1. Sew two corner block units to opposite sides of the center block unit as shown in *Star Block Assembly Diagrams*. Press seams open.
2. Sew two corner block units to the remaining sides of the center block unit to complete one star block. Make nine star blocks with navy print centers and three with gold centers.

QUILT TOP ASSEMBLY

1. Lay out white print F blocks, navy print center star blocks, and gold print center star blocks as shown in *Quilt Top Assembly Diagram*.
2. Sew blocks together in rows; sew rows together to create the quilt top center.
3. Add white print top and bottom borders to the quilt top center.
4. Add white print side borders to complete the quilt top.

FINISHING

1. Divide backing into (2) 90" length panels. Join panels vertically.
2. Layer backing, batting, and quilt top; baste. Quilt as desired.
3. Join 2½" wide binding strips into one continuous piece for double-fold binding. Add binding to quilt.

MAKE 9

MAKE 3

Star Block Assembly Diagrams

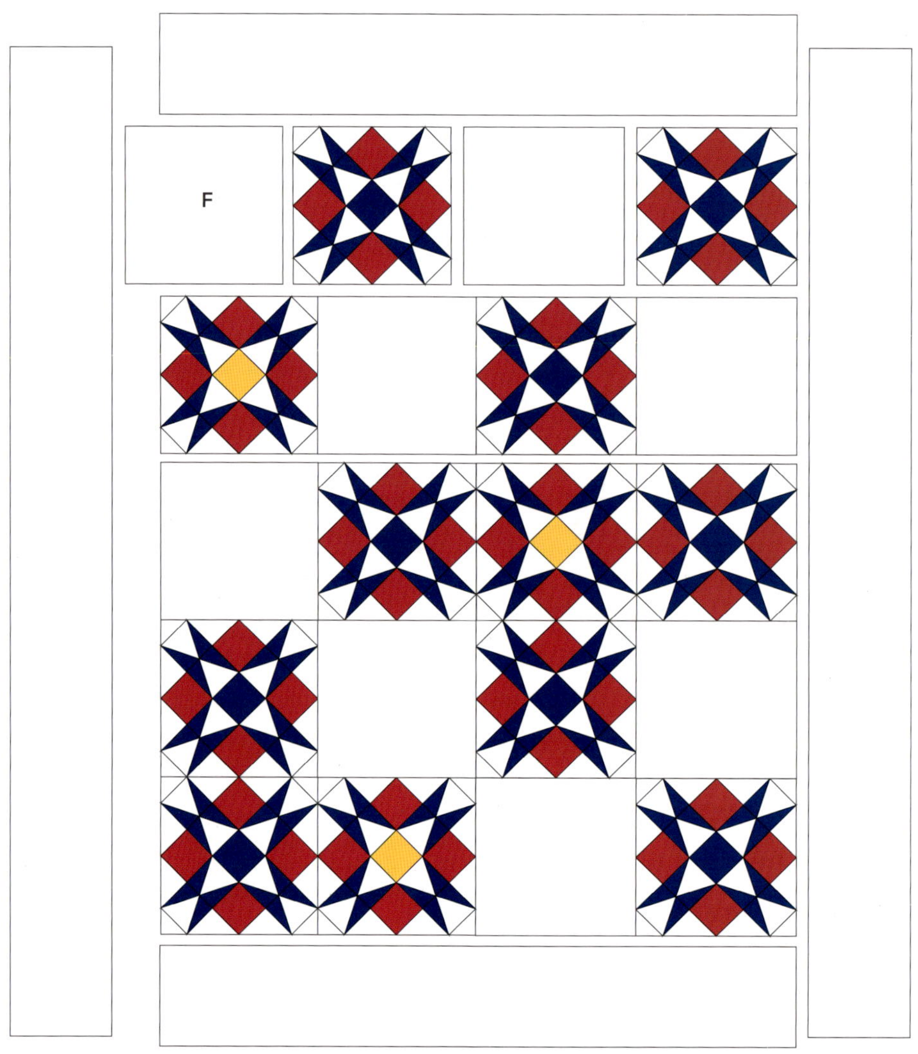

Quilt Top Assembly Diagram

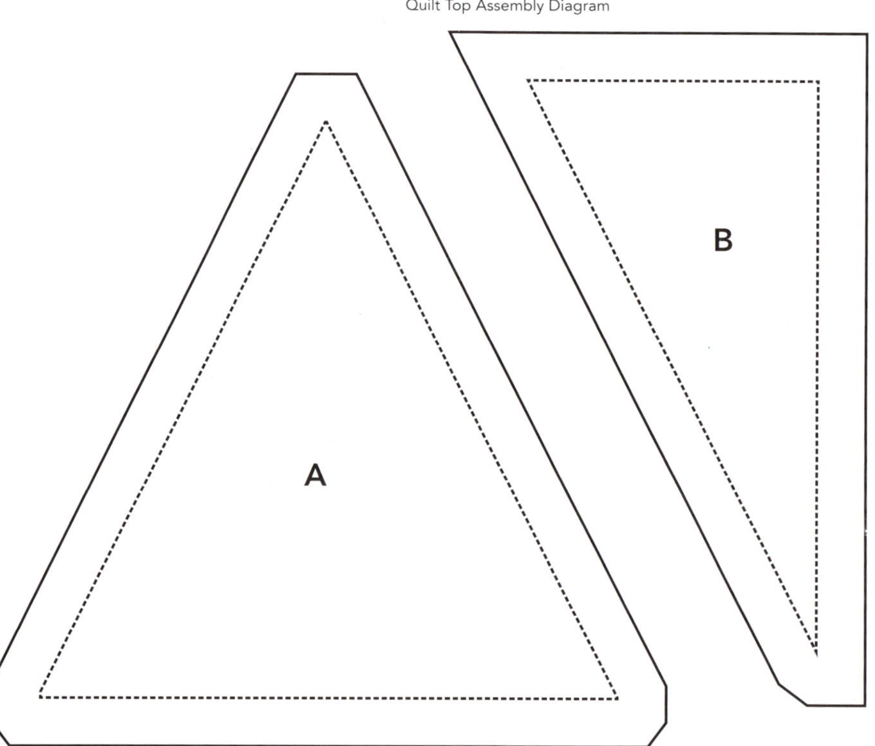

Patriotic Stars

Quilt by Nancy Mahoney • Machine-quilted by Sue Krause

Quilt Size: 61" × 74" | Finished Block Size: 12"

Over the years, I've come to realize that my favorite quilts are ones that look complicated but are actually very simple to make. And if the blocks include a hidden star, it's a winner in my book. Patriotic Stars is just that kind of quilt. The more you look at the quilt, the more secondary designs you see. The sashing not only adds to the design, but it also means you don't have to match any points! *—Nancy*

MATERIALS

16 fat quarters of assorted red prints for blocks

10 fat quarters of assorted navy prints for blocks

½ yard of cream dot for blocks

½ yard of medium blue for blocks

2⅛ yards of cream tone-on-tone for block background and sashing squares

¾ yard of red stripe for sashing

1½ yard navy stars for outer border and binding

Twin-size quilt batting

4¾ yards of backing fabric

CUTTING

Measurements include ¼" seam allowances.

From each of 12 red fat quarters, cut:

- (20) 2" A squares.

From each of 4 red fat quarters, cut:

- (10) 3⅞" G squares.

From each navy fat quarter, cut:

- (1) 3½" strip. From strip, cut (2) 3½" C squares
- (5) 2⅜" strips. From strips, cut (32) 2⅜" F squares

From cream dot, cut:

- (4) 3⅞" strips. From strips, cut (40) 3⅞" B squares.

From medium blue, cut:

- (4) 3½" strips. From strips, cut (80) 2" × 3½" D rectangles.

From cream tone-on-tone, cut:

- (5) 4¼" strips. From strips, cut (40) 4¼" E squares.
- (8) 3½" strips. From strips, cut (80) 3½" C squares.
- (4) 2" strips. From strips, cut (80) 2" A squares.
- (2) 1½" strips. From strips, cut (30) 1½" H squares.

From red stripe, cut:

- (17) 1½" strips. From strips, cut (49) 1½" × 12½" G sashing strips.

From navy stars, cut:

- (7) 4½" strips. Piece strips together to create (2) 4½" × 66½" side borders and (2) 4½" × 61½" top and bottom borders.
- (8) 2¼" strips for binding

STAR POINT UNITS

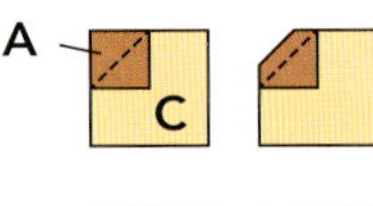

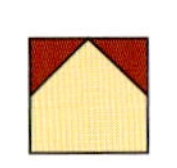
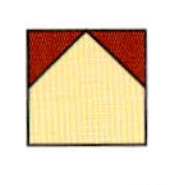

MAKE 80

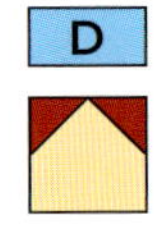

MAKE 80

1. Draw a line diagonally from corner to corner on the backside of the red print A squares.
2. Referring to the *Star Point Unit Diagrams*, place one red A square atop one cream tone-on-tone C square, right sides together. Stitch on the drawn line as shown. Trim ¼" beyond stitching. Press open. Repeat for adjacent corner of cream C square to complete one star point unit. Make 80 star point units.
3. Join one medium blue print D rectangle and one star point unit to complete one side unit (*Side Unit Diagram*). Make 80 side units.

FLYING GEESE UNITS

1. On the wrong side of navy print F squares, draw a diagonal line from corner to corner. Draw lines ¼" away from each side of the previously drawn line as shown in *Flying Geese Unit Assembly Diagrams*.
2. Place two marked F squares on cream tone-on-tone E square, right sides together. Stitch on the outer marked lines. Cut on the centerline and press the seams toward the navy print triangles as shown.
3. Place two marked F squares on the triangle units in step 2 as shown in *Flying Geese Unit Assembly Diagrams*. Stitch on the outer marked lines.
4. Cut on the centerline and press seams toward navy print triangles, as shown, to make four flying geese units.
5. Repeat steps 1 through 4 to make a total of 160 navy print / cream print flying geese units.

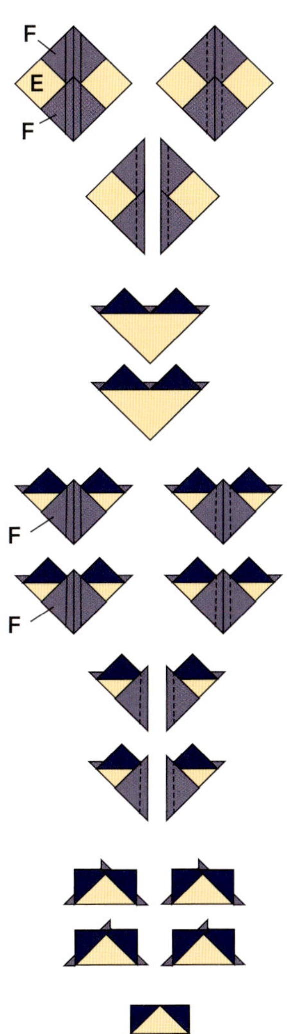

MAKE 160

Flying Geese Unit Diagrams

HALF-SQUARE TRIANGLE ASSEMBLY

1. Draw a diagonal line from corner to corner on the wrong side of the cream dot B squares as shown in *Half-Square Triangle Unit Diagrams*.
2. Draw lines ¼" away from each side of the previously drawn lines as shown.
3. Layer a marked cream dot B square on top of a red print G square, right sides together; stitch on outer marked lines as shown.
4. Cut on the centerlines to make two half-square triangle units.
5. Press seam allowances toward the darker fabric. Make a total of 80 half-square triangle units.

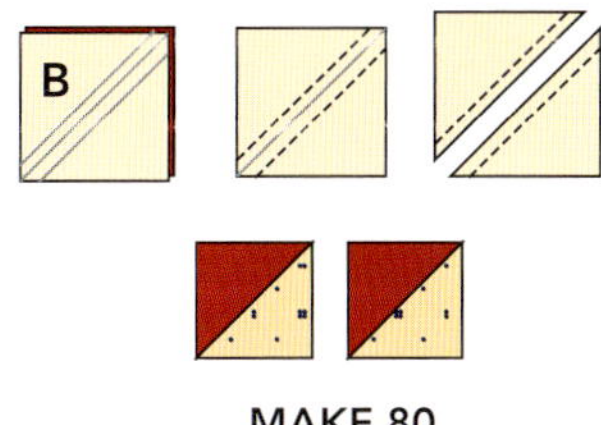

MAKE 80

Half-Square Triangle Unit Diagrams

CORNER UNIT ASSEMBLY

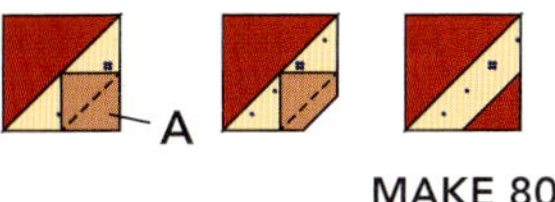

MAKE 80

Unit 1 Diagrams

1. Referring to the *Unit 1 Diagrams*, place one red A square atop one half-square triangle, right sides together. Stitch on drawn line. Trim ¼" beyond stitching. Press the resulting triangle open to complete one Unit 1. Make 80 Unit 1.
2. Lay out two flying geese units, one Unit 1, and one cream tone-on-tone A square as shown in *Corner Unit Diagrams*.
3. Piece units into rows, piece rows together to create one corner unit. Make 80 corner units.

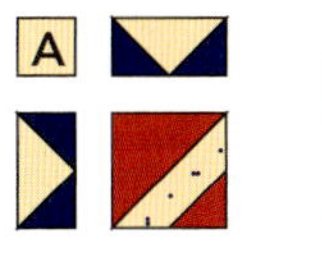

MAKE 80

Corner Unit Diagrams

BLOCK ASSEMBLY

1. Lay out four corner units, four side units, and one navy C square as shown in *Star Block Diagrams*.
2. Sew units into rows; sew rows together to complete star block. Make 20 star blocks.

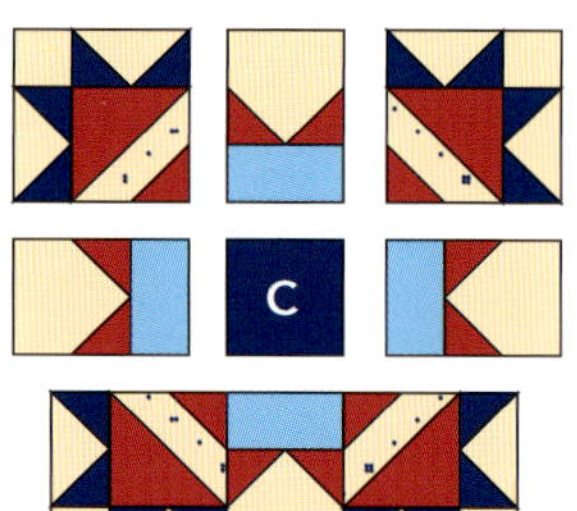

Star Block Diagrams

QUILT TOP ASSEMBLY

1. Lay out star blocks, red G sashing strips, and cream tone-on-tone H sashing squares as shown in *Quilt Top Assembly Diagram*.
2. Sew blocks together in rows, sew rows together to create the quilt top center.
3. Add navy star print side borders to quilt top center. Then add navy print top and bottom borders to complete quilt top.

FINISHING

1. Divide backing into (2) 2⅜-yard- length panels. Join panels vertically.
2. Layer backing, batting, and quilt top; baste. Quilt as desired.
3. Join 2½" wide binding strips into one continuous piece for double-fold binding. Add binding to quilt.

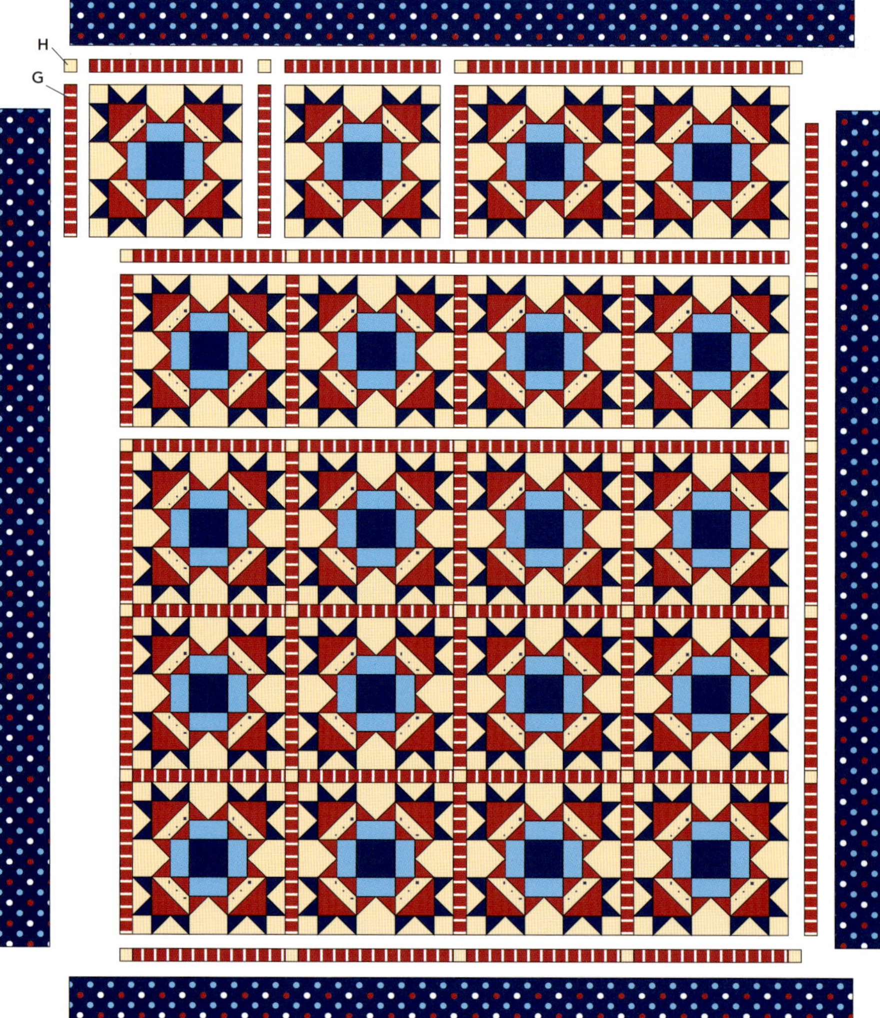

Quilt Top Assembly Diagram

Oh, Say Can You See?

Quilt design and construction by Marti Michell and Sally Joerger • Quilted by Jennifer Kay

Panel by Linda Luckovico and Deborah Edwards for Northcott Fabrics

58" by 70" approx. finished quilt size | 10½" finished size Log Cabin Blocks

Printed fabric panels can and do make a statement alone. However, a panel "embedded" in the warmth and love of a Log Cabin quilt makes an even more beautiful statement. There is no question but that this quilt was made with a purpose. It has a message: Oh, Say Can You See that we honor and appreciate your sacrifices to protect our freedom? *—Marti*

MATERIALS

- 1 printed panel approx. 23" × 45"
- 25 to 45 assorted fabrics to blend with the colors in the panel; any size from a 3" sq. scrap up to 9" × 18" may work
- ½ yard for first border and cornerstones on second border
- ⅝ yard for second border
- ¾ yard for binding
- 3¼ yards for backing
- Full-size quilt batting

SELECTING THE PANEL FOR THIS QUILT

Log Cabin blocks can be made nearly any size with any width of strip. These Log Cabin blocks are made with 1½" finished strips and they are 10½" sq. finished.

That means the useable part of the panel must be divisible by 10.5 in both dimensions. When this panel was purchased, most available panels were approximately 23½" wide by 44" long. Depending on the panel design, it will replace a section of Log Cabin blocks two blocks wide and three blocks long or two blocks wide and four blocks long.

This panel had to fill the four-block-long dimension as there was no way to reduce the length by 10½" without destroying important images. The effect of embedding would have to be created entirely by looking for fabrics with similar colors as the panel, using light-blue sky colors at the top of the quilt and Mt. Rushmore colors at the bottom.

DESIGN DECISIONS

The final design decisions should complement the panel chosen. Think of the panel as the main message and the Log Cabin blocks as the "support group." Because there are always new fabric designs, your panel will probably be different. You may want to use ideas from this quilt or be inspired to create your own.

For me, it is always important to audition ideas on a design wall, not just at the beginning, but also as the quilt progresses.

The panel is off-center because, to me, that is more interesting.

The 1½" strip width was chosen because it was the right proportion to the panel—not overpowering.

The eagle wings, the flag, and Mount Rushmore all have strong diagonal lines from the upper left corner to the lower right corner. The Straight Furrows setting of the Log Cabin blocks reinforces the diagonal design lines in the panel.

The value of the colors in the blocks goes from light at the top to dark at the bottom, again to repeat the panel.

For added interest, half of the Log Cabin blocks have 1½" center squares and half have 4½" finished squares. They, too, create a diagonal design line in the quilt. The combination of the two sizes of center squares and the Straight Furrows setting of the blocks resulted in a slightly different fabric value placement when piecing.

The strips in these Log Cabin blocks rotate clockwise.

No two Log Cabin blocks are the same not only because I prefer scrappy Log Cabin blocks but because assorted fabrics allow the panel to be the statement and help create the embedded look of the panel.

Somewhere between 30 and 45 fabrics are used in the Log Cabin blocks. It may sound like a lot, but it was a small amount of each.

SELECTING FABRICS: LOG CABIN BLOCKS

Starting with the upper left corner I knew I wanted six or eight blocks with light-blue skies. Light blue was the "dark" side of the Log Cabin block so soft white clouds would be the "light" side. I cut a bunch of assorted light cream and light-blue fabrics in assorted lengths needed. I make a lot of scrappy Log Cabin quilts. It won't matter if there are strips left over. Obviously, red would be used for the center square. But then I saw the fabric with the small flags that could be "fussy-cut" to fit in the 4½" center square. Why not alternate the size of the center square?

The blocks going down the left side needed to become darker by the fourth block. When we talk about "dark and light value," it is important to remember that value is relative. For a perfect example, you may notice that some of the same sky-blue fabrics are "dark" at the top of the quilt and "light" toward the bottom of the quilt.

The fussy cut eagles in the 4½" centers were whimsical in the blue sky but didn't look right flying below Mt. Rushmore. In order to continue the diagonal rhythm of alternating two sizes of center squares, it was a simple decision to change the fabric, but which fabric? Put two or three up on the design wall, stand back and look, pick your favorite.

In this quilt, I actually put individual strips for the Log Cabin blocks in order on the design wall and confirmed or replaced colors. It sounds laborious, but in fact, it was somewhat meditative and allowed me to think more about the people who are honored with Quilts of Valor and why we are doing this.

Nonquilters don't realize how the fabrics quilters use often carry stories about the quilter. I have been blessed with having designed many fabric lines. I spotted a scrap of the perfect piece of light-blue fabric for this quilt. It is close to 40 years old but so memorable for me, because that fabric was my first million-yard seller.

MAKING THE CLASSIC LOG CABIN BLOCK

TIP: Scrappy or "L"? Log Cabin and "scrappy" go hand in hand, but an "L" arrangement where the same fabric is used in two consecutive strips is also common. The "L" style is illustrated in the following step by step instructions. To piece this block, arrange strips in order to the left of the sewing machine.

CUTTING AND PIECING

In the directions that follow, all strips are cut 2" wide. The strips are then cut into segments:

- A = 2"
- B = 3½"
- C = 5"
- D = 6½"
- E = 8"
- F = 9½"
- G = 11"

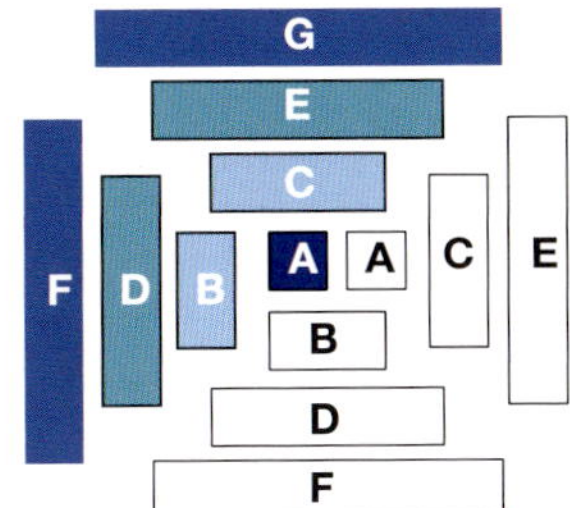

1. Sew the (2) **A** squares together. Press or finger-press away from the center.
2. To go clockwise in the rotation of the block, put the combined **A** squares right side down on the light-colored **B** strip with the **A** center square fabric leading into the machine. Start a little chant: "New piece on the bottom, lead with the center square." We recommend always putting the new piece on the bottom so you can see the seam allowances from previous steps. In the next step, "New piece on the bottom, lead with the center square" is the correct position to make the piecing go clockwise.
3. Sew B to unit. Press seams away from the center square. Good finger pressing should be adequate until you have completed a round of four strips. Don't forget, "New piece on the bottom, lead with the center square."

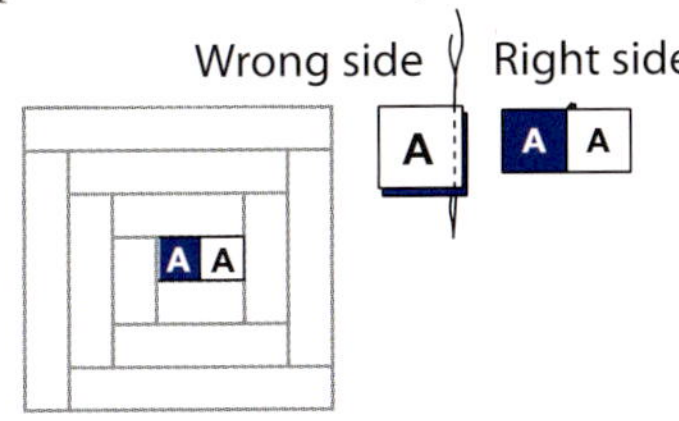

4. Place the sewn unit right side down on the dark strip **B**, with the **A** center square leading into the machine. If you continue to piece with the new strip on the bottom, you can see where you are and control the seam allowances.

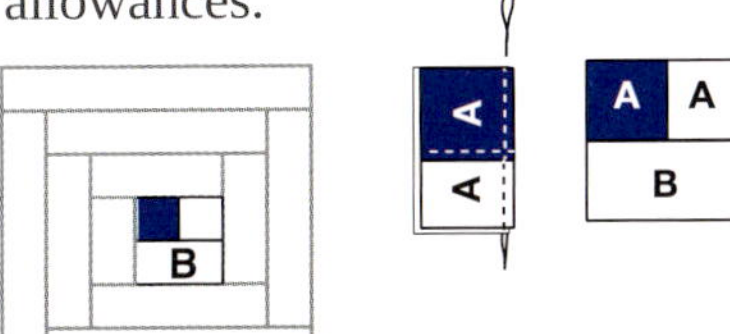

TIP: From this strip on, the new strip will always touch three already-sewn fabric pieces, or, stated another way, the edge of the unit that has two seams.

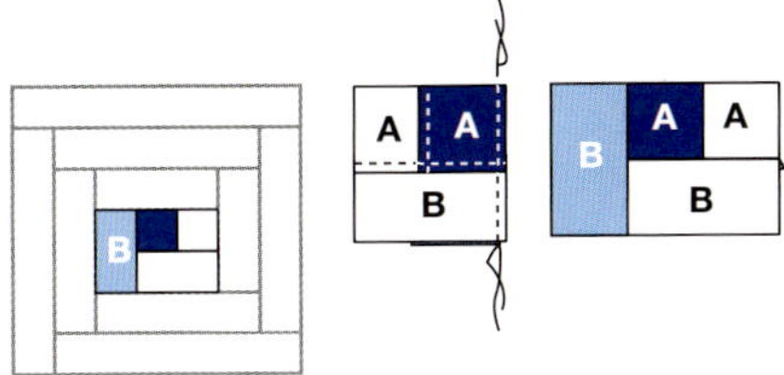

5. Continuing in a clockwise rotation, add the next piece (**C**). Press all four seams away from the center square, using an iron. Continue with "New piece on the bottom," but you are no longer leading with the center square.

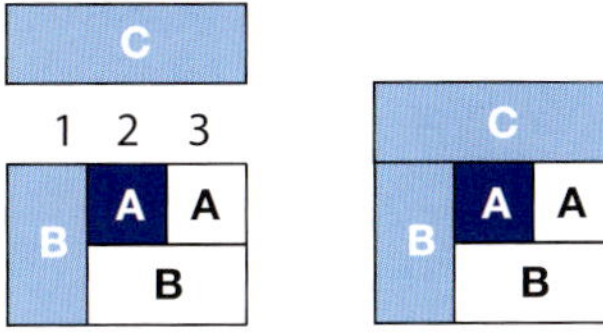

6. Begin the next round with a light piece **C**. Finger-press the seam allowance away from the center.

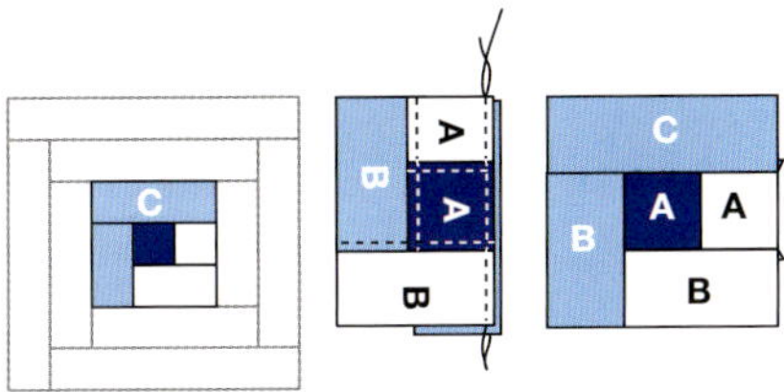

Looking at it from the right side, add subsequent rounds in a clockwise rotation. Finger press the seam allowances away from the center after adding each strip. Use an iron to press after the next round of four strips is completed.

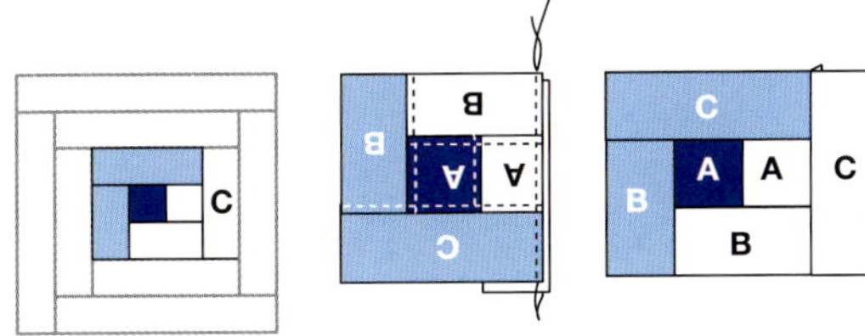

7. Piece units, adding first the light **D** piece …

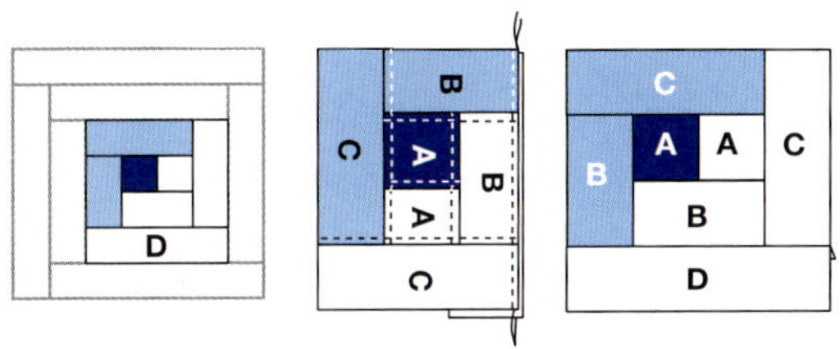

8. … and then the dark **D** piece.

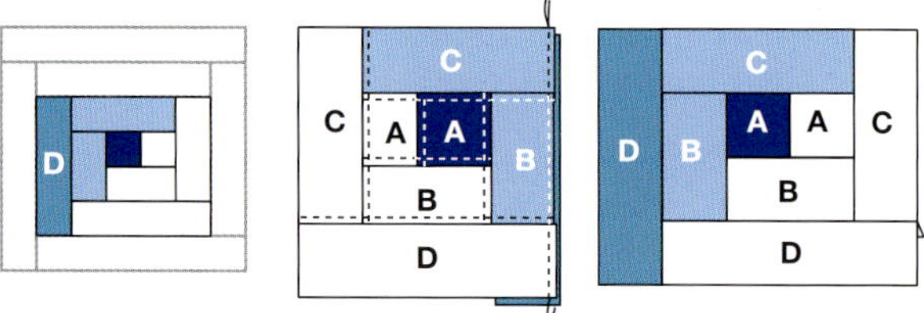

9. Add the dark **E** piece, then light.

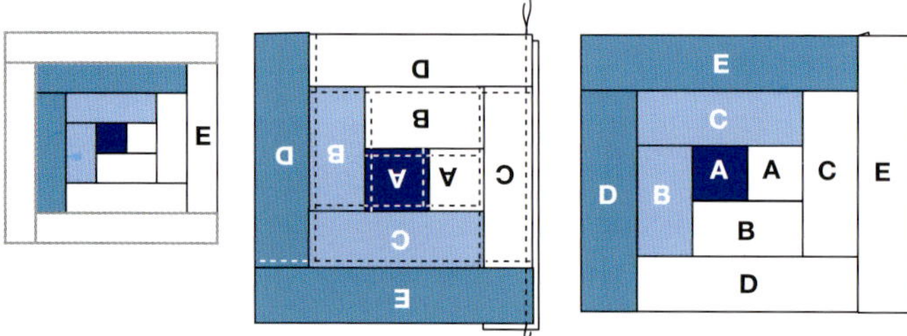

10. Begin the next round with a light piece **F**.

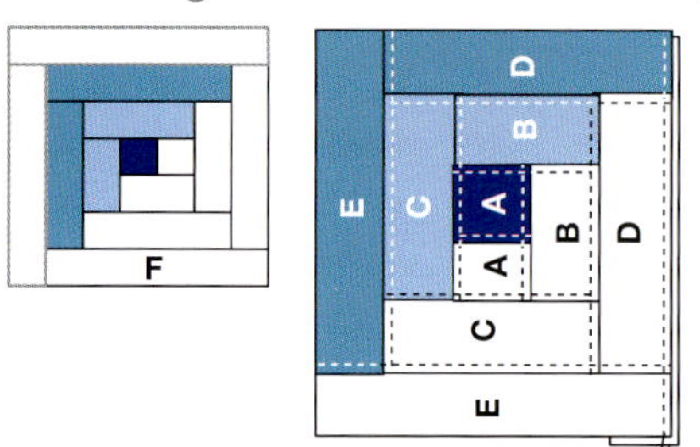

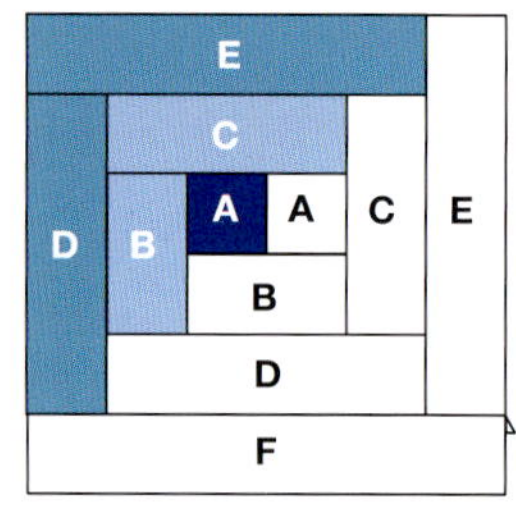

11. Add the dark **F** piece.

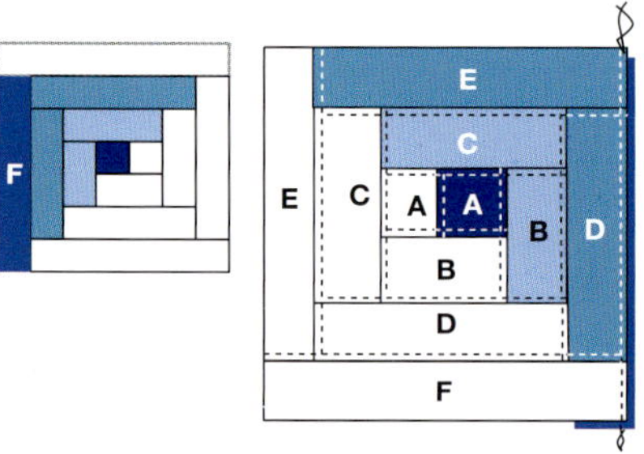

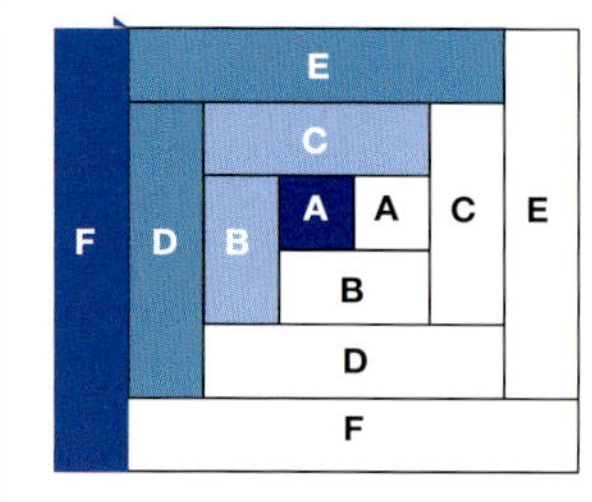

12. Complete the block with a **G** strip.

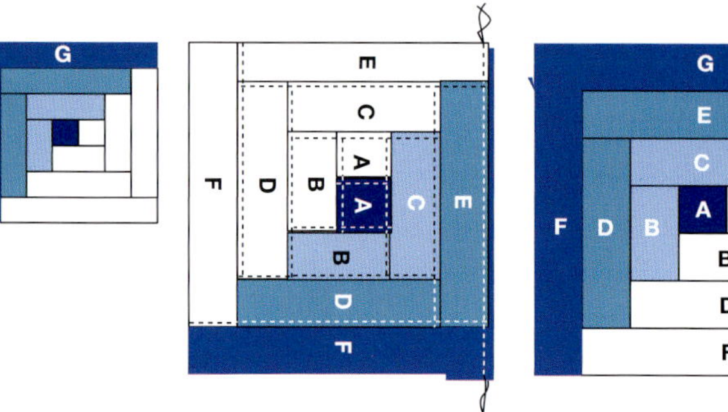

Did you notice that there is only one **G** piece? In order to have a square block, the last strip added is always the longest and the only one of that length. In the above illustration, that is piece **G**. Confirm blocks are 11" square.

OPTIONAL BLOCKS WITH LARGE CENTER SQUARE

To make some of the blocks with larger centers, cut a 5" square. The first strip added will be a light C. The next two strips will be dark Ds. NOTE: The large center square may be directional fabric.

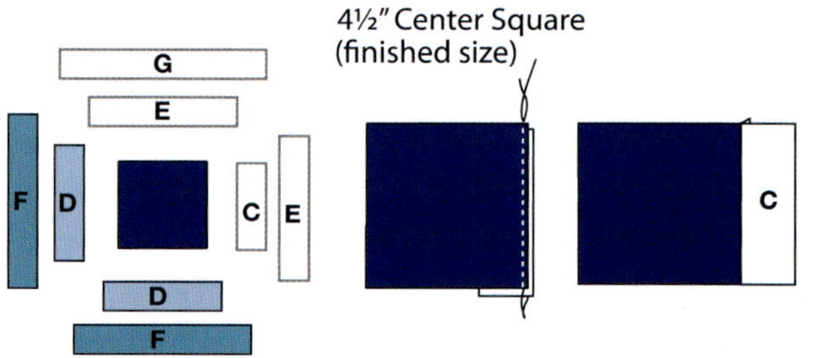

MAKING THE QUILT TOP

The Log Cabin blocks are 10½" square finished. That means the mathematically correct cut size for the panel is 21½" by 42½". The fearless quilter will cut the panel down to size and make the blocks fit. I chose to mark the dimension on the panel with a water erasable marking pen. After all of the quilt blocks were made, they were joined into the four sections shown (see illustration).

- Check the measurements of each section.
- Add the sections in numerical order. As the sections were added, the raw edge of the blocks would align with one of the drawn lines on the panel.
- When complete, trim excess fabric away from the panel.
- The borders, also auditioned on the design wall, are 1¼" finished width for the first border and 1½" finished for the second border. You may want different widths for your borders.
- The finished quilt is approximately 58" × 70" but could easily have another border for additional size.

MAKING THE BACKING

1. Trim off the selvedges.
2. Cut one piece 2 yards & 6" long. Cut remaining fabric in half lengthwise (two pieces approx. 21" × 39").
3. Join sections as shown.

Backing

42″ x 78″
2 yards 6 inches

22″ x 39″

22″ x 39″

LAYER AND QUILT AS DESIRED.

Awarding This Quilt

My grandfather,* the last veteran in my immediate family, enlisted in Company 1 of the 18th Regiment, Iowa Volunteer Infantry, in response to an appeal by President Abraham Lincoln in 1862. Since I do not have surviving veterans in my family, when it comes time to award this quilt, it would be fitting if it is awarded to a veteran who does not have surviving family members.

* Yes, I do mean my grandfather, not a great- or great-great-grandfather. We have very long generations in my family. My grandfather was 56 when my father was born, and my father was 38 when I was born.

Freedom's Path

Quilt designed and made by Scott Murkin

Quilt Size: 60" × 78" | Finished Block Size: 6"

Each veteran's service means uniquely personal things to them, and Scott wanted to make a design that had a somewhat universal appeal that would be appropriate in most or all settings. The preference was for something that was a joy to look at but not overly fussy either in presentation or construction. The design clearly evokes the feeling of "stars and stripes" without being too literal about either. Most scrappy-style designs benefit from incorporation of a wide variety of visual textures—plaids, dots, paisleys, florals, stripes, and other geometrics as well as a variety of print scales, depending on the size of the pieces.—*Scott*

MATERIALS

1½ yards of mixed white prints OR 6 fat quarters

2¼ yards of mixed red prints OR 11 fat quarters

2¼ yards of mixed navy prints OR 11 fat quarters

⅝ yard of binding print

Twin-size quilt batting

4 yards of backing fabric

CUTTING

Measurements include ¼" seam allowances.

From white prints, cut:

- (130) 3½" B squares

From red prints, cut:

- (66) 6½" A squares (64) 1" × 6" C rectangles.

From blue prints, cut:

- (64) 6½" A squares (66) 1" × 6" C rectangles.

From binding print, cut:

- (8) 2¼" strips for binding

BLOCK ASSEMBLY

1. Draw a line diagonally from corner to corner on the reverse side of each white print B square, as shown in *Block Diagrams*.
2. Layer a white print B square atop a red print A square, with right sides facing as shown.
3. Stitch on marked line. Trim ¼" beyond the stitch line and press toward the corner triangle.
4. Measure 4¼" from the stitch-and-flip seam you just completed. Trim off the opposite corner. Save trimmed corner.
5. With right sides together, sew a navy print strip on the newly cut edge. Press toward the strip. Trim the strip even with the edges of the block. Hint: you can trim with any ruler, but a 6½" ruler (the size of the unfinished block) makes the trimming efficient and accurate.
6. Sew the previously trimmed corner onto the block and press toward the navy print strip. Make 66 red blocks with navy stripes.
7. In the same manner, make 64 navy blue blocks with red stripes.

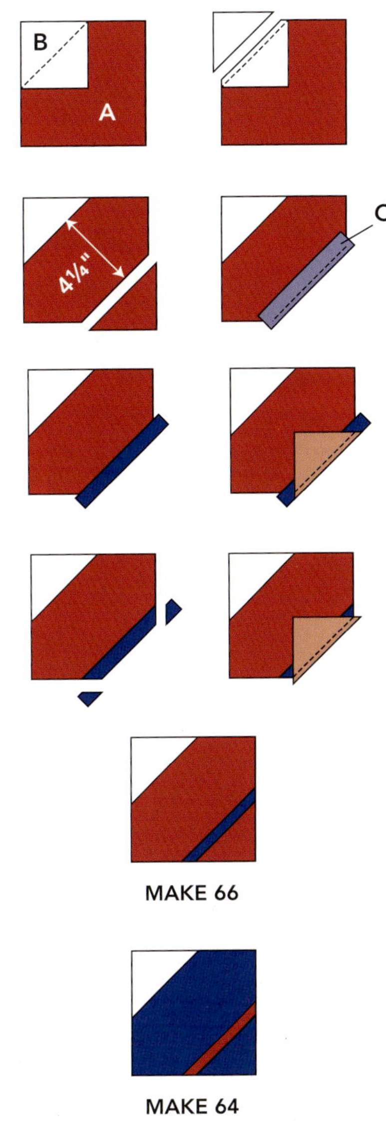

Block Diagrams

QUILT TOP ASSEMBLY

1. Lay out blocks as shown in the *Quilt Top Assembly Diagram*.
2. Sew blocks together in rows; sew rows together to create the quilt top.

FINISHING

1. Divide backing into (2) 72" length panels. Join panels horizontally.
2. Layer backing, batting, and quilt top; baste. Quilt as desired.
3. Join 2¼" wide binding strips into one continuous piece for double-fold binding. Add binding to quilt.

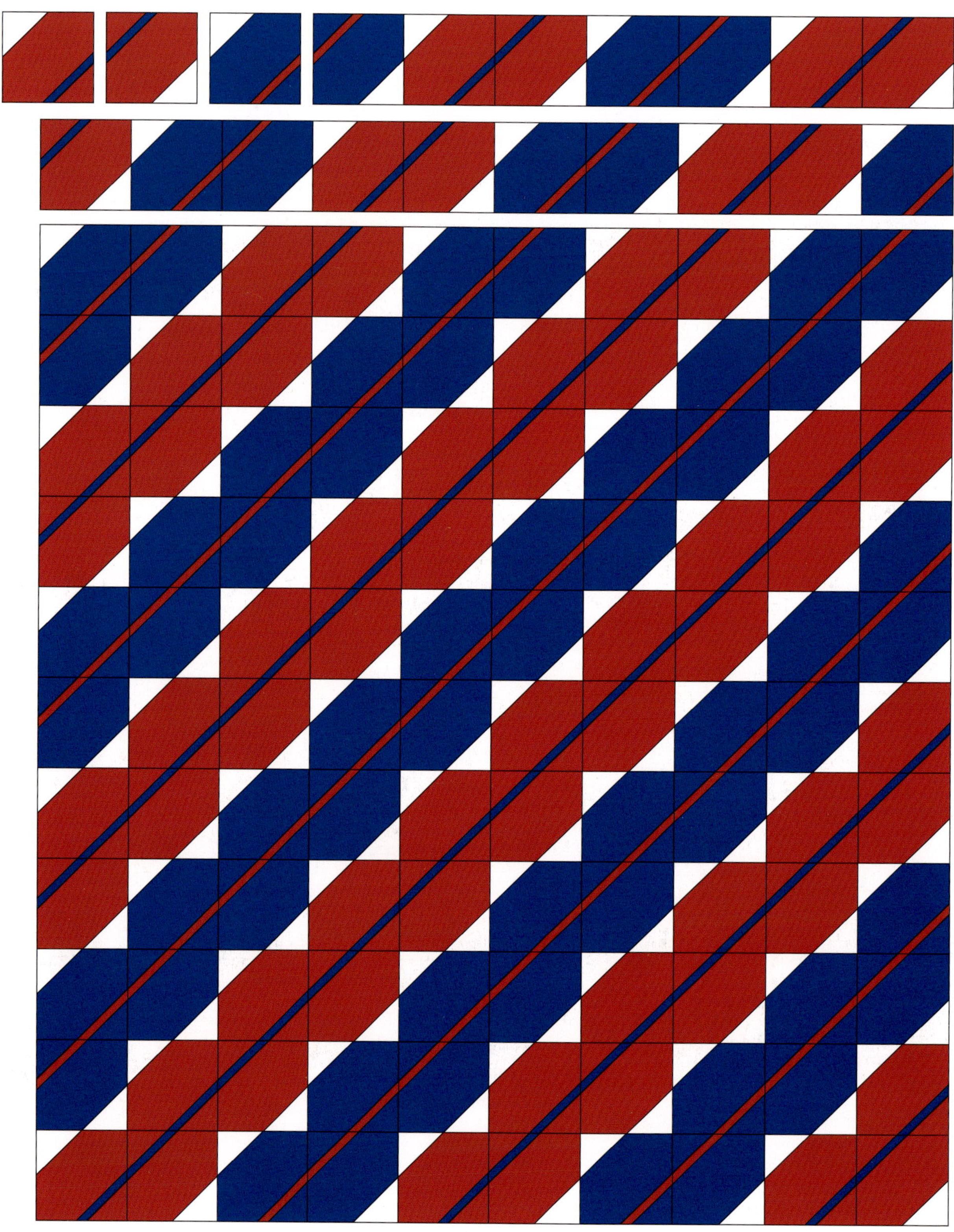

Quilt Top Assembly Diagram

Pieces of Pride

Quilt designed by Paula Nadelstern • Quilt made by Peggy True

Quilt Size: 68" × 68" | Finished Block Size: 4"

This quilt was inspired by a Paula Nadelstern pattern. It was fussy cut to highlight the fabric designs. You can easily make a patriotic version using your own stash of red, white, and blue prints (see page 87). The original design was known as Thumbnail.—*Paula*

MATERIALS

- 2¾ yards of black print (includes binding)
- 2⅛ yards of scraps OR (144) 4½" squares
- ⅜ yard of multiprint
- ⅛ yard focus print
- Full-size quilt batting
- ¼ yard lightweight fusible web
- 4½ yards of backing fabric

CUTTING

Measurements include ¼" seam allowances.

From black print, cut:

- (38) 1½" strips. From 15 strips, cut (132) 1½" × 4½" B rectangles. Piece the remaining strips together to create (13) 1½ " × 59½" C rectangles and (2) 1½" × 61½" D rectangles.
- (4) 2½" strips. From 2 strips, cut (8) 2½" × 6½" E rectangles. From remaining 2 strips, cut (4) 2½" × 19½" F rectangles.
- (6) 2" strips. Piece strips together to create (4) 2" × 61½" G rectangles.
- (1) 4" strip. From strip, cut (4) 4" H squares.
- (8) 2¼" strips for binding

From scrap prints, cut:

- (144) 4½" A squares

From multiprint, cut:

- (4) 2½" strips. From strips, cut (8) 2½" × 15½" I rectangles.

From focus print, cut:

- (4) 3" motifs (fussy cut)

CORNER BLOCK ASSEMBLY

1. Apply lightweight fusible web to the back of the focus fabric.
2. Cut out four motifs that are approximately 3" square.

Appliqué Diagram

3. Fuse motifs to the center of the black print H squares as shown in the *Appliqué Diagram*. Stitch around the edges of the motifs to secure them in place using a decorative stitch.

PIECED BORDER ASSEMBLY

1. Lay (2) black print E rectangles, (1) black print F rectangle, (1) black print G rectangle, and (2) multiprint I rectangles as shown in *Pieced Border Diagrams*.
2. Sew black print E rectangles, black print F rectangle, and multiprint I rectangles as shown to create a row.
3. Attach black print G rectangle to the pieced row to complete a pieced border. Make four pieced borders.

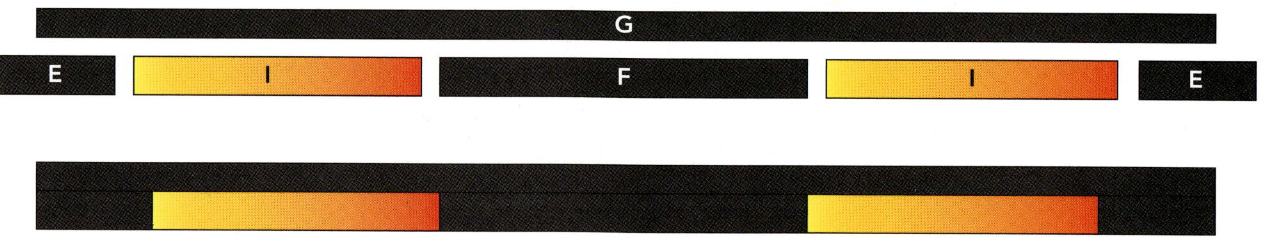

Pieced Border Diagrams

QUILT TOP ASSEMBLY

1. Lay out scrap print A squares, black print B rectangles, and black print C rectangles as shown in the *Quilt Top Assembly Diagram*.
2. Sew pieces together in rows; sew rows together to create the quilt top center.
3. Add black print D rectangles to either side of the quilt top center.
4. Attach a pieced border to either side of the quilt top center.
5. Sew a corner square to either end of the remaining pieced borders.
6. Attach these pieced border sections to the top and bottom of the quilt top center to complete the quilt top.

FINISHING

1. Divide backing into (2) 81" length panels. Join panels vertically.
2. Layer backing, batting, and quilt top; baste. Quilt as desired.
3. Join (8) 2¼" wide binding strips into one continuous piece for double-fold binding. Add binding to quilt.

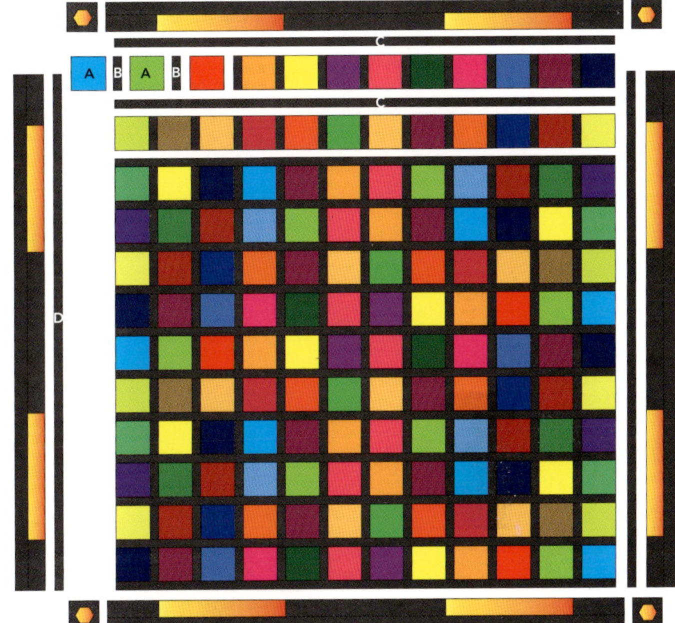

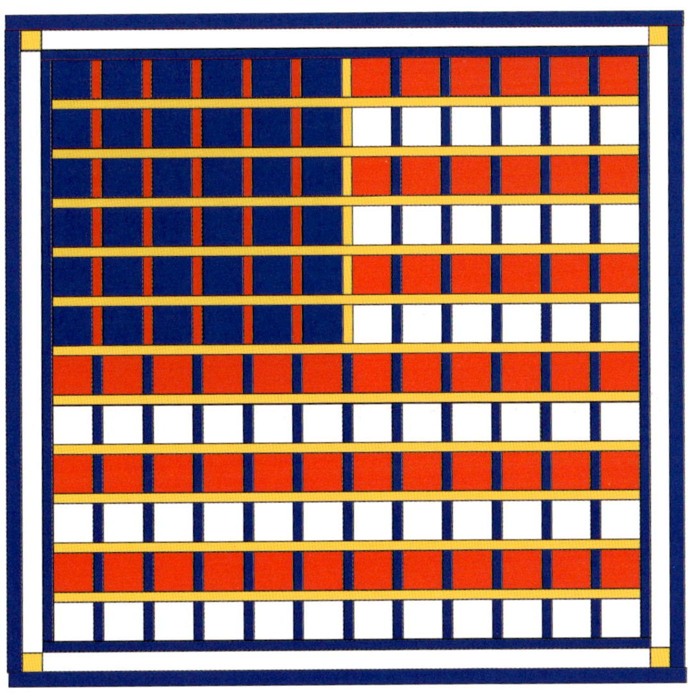

An Alternate Colorway

Flurry

Quilt designed and quilted by Gina Perkes
Pieced by Gina Perkes and Arleen Logan (Gina's grandmother)

Quilt Size: 70" × 72"

I designed Flurry as a featured quilt for my monthly event I hold in Arizona and on Facebook called Gina's Demo Day. The goal is to create simple quilts for new quilters to make while learning new techniques each month. Flurry can reflect different seasons simply by changing the applique shapes. I've made this quilt with snowflakes for winter and leaves for fall. It's an incredibly versatile quilt providing an opportunity to enjoy the beauty of ombré fabrics. —*Gina*

FABRIC

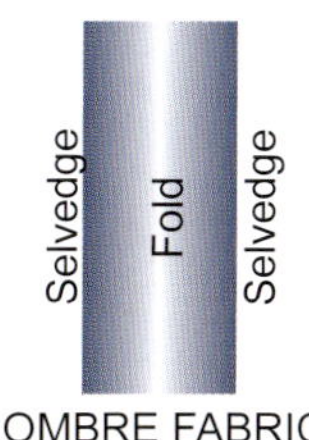

OMBRE FABRIC

TIP: Gina selected ombré fabrics that change from dark at one selvedge to light at the center, then to dark again on the opposite selvedge, as shown in *Ombré Fabrics* illustration. She chose a red for the blocks and a blue for the sashing strips.

2¼ yards blue ombré for vertical sashing strips

1½ yards red ombré for block corners

(24) 2½" × width of fabric (WOF) strips of assorted grays for block centers OR 1½ yards of solid fabric instead of strips

2¼ yards of 103" wide backing fabric OR 4¾ yards 42"–44" wide fabric for backing

¾ yard for binding

TOOL

TRI RECS BLOCK

The Tri Recs™ Tool by Darlene Zimmerman and Joy Hoffman is ideal for cutting the blocks in this quilt. To make a square block as shown in *Tri Recs Block*, you will use two templates: a triangle called TRI TOOL for the center, and a RECS TOOL for the sides.

CUTTING

For Block Background, from the red ombré fabric, cut:

- (8) 6½" strips across the folded width of fabric

1. Use the RECS tool to cut (2) of each shade from each folded strip, rotating the tool as shown in *Cutting Diagram for RECS Tool.*
2. Cut the folded strips individually for accuracy.
3. Be sure to trim the angled point on the top of the RECS tool; it will help later with alignment.
4. The lightest color is referred to as #1, the darkest as #10. As you cut the RECS shapes from the strips, stack them according to shade.
5. After cutting all (8) strips, number the stacks #1 (lightest) through #10 (darkest).
6. You will have (10) stacks of (16) pieces per stack.

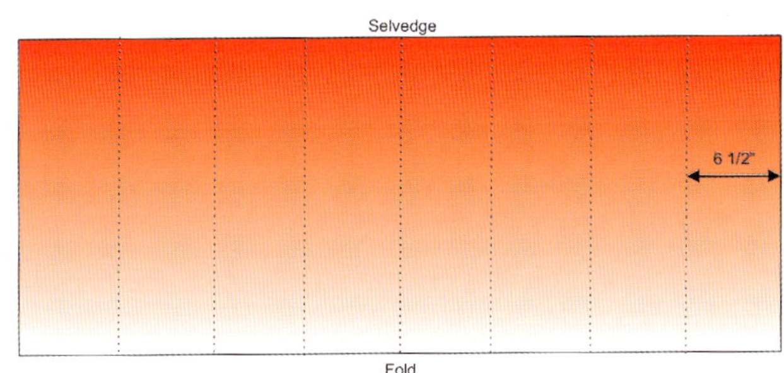

CUTTING DIAGRAM FOR OMBRE STRIPS

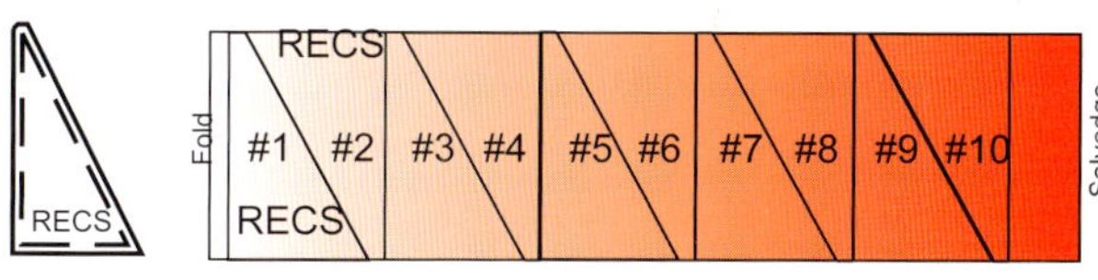

CUTTING DIAGRAM FOR RECS TOOL

For Block Center Triangle, use the (24) assorted 2½" × WOF strips

1. Sew strips into (8) sets of (3) strips each.
2. Press seams open.

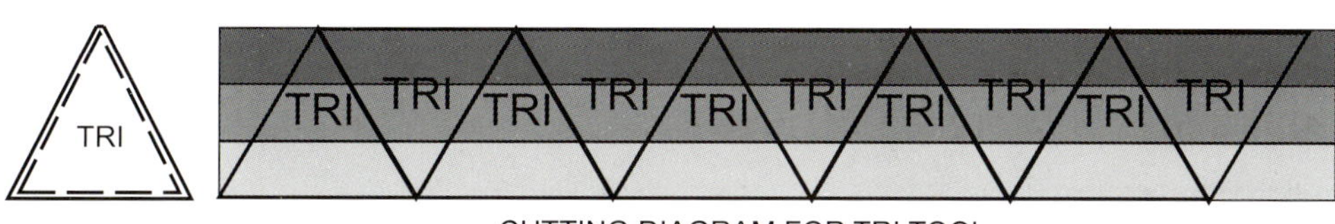

CUTTING DIAGRAM FOR TRI TOOL

From (8) strip sets OR from (8) 6" strips of solid fabric

1. Use the TRI tool to cut the triangles as shown in *Cutting Diagram for TRI Tool.*
2. Each solid strip or strip set will yield (10) triangles.
3. Cut one triangle at a time for accuracy.
4. You will have (80) TRI units.

ASSEMBLING THE BLOCKS

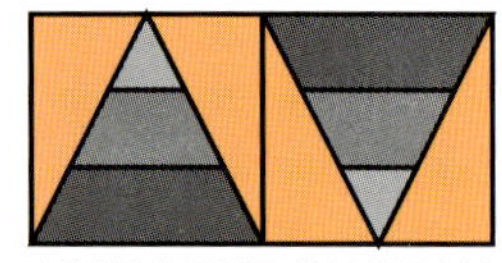

UNIT A PAIR DIAGRAM

Adding REC units to TRI Units

1. Begin sewing RECS sides to TRI units. This step can be chain-pieced; however, it is important to keep RECS shades together. Complete all of shade #1 before moving on to shade #2. Keep stacks organized.
2. Position RECS piece to triangle as shown and sew ¼" seam. Press seam toward RECS.
3. Sew second side of RECS to TRI unit. Keep like shades together.
4. Press seam allowance toward RECS.

Joining TRI-RECS Units into Pairs

The Unit A and Unit B blocks will be attached in pairs of two that contain the same shade RECS, but with the TRIs "pointing" in opposite directions. Please note that in Unit A, the left block points up, as shown in *Unit A Pair Diagram.* In Unit B, the left block points down, as shown in the *Unit B Pair Diagram.*

UNIT B PAIR DIAGRAM

- Make pairs of Unit A blocks as follows, being sure to keep the shades organized:

Shade/Block	#1/A	#2/A	#3/A	#4/A	#5/A	#6/A	#7/A	#8/A	#9/A	#10/A
Blocks Needed	2	1	2	1	2	2	2	2	2	2

- Make pairs of Unit B blocks as follows, being sure to keep the shades organized:

Shade/Block	#1/B	#2/B	#3/B	#4/B	#5/B	#6/B	#7/B	#8/B	#9/B	#10/B
Blocks Needed	1	2	1	2	2	2	2	2	2	2

JOINING THE PAIRS INTO COLUMNS

Join the pairs of Units A and B blocks into (3) columns of (12) units each. Notice that the A and B units alternate.

ASSEMBLING THE QUILT

1. Measure the lengths of the three columns. Record the smallest measurement.
2. Tear ombré fabric lengthwise into (4) 9" wide strips. Pay attention to the sections you are tearing. Tear the outer sections from the darkest sections of the fabric. Tear the inner sections from the lightest sections of the fabric.
3. Cut the length of the strips to the recorded measurement of the columns.
4. Join columns as shown. Press seams toward the ombré fabric.

STAR APPLIQUÉ

TIP: Gina recommends using different simple appliqué motifs for different seasons, holidays, or whatever is the theme of your quilt. She chose stars for this patriotic-themed quilt but use whatever design and technique you like.

Use the *Star Appliqué Template* to create different sizes of stars. Hand- or machine-stitch the stars in a diagonal swath across the quilt. Refer to original photo for approximate placement.

ASSEMBLING THE COLUMNS

FINISHING

1. Divide 42"–44" wide backing into (2) 78" length panels. Join panels vertically. Cut down wide backing fabric to 78" × 80".
2. Layer backing, batting, and quilt top; baste. Quilt as desired.
3. Join 2¼" wide binding strips into one continuous piece for double-fold binding. Add binding to quilt.

STAR APPLIQUE TEMPLATE

A Symbol of Hope

Quilt designed and made by Sue Reich • Quilted by Pat Hluska

Finished Size: 64" × 72" with 4" border

About the same time as I was creating quilt patterns using large hexies, I started to make Quilts of Valor. The anchor hexie was one of the first patterns I created. When a Navy veteran is awarded a quilt made with this motif, there's an immediate recognition and personalization of his/her military service. The anchor symbolizes hope and steadfastness; thus the title I've assigned to this design. Piecing this quilt goes very quickly. I usually cut the hexagons the night before. Within the next day and a half to two days, the top is completed. The negative ground provides space for great quilting designs. The finished product is a dramatic, patriotic quilt created to show gratitude to a Navy veteran or service member. —*Sue*

MATERIALS

- $2\frac{5}{8}$ yards white for background whole hexies
- $1\frac{5}{8}$ yards blue for anchor hexies
- $\frac{5}{8}$ yard red for binding and outer half hexies
- $3\frac{1}{2}$ yards for backing
- Full/double size quilt batting, or scraps for quilt-as-you-go method

TIP: This quilt can be assembled as a quilt-as-you-go project, where each hexagon is quilted to scraps of batting (but not backing). After the prequilted blocks are attached together, the entire top can be quilted "in the ditch" around each hexie. Or, the top can be assembled as a regular quilt top and then layered with batting and backing. As with any quilt, it can be made in any colors; however, the red, white, and blue fabric references in this pattern are intended to distinguish the different elements of the quilt.

An alternate design option is Thank You for Your Service; it uses the same hexagon template and piecing techniques. See page 97.

MAKE YOUR OWN TEMPLATE

There are many sizes of hexagon cutting templates available. For this quilt, you need a template for cutting hexagons that are 8" finished size (measured from one flat side to the opposite flat side). The unfinished hexagon will measure 8½" side-to-side because of the added ¼" seam allowance. You can also make your own hexagon template (without seam allowances):

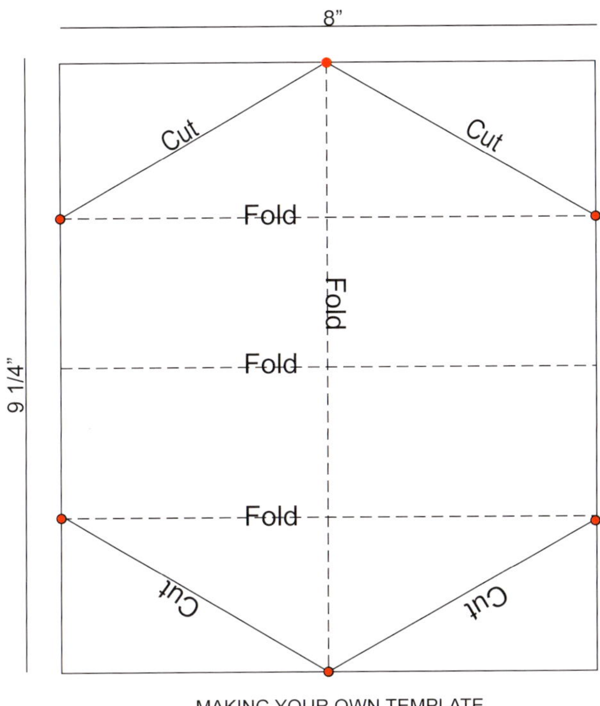

MAKING YOUR OWN TEMPLATE

1. Trim a piece of paper or card stock to measure 8" × 9¼".
2. Fold the sheet in half top to bottom and then side to side.

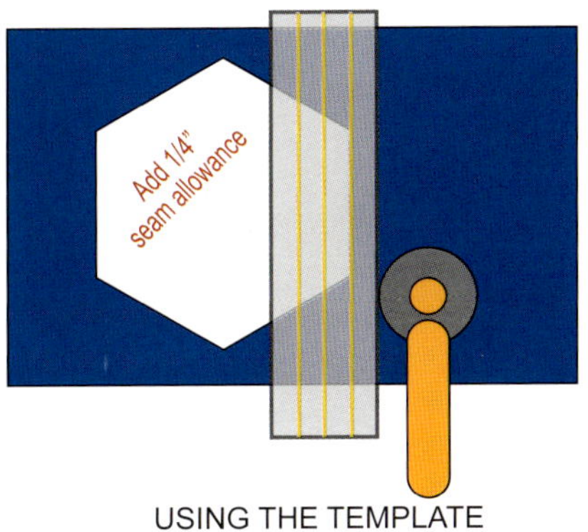

USING THE TEMPLATE

3. Mark a point at the center top and bottom edge of the sheet.
4. Fold the sheet again to divide the sheet into four horizontal quarters.
5. Mark a point at the beginning and end of these two horizontal lines at the edge of the paper.
6. Refer to the illustration *Making Your Own Template* to draw lines to connect each of these points to the top center.
7. Trim off the corners.

When you use this template to cut one or more layers of fabric:

1. Use flat flower head pins to hold the template to the fabric.
2. Use a ruler and rotary cutter to cut out the shapes, being careful to lay the ¼" line on the edge of the paper template before you cut, as shown in *Using the Template* illustration.
3. Note: If you decide to use the quilt-as-you-go technique, you will use this same template to cut hexagons of batting, but without the added seam allowance.

CUTTING

From white fabric, cut:

- (38) Full Hexies

From blue fabric, cut:

- (20) Full Hexies

From red fabric, cut:

- (8) Left/Right (trapezoid-shaped) Half Hexies
- (16) Top/Bottom (pointed roof-shaped) Half Hexies

Note: Fold the template in half to create the Left/Right or Top/Bottom Half Hexie. Remember to add ¼" seam allowance!

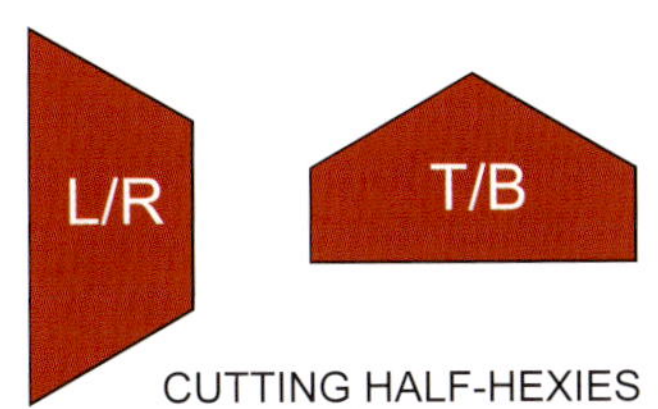

CUTTING HALF-HEXIES

A good idea is to use a pencil or fabric-marking pen to make a dot at the beginning/end of each seamline on the back of the hexies. Find this line by finger-pressing the fabric. You will stop and start at these points as you sew the hexies later.

ASSEMBLING THE QUILT

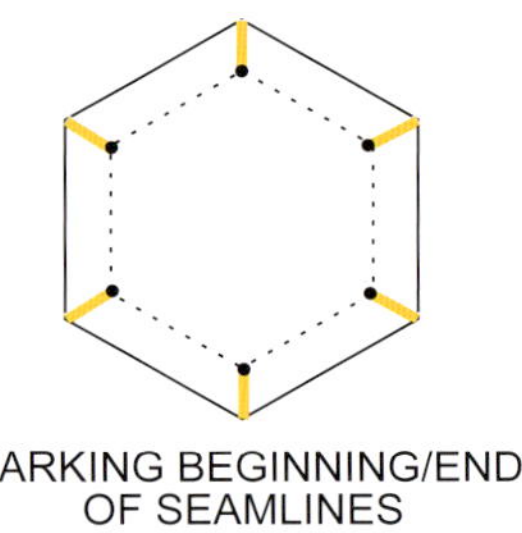
MARKING BEGINNING/END OF SEAMLINES

Attaching Hexies

Whether you attach the hexies by hand or machine, you will start and stop at the beginning of each seamline.

Sewing by Hand

1. Place hexies right sides together. Use your needle to anchor the beginning of the seamline.
2. Pin the end of the seamline, making sure to line up the dots as shown in the *Sewing by Hand* illustration.
3. Knot your thread at the beginning, sew to the end of the seamline, and then knot again.
4. All seams are done in this same manner.

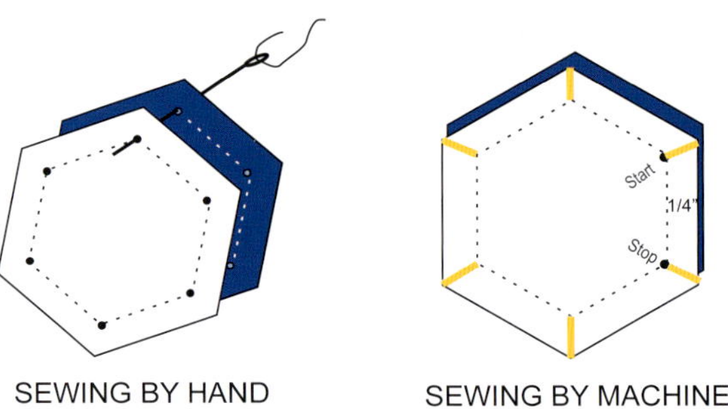

SEWING BY HAND SEWING BY MACHINE

Sewing by Machine

1. Start at the marked intersection as shown in *Sewing by Machine* illustration; stitch two stitches forward, then two stitches backward; and then continue to the end of the seamline.
2. At the end, stop at the marked intersection and backstitch two stitches.
3. Cut the thread.
4. All seams are done in this same manner.

Quilt-as-You-Go Technique

1. Cut hexies of batting for each full or half hexagon using the same template, but **DO NOT** add a ¼" seam allowance.
2. Center a piece of batting on the back of each hexagon.
3. Quilt as desired.
4. Follow the illustration to attach one prequilted hexie at a time to the quilt. The batting will fit snugly into the seam allowance as you attach one hexie to another during assembly.
5. Press the seams open as you go to flatten the seams and help keep the batting in place.

Whether you are assembling the quilt by hand or on a sewing machine, follow the order shown in *Attaching the Hexies* illustration to attach the hexies one at a time.

Attach the Top/Bottom Half Hexies after the main body of the quilt is assembled. Trim off the excess at the corners.

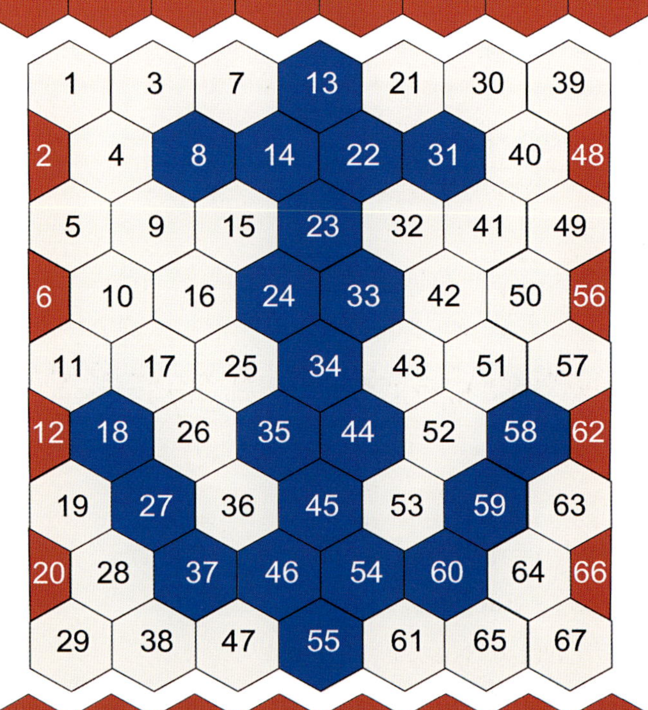

ADDING A BORDER

1. If you quilted the hexies individually, cut 4" strips of batting.
2. Attach the batting strips to the four edges of the completed top with a zigzag stitch.
3. Measure the quilt top to bottom and cut 4½" strips to this length.
4. Add these strips to the left and right sides of the quilt.
5. Measure the quilt from left to right and cut 4½" strips to this length.
6. Add these strips to the top and bottom sides of the quilt.

FINISHING THE QUILT

Backing and Batting

The quilt should now measure about 64" × 72".
Adding 8" to each measurement indicates a backing size of 71" × 80".
If you have already added the batting as part of the quilt-as-you-go technique, just layer the top with the prepared backing. Quilt in the ditch to attach the top to the backing.
Otherwise, quilt the top, batting, and backing as desired.
Add binding to complete the quilt.

ALTERNATE DESIGN

The patriotic fabric in this quilt was inspired by an embroidered words quilt I made to honor the branches of the military, Thank You for Your Service, quilted by Pat Hluska (see photo on page 94). In 2018, Northcott Fabrics, our Quilt of Valor Foundation partner, designed this fabric line with many of the mottos and logos, expressions of gratitude for service, and Welcome Home messages expressed on my quilt. With the passing of the World War II– and Korean War–era veterans, Quilts of Valor Foundation is awarding more and more quilts to Vietnam-era soldiers. Time and again, the veterans share that for the first time in over 50 years, they have been welcomed home and thanked for their service. Quilts of Valor Foundation is a service organization whose main purpose is to recognize military service and express gratitude for defending our country. It is a true honor to serve our nation making Quilts of Valor. —*Sue*

Use the same hexagon template and piecing techniques to create the following design.

ALTERNATE DESIGN

For this design, you will need:

White for Background:

- (38) Whole Hexies
- (8) Top Half Hexies
- (4) Bottom Half Hexies
- (3) Left-Side Half Hexies
- (4) Right-Side Half Hexies

Medium Blue for Outer Ring of Large Hexies:

- (17) Whole
- (1) Bottom
- (1) Left

Print for Second Ring of Large Hexies and Outer Ring of Smallest Hexies:

- (13) Whole
- Bottom

Light Blue for Inner Ring of Corner Hexie:

- (2) Whole
- (2) Bottom Half
- (1) Left Half

Red for Centers:

- (2) Whole
- (1) Right Half

Thank You for Your Courage

Quilt designed by Shannon Shirley • Machine-quilted by Brenda Edwards

Quilt Size: 72" × 72" | Finished Block Size: 8"

Growing up in an Air Force family, I was taught to honor those who serve our country in all branches of the military. When asked to design a quilt for Quilts of Valor, I was more than happy to oblige. Thank you to all that have served or are currently serving. —*Shannon*

MATERIALS

¾ yards each of four assorted cream prints

½ yards each of four assorted red prints

½ yards each of four assorted blue prints

1¼ yards of multistripe

⅝ yard of binding print

Full-size quilt batting

4½ yards of backing fabric

CUTTING

Measurements include ¼" seam allowances.

From each cream print, cut:

- (2) 9½" strip. From strip, cut:
  - (8) 9½" A squares
- (3) 1¾" strips. From strips, cut:
  - (8) 1¾" × 12" strips

From each red print, cut:

- (1) 9½" strip. From strip, cut:
  - (4) 9½" A squares
- (2) 1¾" strips

From strips, cut (4) 1¾" × 12" strips.

From each blue print, cut:

- (1) 9½" strip. From strip, cut:
  - (4) 9½" A squares
- (2) 1¾" strips. From strips, cut:
  - (4) 1¾" × 12" strips

From multistripe, cut:

- (8) 4½" strips. Piece strips together to create (2) 4½" × 72½" top and bottom borders and (2) 4½" × 64½" side borders.

From binding print, cut:

- (8) 2¼" strips for binding

BLOCK ASSEMBLY

1. With (cream, red, and blue) A squares right sides up, make a diagonal cut 2¼" from the upper right corner and 2¼" from the lower left corner, as shown in the *Block Assembly Diagrams*.
2. Take a cream print A square that has been cut and lay a red B rectangle atop the left portion of it with right sides together. Sew the pieces together as shown. Press seam open.
3. Align the right portion of the cream square with the edge of the red strip as shown. Sew the pieces together. Press seam open.
4. Trim the pieced block to 8½" as shown. Make 16 cream blocks with a red strip.
5. In the same manner, make 16 cream blocks with blue strip, 16 red blocks with cream strip, and 16 blue blocks with cream strip.

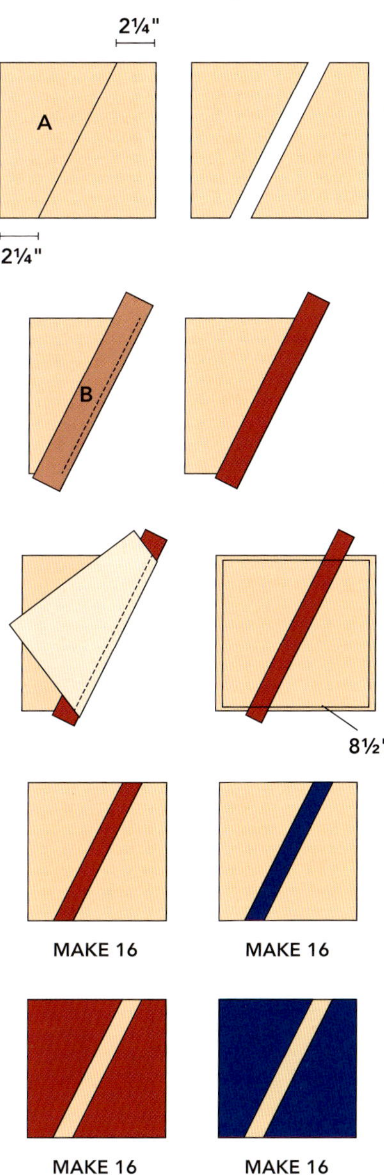

QUILT TOP ASSEMBLY

1. Lay out blocks as shown in the *Quilt Top Assembly Diagram*.
2. Sew blocks together in rows, sew rows together to create the quilt top center.
3. Add multistripe side borders to either side of quilt top center.
4. Add multistripe top and bottom borders to complete the quilt top.

FINISHING

1. Divide backing into (2) 81" length panels. Join panels vertically.
2. Layer backing, batting, and quilt top; baste. Quilt as desired.
3. Join 2¼" wide binding strips into one continuous piece for double-fold binding. Add binding to quilt.

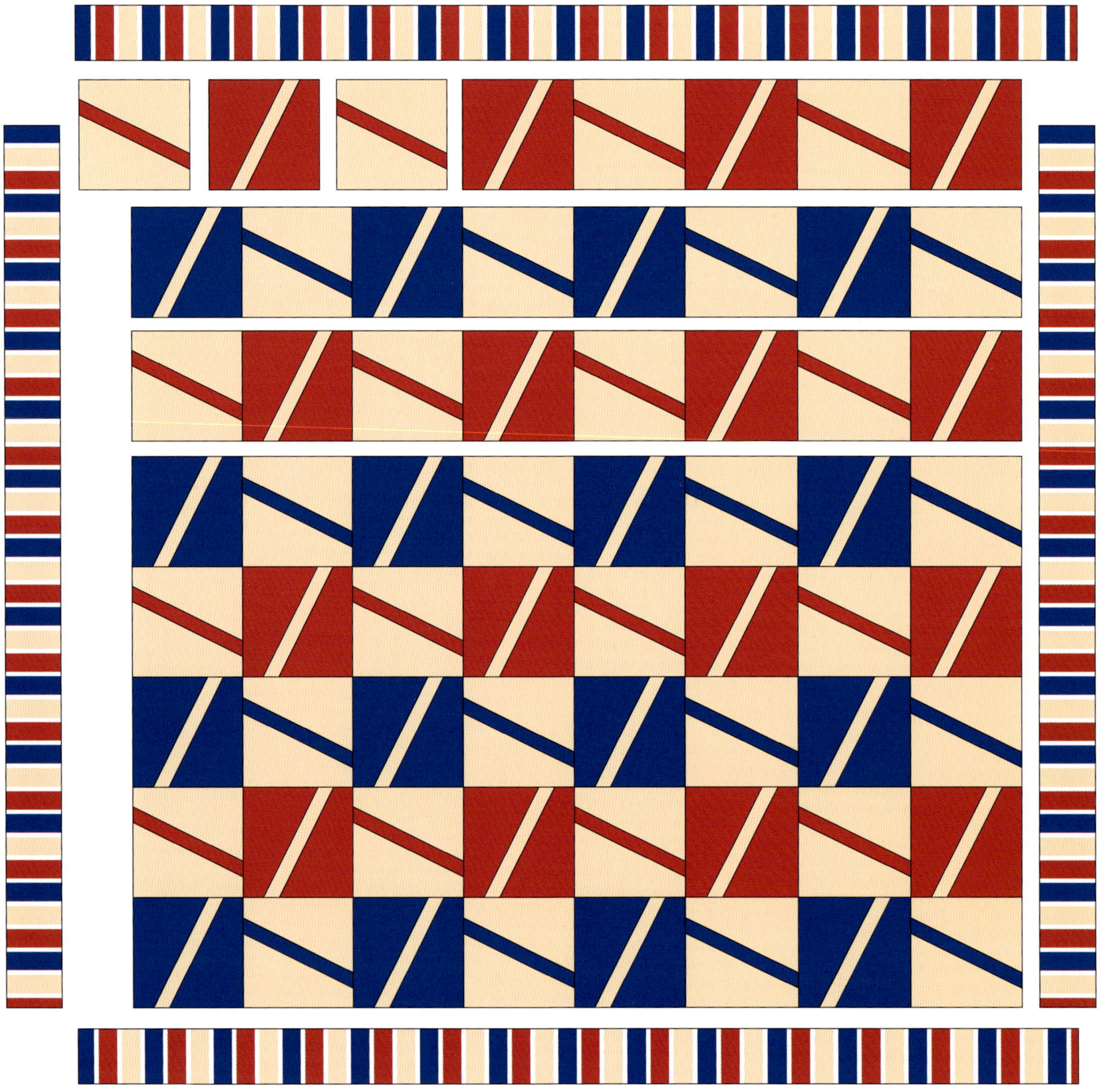

Quilt Top Assembly Diagram

Stars of Appreciation

Quilt designed by Pat Sloan • Fabric designed by Pat Sloan and provided by Benartex Fabric
Pieced and quilted by Betty Jenkins

Quilt Size: 66" × 80" | Block Size: 12" | Sashing: 2" | Border: 4"

It's been thrilling to watch Quilts of Valor grow into an important ambassador of the very best of quilting. When designing a quilt for this book, I knew it had to be a star. Stars for hope, stars for courage, stars to show our appreciation for the work done for our country. Thank you to everyone for making a quilt available to our friends who have given so much to our country. *—Pat*

This quilt was inspired by Pat's pattern Movie Theater.

MATERIALS

- 2½ yards Cream Ponds (Benartex 10184-07)
- 1 yard Red Benches (10183-10)
- 2 yards Blue Ponds (10184-50)
- 1⅛ yards Sky Blue Pathways (10185-05)
- 5 yards backing
- ¾ yard binding
- 74" × 88" batting

CUTTING

Cream Ponds

For Blocks, cut:

- (80) 3" squares for HSTs
- (80) 2½" × 4½" rectangles

For Sashing, cut:

- (49) 2½" × 12½" rectangles

Red Benches

For Blocks, cut:

- (120) 2½" squares

For Sashing Cornerstones, cut:

- (30) 2½" squares

For Outer Border Corners, cut:

- (4) 4½" squares

Blue Ponds

For Blocks, cut:

- (120) 2½" squares
- (80) 3" squares for HSTs
- (80) 2½" × 4½" rectangles

Sky Blue Pathways

For Outer Border, cut:

- (7) 4½" × WOF strips

Piece these together, end to end, and cut into:

(2) 4½" × 58½" for Top/Bottom

(2) 4½" × 72½" for Left/Right

Binding

- Cut (8) 2½" × WOF strips, joined together end to end with diagonal seam.
- Press joining seams open and press strip in half lengthways.

MAKING THE BLOCKS

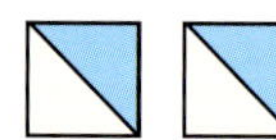

MAKING HST UNITS

Half-Square Triangles

- Use the 3" blue and cream squares to make (160) HSTs. Refer to *Making HST Units* illustration.

1. Draw a diagonal line on the back of the cream squares.
2. Layer cream+blue squares right sides together.
3. Sew ¼" seam on both sides of the drawn line.
4. Cut on the drawn line for two HSTs.
5. Press open or toward blue.
6. Trim HST to 2½" square, if necessary.

Rail Fence Units

- Use rectangles to make (80) Rail Fence units. See *Rail Fence* illustration.

1. Sew blue and cream 2½" × 4½" rectangles together.
2. Press seams open or toward blue.

Corner Units

- Use the blue+cream HSTs, 2½" red squares, and 2½" blue squares to make (80) Corner Units. See *Corner Unit* illustration.

1. Attach blue square to HST, paying attention to the orientation of the HST.
2. Attach another HST to the red square.
3. Press the seam allowance toward the squares.
4. Attach the (2) units to make the Corner Unit, nesting the seam allowances.
5. Trim to 4½" square, if necessary.

Four-Patch Units

- Use (40) 2½" red squares and (40) 2½" blue squares to make the center four-patch units. Refer to *Four Patch* illustration.

1. Attach pairs of red and blue squares together.
2. Press seam allowance toward darker fabric.
3. Attach the two sides nesting the seams, to make a Four-Patch unit.

RAIL FENCE UNIT

CORNER UNIT

FOUR PATCH

ASSEMBLING THE BLOCKS

- Refer to *Block Assembly* to put the blocks together.

1. Make (2) rows consisting of (2) Corner Units and (1) Rail Fence.
2. Press seams toward Rail Fence.
3. Make (1) row consisting of (2) Rail Fence Unit and the center Four-Patch.
4. Press seams toward Rail Fence.
5. Attach the rows, nesting the seams and being careful to turn rows 1 and 3 correctly.

BLOCK ASSEMBLY

ASSEMBLING THE SASHING

Sashing

- Refer to *Sashing* illustration.

1. Attach (30) 2½" red squares between (24) 2½" × 12½" cream rectangles to make (6) Sashing units.
2. Press seam allowances toward the cream sashing rectangles.

Block Rows

- Refer to *Block Row and Sashing* illustration.

1. Attach (4) completed blocks with (5) 2½" × 12½" cream rectangles to make (5) Block rows.
2. Press seam allowances toward the cream sashing rectangles.

ASSEMBLING THE QUILT

- Refer to *Quilt Assembly* illustration.

1. Alternate Sashing Rows and Block Rows, being careful to pin and match seam lines.
2. Press seams open.
3. Measure through the center of the quilt from top to bottom to get the actual length of the top.
4. Measure through the center of the quilt from left to right to get the actual width.
5. Use the length measurement to cut the left and right borders from the 4½" Outer Border fabric.
6. Attach these left/right borders.
7. Use the width measurement to cut the top and bottom borders.
8. Add 4½" red corner squares to each end.
9. Attach to top/bottom to complete quilt top.

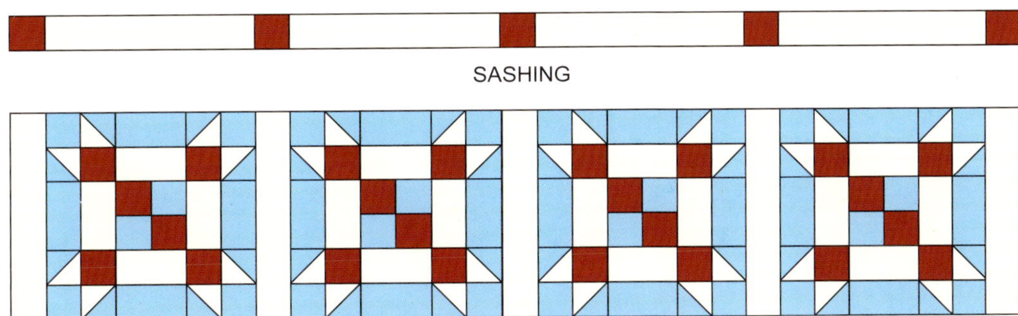

SASHING

BLOCK ROW AND SASHING

FINISHING

- Layer top, batting, and backing.
- Quilt as desired.

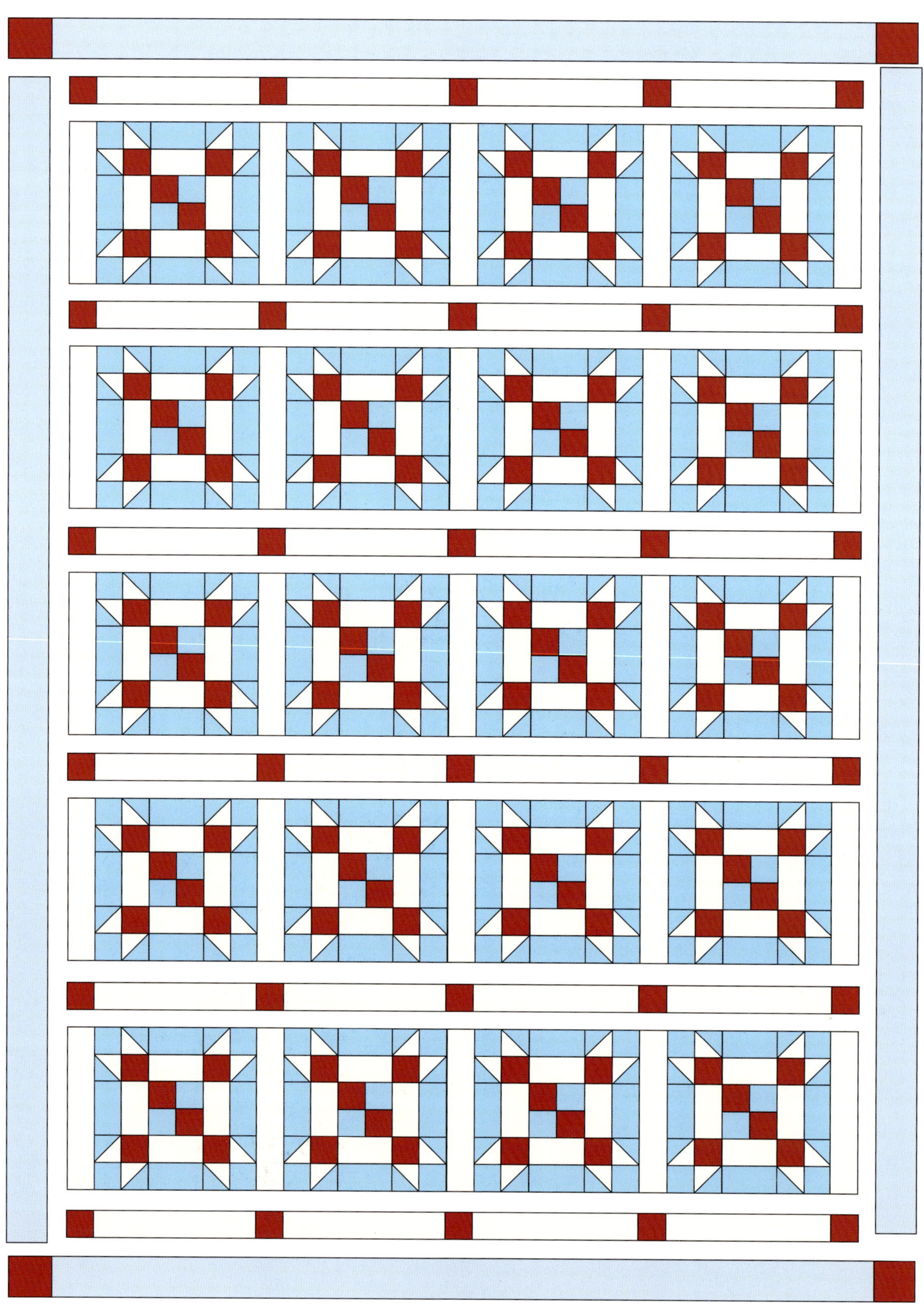

QUILT ASSEMBLY

Flags for Our Fathers

Quilt designed and quilted by Kris Vierra • Pieced by Debbie Tribble

Quilt Size: 63" × 78" with 2" border

My father was a B-52 pilot and served in Strategic Air Command. My husband served in the Army during Vietnam. My father-in-law served in the Navy during World War II. We have three sons: the two youngest served in the Marine Corps, and our oldest is currently serving as a police officer. Service seems to be a common theme. I am honored to be a part of this salute to servicemen and servicewomen. —*Kris*

MATERIALS

1¾ yards blue

2¼ yards white

2¾ yards red

5 yards for backing

¾ yard for binding

71" × 86" batting

In addition to regular cutting and sewing tools, a Diagonal Set Ruler will be helpful in cutting the triangles that set the Variable Star blocks columns. You will need a ruler that works for 10" finished size blocks such as Fons & Porter™ "Easy Diagonal Sets Ruler" or From Marti Michell™ "Diagonal Set Triangle Ruler for 2½" to 10" Blocks."

Cutting and Assembling Blocks

FLAG STRIPE BLOCKS

Note: Cut 2½" × WOF strips for A and B Strip Sets, which will be cut into straight segments.

Cut 2¼" × WOF strips for C and D Strip Sets, which will be cut into 60° angled segments.

Press all seam allowances toward the blue or red fabric.

Strip Set A

Cut 2½" × WOF strips.

1. Cut (3) blue.
2. Cut (6) white.
3. Cut (6) red.
4. Make (3) strip sets in the following order: blue/white/red/white/red.
5. Press seam allowances toward red or blue strip.
6. Cut each strip set into 3⅞" segments.
7. You will need (24) segments.

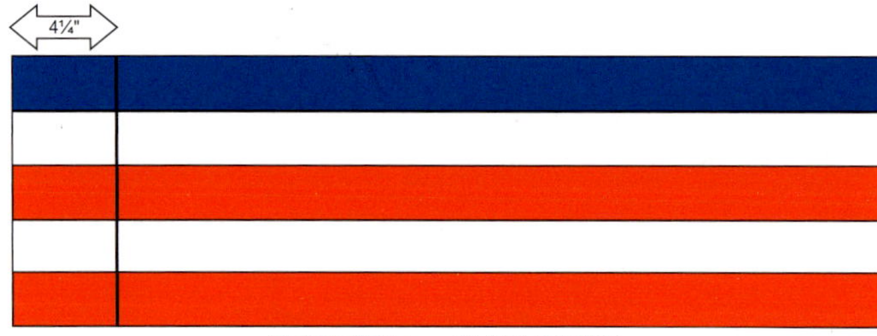

STRIP SET A - (5) 2½" STRIPS

Strip Set B

Cut 2½" × WOF strips.

1. Cut (3) red.
2. Cut (4) white.
3. Join red strips end to end. Cut long strip in half (each approx. 60" long).
4. Join white strips end to end. Cut long strip into thirds (each approx. 54" long).
5. Make (1) strip set from these long strips in the following order: white/red/white/red/white.
6. Cut each strip set into 4¼" segments.
7. You will need (12) segments.

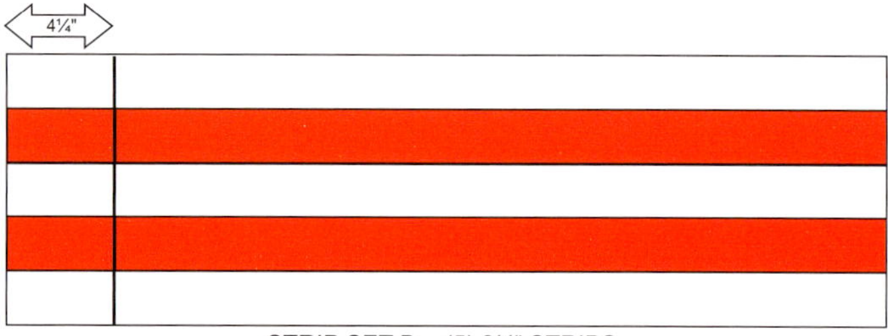

STRIP SET B - (5) 2½" STRIPS

Strip Set C

Cut 2¼" × WOF strips

1. Cut (6) white.
2. Cut (6) red.
3. Make (2) strip sets in the following order: white/red/white/red/white/red.
4. Cut 60° off one end (notice that the white segment becomes a point).
5. Cut remainder of strip set into 4¼" segments, measured from the cut line.
6. You will need (12) segments. The points will be trimmed off later.

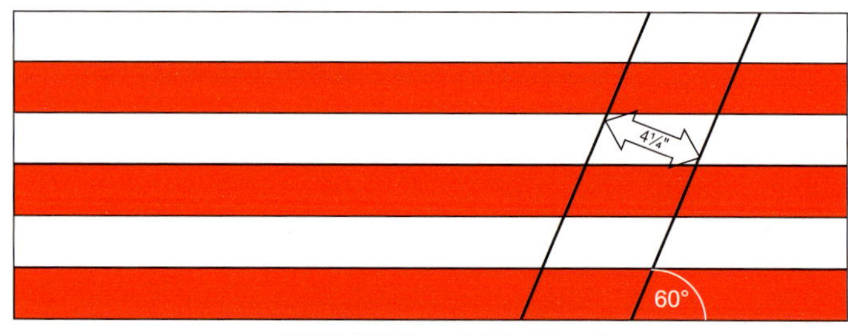

STRIP SET C - (6) 2¼" STRIPS

Strip Set D

Cut 2¼" × WOF strips

1. Cut (2) blue.
2. Cut (6) white.
3. Cut (4) red.
4. Make (2) strip sets in the following order: blue/white/red/white/red/white.
5. With blue strip at the top, cut 60° off one end. (Notice that blue segment becomes a point.)
6. Cut remainder of strip into 4¼" segments, measured from the cut line.
7. You will need (12) segments. The points will be trimmed off later.

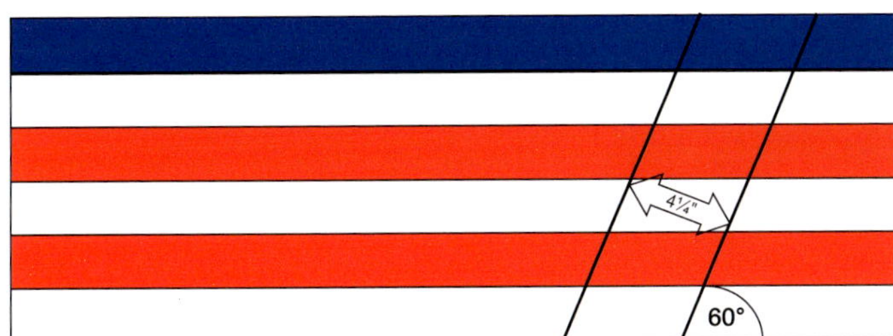

STRIP SET D - (6) 2¼" STRIPS

Assembling the Flag Stripe Block

1. Attach segments as illustrated in *Attaching Flag Stripe Block Segments*, matching strip intersections.
2. After all (5) segments in each block are attached, trim off the angled pieces as shown in *Trimming the Flag Stripe Block*. Trim off ¼" from top and bottom to adjust the length of the block to 18 ½".
3. Press seams open.
4. Cut block should measure 10½" × 19".
5. Make (12) blocks.

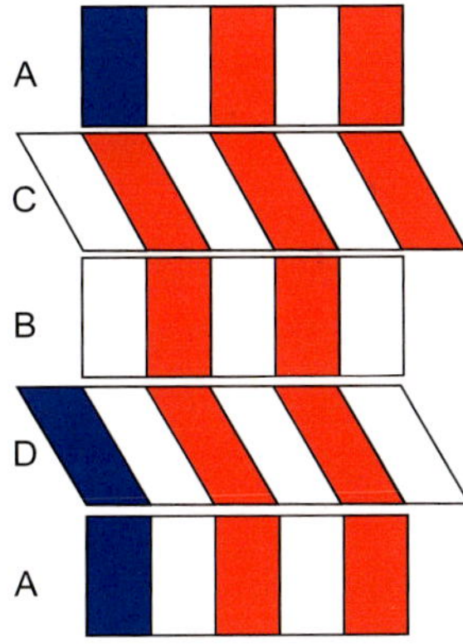

ATTACHING FLAG STRIPE BLOCK SEGMENTS

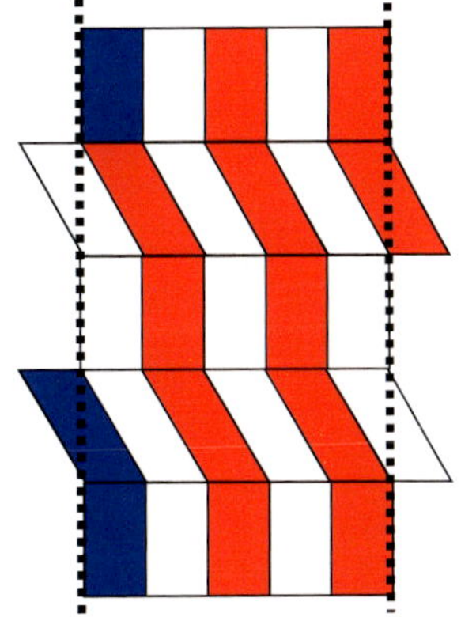

TRIMMING THE FLAG STRIPE BLOCK

VARIABLE STAR BLOCKS

From blue fabric, cut:

- (2) 5½" × WOF strips

  Subcut (10) 5½" squares for block centers.

From white fabric, cut:

- (3) 3" × WOF strips

  Subcut (40) 3" squares for block corners.

- (3) 5½" × WOF strips

  Subcut (40) 3" × 5½" rectangles for Star Points background.

From red fabric, cut:

- (7) 3" × WOF strips

  Subcut (80) 2½" red squares for Star Points.

Making Flying Goose Units / Star Points

Make the star points for the Variable Star blocks. Refer to *Flying Goose / Star Points* illustration.

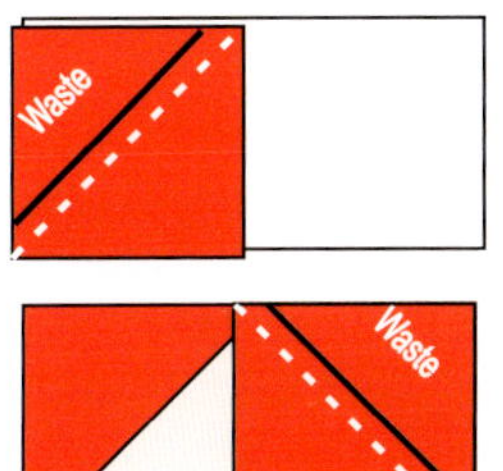

FLYING GOOSE / STAR POINTS

1. Place a square at the left end of the rectangle, right sides together.
2. Sew a diagonal seam from corner to corner.
3. Trim the outer corner, leaving ¼" seam allowance.
4. Press seam allowance open.
5. Add another square to the right end of rectangle.
6. Sew diagonal seam corner to corner, crossing the first seam.
7. Trim outer corner, leaving ¼" seam allowance.
8. Press seam allowance open.

Assemble the Variable Star Blocks

ASSEMBLING THE STAR BLOCKS

Assemble the block as shown in *Assembling the Star Blocks* illustration.

1. Attach white corner squares to each side of Flying Goose unit.
2. Press seam allowances toward corners.
3. Attach Flying Goose units to each side of blue center square, making sure that the "points" are in the correct position.
4. Press seam allowances toward center square.
5. Attach the rows together to make the block, nesting the seams, and again making sure that the "points" are correct.
6. The blocks should measure 10½" square unfinished. Make (10) blocks.

SETTING TRIANGLE STRIP SETS

CUTTING SETTING TRIANGLES

From red, cut:

- (4) 4" × WOF strips

From blue, cut:

- (4) 4" × WOF strips

1. Assemble strips into (4) red/blue strip sets. Press seam open.
2. Use a diagonal set ruler to cut setting and corner triangles. Use the 10" line as the base.
3. From one end of each strip set, cut (1) blue base corner triangle.
4. From each strip set, cut (4) large setting triangles, alternating direction of triangle with each cut.
5. From the other end of each strip set, cut (1) red base corner triangle.

ASSEMBLING THE QUILT BORDERS

From red, cut:

- (4) 2½" × WOF strips for border

  Attach end to end to form long strip

From blue, cut

- (4) 2½" × WOF strips for border.

  Attach end to end to form long strip

Refer to illustration *Assembling Quilt Top.*

FLAG STRIPE BLOCK COLUMNS

- Assemble (3) vertical columns of (4) blocks each from Flag Stripe Blocks.

VARIABLE STAR BLOCK COLUMNS

- Assemble (2) vertical columns of (5) Variable Star Blocks and Setting Corner Triangles.

ADDING THE BORDERS

1. Measure through the center of the top from top to bottom to get the length for the side borders.
2. Cut (1) Left Red strip and (1) Right Blue strips to this length and attach to the sides.
3. Measure through center from left to right, including the borders you just added.
4. Cut (1) Top Red strip and (1) Bottom Blue strip to this length and attach.

FINISHING

- Layer top, batting, and backing.
- Quilt as desired.
- Add binding.
- Remember to label your quilt.

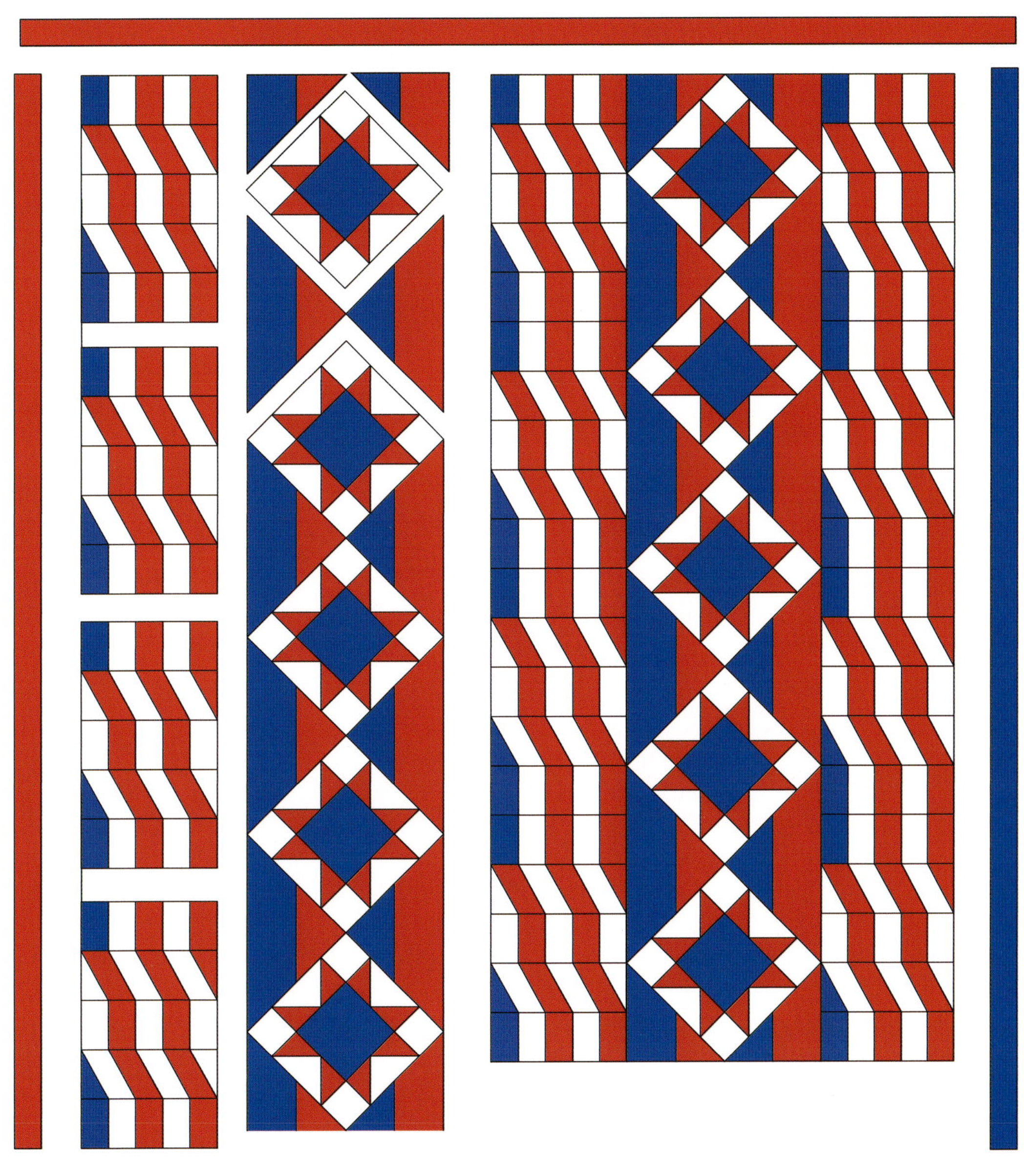

ASSEMBLING QUILT TOP

Shine On

Quilt designed and pieced by Victoria Findlay Wolfe • Machine-quilted by Deb Peterson

Quilt Size: 72" × 84"

Victoria used easy shapes to play with movement within each individual block and also within the background of her design. Half-square triangles have so many fun options that can change the movement of a quilt. Mastering the technique of making more than one half-square triangle at a time speeds this quilt along and makes for a dramatic finished piece. Hit your scrap bins and PLAY!—*Sue Reich*

MATERIALS

- 2¾ yards light-blue solid
- 3½ yards white solid
- ¾ yards navy solid
- ¼ yards royal blue solid
- 1¼ yards red solid
- 5 yards for backing

MAKING HALF-SQUARE TRIANGLE UNITS

1. Draw a diagonal line from the upper left corner to the lower right corner on the wrong side of the white solid A squares, as shown in the diagrams below.
2. Draw lines ¼" away from each side of the previously drawn lines as shown.
3. Layer a marked white A square on top of a light-blue solid A square, right sides together; stitch on outer marked lines as shown.
4. Cut on the centerlines to make two half-square triangle units.
5. Press seam allowances toward the light-blue fabric. Make a total of 94 white solid / light-blue solid half-square triangle units.
6. In the same manner, use white solid and navy solid C squares to make 84 half-square triangle units. Use white solid and royal blue solid C squares to make 16 half-square triangle units.

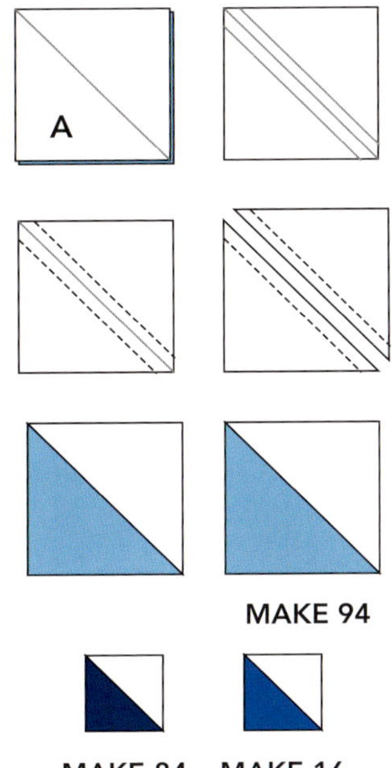

CUTTING

Measurements include ¼" seam allowances.

From light-blue solid, cut:

- (8) 6⅞" strips. From strips, cut (47) 6⅞" A squares.
- (5) 6½" strips. From strips, cut (22) 6½" E squares.

From white solid, cut:

- (2) 7¼" strips. From strips, cut (9) 7¼" B squares.
- (8) 6⅞" strips. From strips, cut (47) 6⅞" A squares.
- (5) 3⅞" strips. From strips, cut (50) 3⅞" C squares.
- (4) 3½" strips. From strips, cut (36) 3½" D squares.

From navy solid, cut:

- (5) 3⅞" strips. From strips, cut (42) 3⅞" C squares.

From royal blue solid, cut:

- (1) 3⅞" strip. From strips, cut (8) 3⅞" C squares.

From red solid, cut:

- (4) 3⅞" strips. From strips, cut (36) 3⅞" C squares.
- (9) 2¼" strips for binding.

MAKING PINWHEEL BLOCKS

1. Lay out four white solid / navy solid half-square triangle units as shown in *Pinwheel Block Diagrams*.
2. Sew units into rows; sew rows together to create one pinwheel block. Make a total of 21 white solid / navy solid pinwheel blocks.
3. In the same manner, make four pinwheel blocks using white solid / royal blue half-square triangle units.

Pinwheel Block Diagrams

MAKING STAR POINT UNITS

1. On the wrong side of red solid C squares, draw a diagonal line from corner to corner. Draw lines ¼" away from each side of the previously drawn line, as shown in *Star Point Unit Assembly Diagrams*.
2. Place two marked C squares on white solid B square, right sides together. Stitch on the outer marked lines. Cut on the centerline and press the seams toward the red solid triangles as shown.
3. Place two marked C squares on the triangle units in step 2, as shown in *Star Point Unit Assembly Diagrams*. Stitch on the outer marked lines.
4. Cut on the centerline and press seams toward red solid triangles, as shown, to make four star point units.
5. Repeat steps 1 through 4 to make a total of 36 red solid / white solid star point units, as shown in *Star Point Unit Assembly Diagrams*.

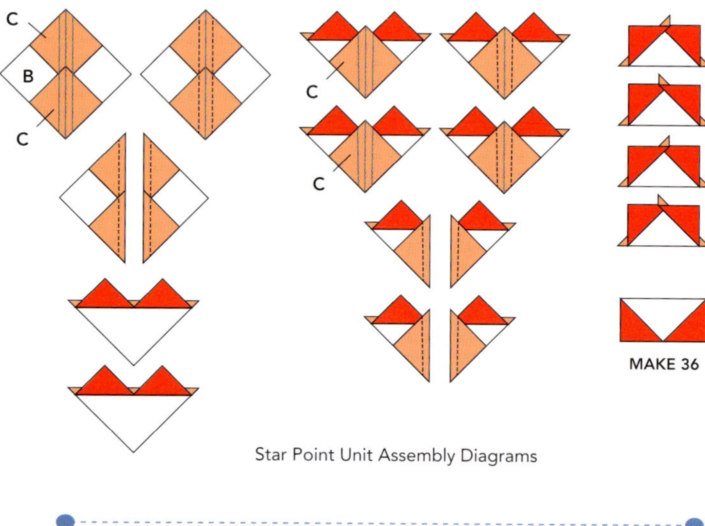

Star Point Unit Assembly Diagrams

STAR BLOCK ASSEMBLY

1. Lay out four white solid D squares, four star point units, and one white solid / navy solid pinwheel block, as shown in *Star Block Diagrams*.
2. Sew units into rows; sew rows together to create one star block. Make a total of five star blocks with a white solid / navy solid pinwheel block in the center.

VICTORIA'S TIP: After sewing units into rows, the points should be ¼" from the edge, no more and no less. If they aren't in the correct place at this point, fix it NOW so they will be in the right spot later.

3. In the same manner, make four star blocks using white solid / royal blue pinwheel blocks as the center.

Star Block Diagrams

QUILT TOP ASSEMBLY

1. Lay out white solid / light-blue triangle-square units, light-blue E squares, pinwheel blocks, and star blocks, as shown in the *Quilt Top Assembly Diagram* on page 113.
2. Sew blocks together to create rows.
3. Sew rows together to complete the quilt top.

FINISHING

4. Divide backing into two (90") length panels. Join panels vertically.
5. Layer backing, batting, and quilt top; baste. Quilt as desired.
6. Join 2¼" wide binding strips into one continuous piece for double-fold binding. Add binding to quilt.

Quilt Top Assembly Diagram

The Patriot's Quilt

Pieced by Sue Reich • Quilted by Debbie Newill

Finished Quilt Size: 65" × 85" | Finished Size with 2½" Borders

The 5.5" squares in this quilt provide the opportunity to use large motif fabrics effectively as the eye moves across the quilt from pinwheels to symbols of patriotism. It's a great fabric for fussy cutting favorite images.—*Sue*

FABRIC REQUIRED

Measurements include ¼" seam allowance. Fabric is assumed to be first-quality quilting-weight fabric with at least 42" usable width. Strips are cut across the width of the fabric (WOF).

Red: 1¾ yards

White: 1¾ yards

Blue: 1¾ yards

Blue for border: ⅞ yard if border strips are pieced, 2⅜ yards needed for unpieced strips

Backing: 73" × 93"

Binding: ¾ yard

CUTTING AND MAKING QUILT UNITS

This quilt is based on a quilt from the early 1900s, and there are several ways to make it. Instead of blocks, we decided to construct the quilt in vertical strips of squares, rectangles, and pinwheels. Your first job is to cut and assemble all the units. You will need:

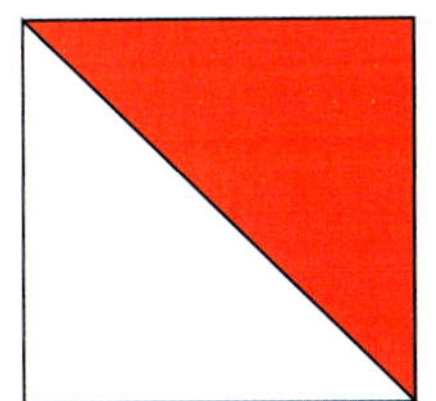

For (96) Half-Square Triangle Units:

- Cut (2) red 6¾" × WOF strips, then cut strips into (12) 6¾" squares.
- Cut (2) white 6¾" × WOF strips, then cut strips into (12) 6¾" squares.

For (82) Rail Fence Units:

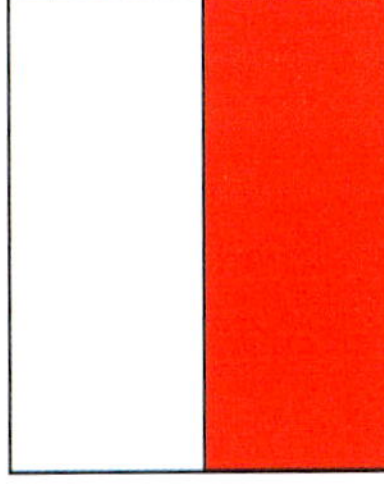

- Cut (12) red 3" × WOF strips.
- Cut (12) white 3" × WOF strips.
- Sew red and white pairs of these strips together on the long edge.
- Press seam allowance toward darker fabric.
- Cut each red + white strip set into 5½" segments.
- You will need a total of (82) segments, which should measure 5½" square.

For (65) Blue Squares

- Cut (10) blue 5½" × WOF strips, then cut the strips into (65) 5½" squares.

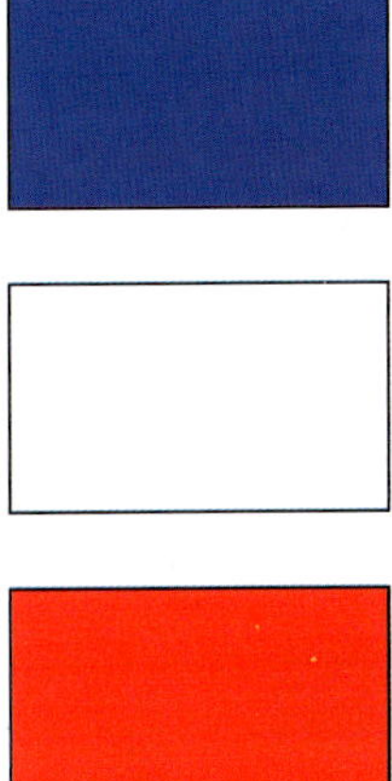

Rectangles::

- Cut (2) blue 3" × WOF strips, then cut the strips into (14) 3" × 5½" rectangles.
- Cut (2) white 3" × WOF strips, then cut the strips into (14) 3" × 5½" rectangles.
- Cut (2) red 3" × WOF strips, then cut the strips into (14) 3" × 5½" rectangles.

Make Eight-at-a-Time Half-Square Triangles

There are a dozen ways of making HSTs. For this pattern, try using this technique, because if you measure, mark, sew, and cut carefully, you won't need to trim each of the individual (96) HST units. They will all come out the correct size.

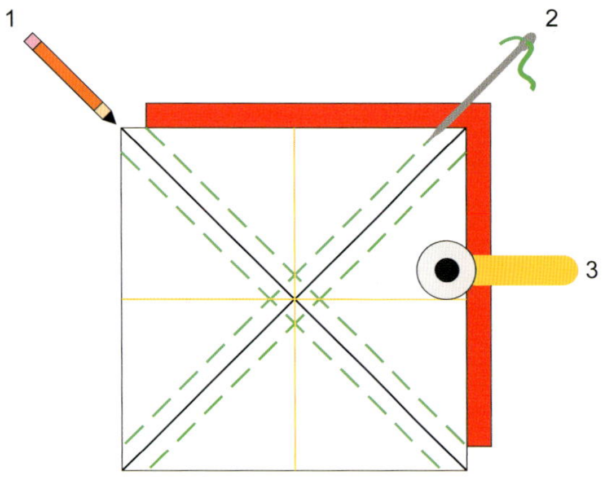

1. Draw diagonal lines from corner to corner in each direction on the back of the lighter fabric.
2. Place 6¾" red and marked white squares right sides together.
3. Sew exactly ¼" from each side of the drawn line in both directions.
4. First cut: through the center, each direction, to make 4 squares.
5. Second cut: on the drawn lines to separate the HSTs.
6. Press seam allowances toward the darker fabric.
7. No need to trim off the "ears."
8. Units should measure 3" square.

Make Pinwheel Units

Paying close attention to the orientation of the HSTs, use the HSTs to make:

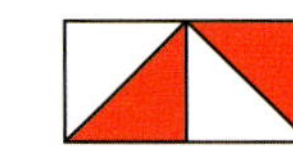

- (18) Pinwheel Units
- (10) Double HST Units

Set aside remaining (4) HSTs.

ASSEMBLE THE COLUMNS

There are only four strip designs to assemble for this quilt:

- **A.** Make (2) of these—one for each side of the quilt. Note that you will use one on the left side as pictured and the other strip on the right side but rotated 180 degrees.
- **B.** Make (6) of these. Half of these also are rotated 180 degrees, as illustrated.
- **C.** Make (3) of these strips. These strips are not rotated.
- **D.** Make (2) of these strips. These strips are not rotated.

After you assemble the columns, attach the columns to each other as shown.

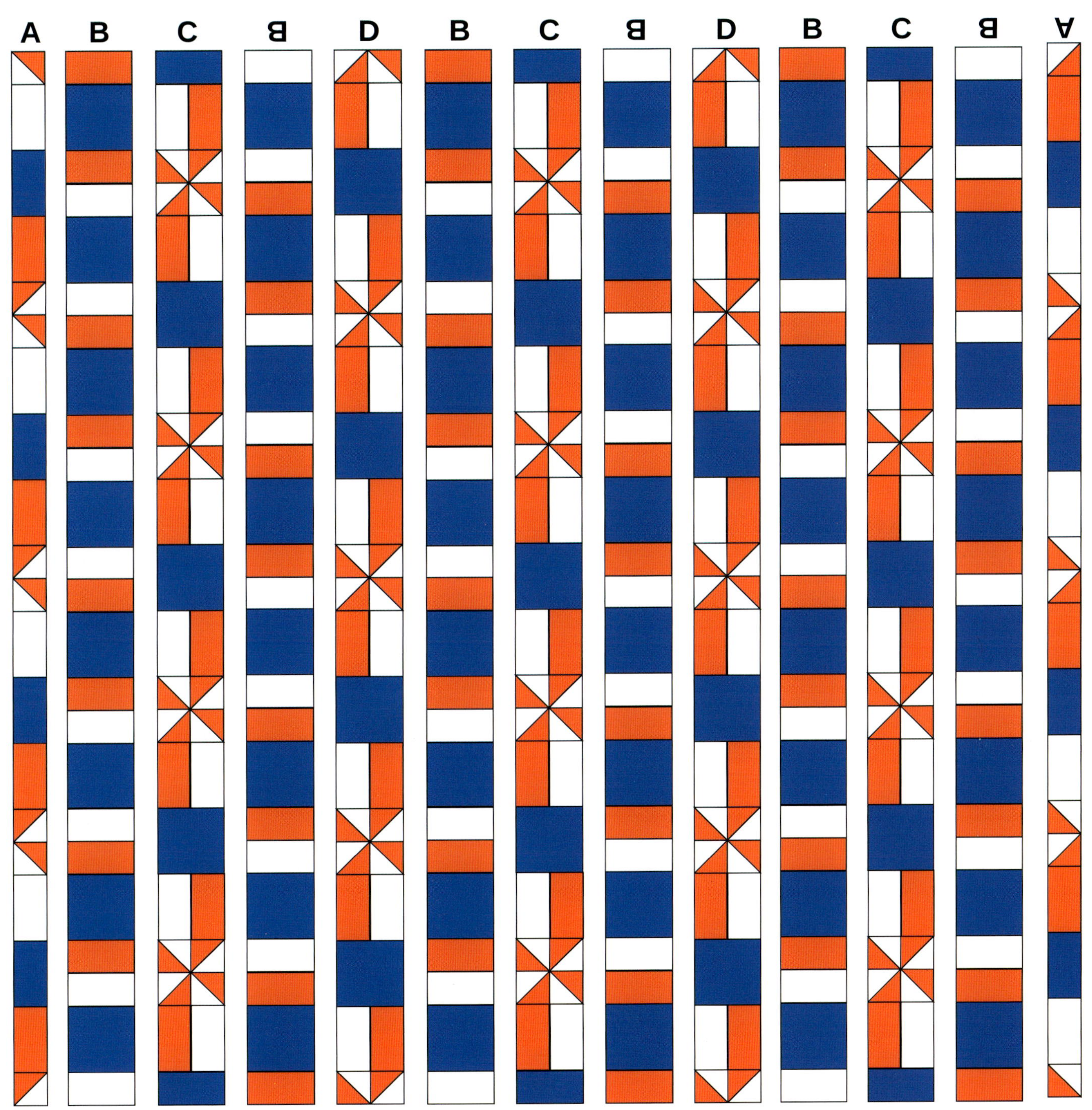
A
B
C
B
D
B
C
B
D
B
C
B
A

ADD BORDER

These cutting instructions are for cutting WOF strips that will be pieced together to make long strips. If you don't want to piece the border fabric, you'll need 2⅜ yards

- Cut (8) 3" strips across WOF and join end to end.
- Measure finished quilt top.
- From the long strips, you should need to cut:
- For left/right borders: cut (2) 80½" lengths.
- For top/bottom borders: cut (2) 65½" lengths.
- But make adjustments, if necessary, for your specific measurements.

FINISHING

1. Quilt top should now measure 65½" × 85½".
2. Create a backing that is 8" larger than this top: 73" × 93".
3. After layering the quilt top, batting, and backing, quilt as desired.
4. Cut binding fabric into (8) 2¼" × WOF strips.
5. Join these strips with a diagonal seam; press in half for double-fold binding.
6. To attach binding to quilt, first decide if you will hand-finish or machine-finish the binding.
7. If you hand-finish, attach the raw edges of the binding to the front raw edges of the quilt, press around to the back, and then whipstitch the binding to the back.
8. If you machine-finish, attach the raw edges of the binding to the raw edges of the back of the quilt, press around to the front, and then stitch very close to the folded edge on the front.

Stitch by Stitch, We Remember

Pieced by Betsy Hockenberry • Quilted by Nancy King

Finished Size: 60" × 84" with (24) 12" Blocks and (2) 3" Borders

The perfect fabric was used in creating this quilt to give motion to the stretched star designs. Stars are the most popular design element incorporated in quilts for our veteran and military service members.—*Sue Reich*

NOTE ON FABRIC: The blue fabric is cut from a striped fabric. Usually, stripes run the length of the yardage. Controlling the direction of the stripes is easy and really "makes" the quilt.

FABRIC REQUIRED

Red: 1 yard

White: 2¼ yards

Blue (lengthwise stripe): 1½ yards

Blue for border: ⅞ yard

Red for border: ⅞ yard

Cut each border fabric into (8) 3½" × WOF strips. Join strips end to end and set aside until after the top is assembled.

Red for binding: ¾ yard

Backing: 68" × 92"

CUTTING FOR THE BLOCKS

From Red:

- Cut (9) 3½" × WOF strips, then cut strips into (96) 3½" A squares.

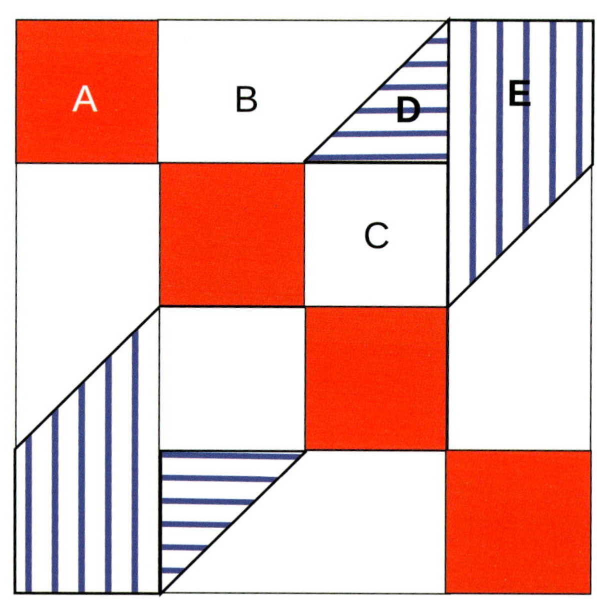

From White:

- Cut (16) 3½" × WOF strips, then cut strips into (96) 3½" × 6½" B rectangles.
- Cut (5) 3½" × WOF strips, then cut strips into (48) 3½" C squares.

From Blue (stripe runs lengthwise on fabric):

- Cut (5) 3½" × WOF strips, then cut strips into (48) 3½" D squares.
- Cut (5) 6½" × WOF strips, then cut strips into (48) 3½" × 6½" E rectangles.

ASSEMBLING THE BLOCKS

Make (48) B + D Units

1. Place a blue D square right sides together on end of white B rectangle, as shown in diagram. Be sure to orient the stripes as shown.

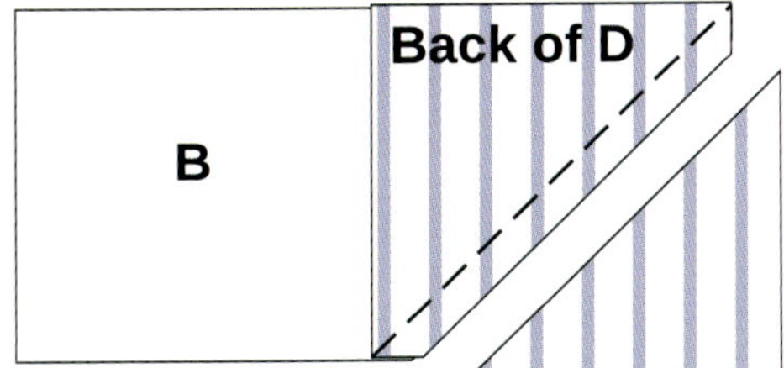

2. Sew diagonal seam from corner to corner.
3. Trim off and discard outer corner, leaving ¼" seam allowance.
4. Press seam allowance open.
5. Notice that the stripe in the fabric runs parallel to the long side of the B rectangle.

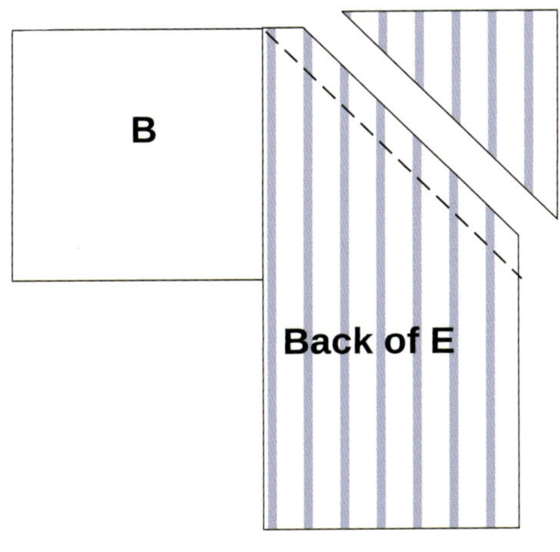

Make (48) B + E Units

1. Place a blue E rectangle right sides together on end of white B rectangle, as shown in diagram. Be sure to orient the stripes as shown.
2. Sew diagonal seam from corner to corner.
3. Trim off and discard outer corner, leaving ¼" seam allowance.
4. Press seam allowance open.
5. Notice that the stripe in the fabric runs parallel to the long side of the B rectangle.

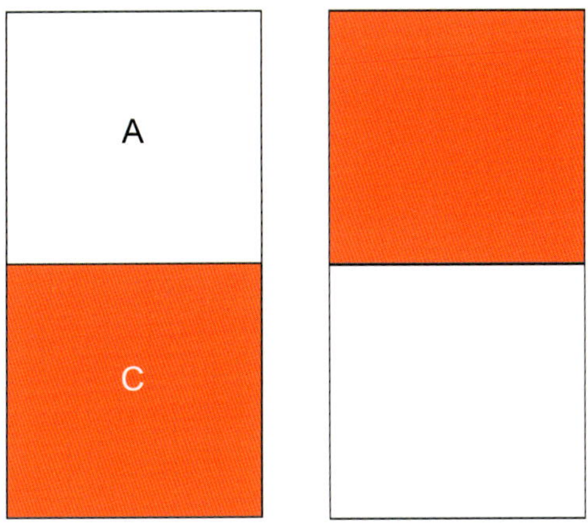

Make (24) A + C Four-Patch Units

1. Sew together (48) pairs of red and white 3½" squares.
2. Press seam allowance toward red fabric.
3. Attach pairs, matching seamline, to make (24) Four-Patch Units.

1. Use remaining red A squares to assemble units as shown to complete block.
2. Make (24) blocks.

ASSEMBLE QUILT TOP AND ADD BORDERS

Attach blocks in (6) rows of (4) blocks each, being careful to match the seams and turn the blocks in the same direction.

Measure through the center of the quilt from top to bottom. The measurement should be 72½" for the left and right blue borders. Cut the presewn border strips to the correct length and attach to quilt top.

Measure through the center from left to right, including the borders just added. This measurement should be 54½" for the top and bottom blue borders. Cut the presewn strips to the correct length and attach to the quilt top.

Repeat for the left/right red borders (should be 78½") and for the top/ bottom red borders (should be 60½").

FINISHING

1. Quilt top should now measure 60½" × 84½".
2. Create a backing that is 8" larger than this top: 68" × 92".
3. After layering the quilt top, batting, and backing, quilt as desired.
4. Cut binding fabric into (8) 2 ¼" × WOF strips.
5. Join these strips with a diagonal seam; press in half for double-fold binding.
6. To attach binding to quilt, first decide if you will hand-finish or machine-finish the binding.
7. If you hand-finish, attach the raw edges of the binding to the front raw edges of the quilt, press around to the back, and then whipstitch the binding to the back.
8. If you machine-finish, attach the raw edges of the binding to the raw edges of the back of the quilt, press around to the front, and then stitch very close to the folded edge on the front.

Unity in Red, White, and Blue

Pieced and quilted by Ann Davis

Finished Size: 68" × 83"; (20) 10½" Finished Size Pieced Blocks | 1" Border and 3½" Border

Nine-patch variation blocks set on point alternating with solid fabric blocks create a quilt that looks complex but is actually simple to make. This would be a great design for beginning quiltmakers.—*Sue Reich*

FABRIC REQUIRED:

Fabric calculations are based on a usable fabric width of at least 40". Strips are cut across the width of the fabric (WOF).

Red: 1⅞ yard

White: 3¼ yards

Blue: 1½ yard

Blue for inner border: ½ yard

Red for outer border: 1 yard

For binding: ¾ yard red

For backing: 76" × 91"

CUTTING

For Borders:

- Cut blue inner border fabric into (8) 1½" × WOF strips.
- Cut red outer border fabric into (8) 4" × WOF strips.
- Join strips of each color end to end and set aside until after the top is assembled.

For Pieced Blocks, Setting Squares, and Side/Corner Triangles:

- Cut (8) red 4" × WOF strips, then cut strips into (80) 4" A squares.
- Cut (2) blue 4" × WOF strips, then cut strips into (20) 4" B squares.
- Cut (3) blue 8¾" × WOF strips, then cut strips into (10) 8¾" squares for C + D half-square triangles (HSTs).
- Cut (3) white 8¾" × WOF strips, then cut strips into (10) 8¾" squares for C + D HSTs.

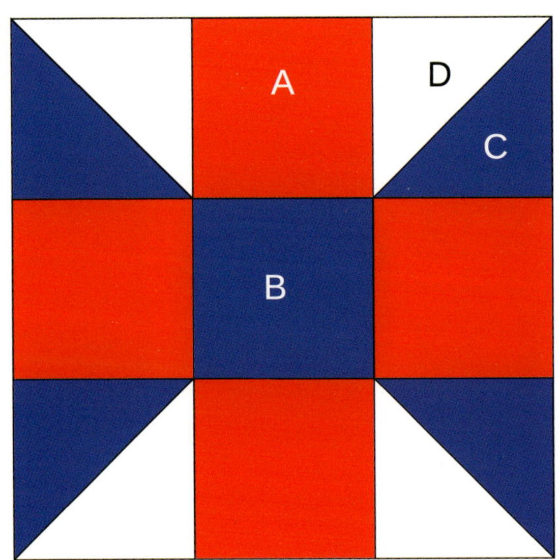

For Setting Squares:

Cut (4) white 11" x WOF strips, then cut strips into (12) 11" squares. Pin a note to these squares saying, "Setting Squares."

For Side-Setting Triangles:

NOTE: Setting squares are the plain white squares that separate the pieced blocks. Side/corner triangles are white triangles for the quilt's edges.

1. Cut (2) white 16⅛" × WOF strips, then cut strips into (4) 16⅛" squares.
2. Cut squares in half twice on the diagonal to make (16) side-setting triangles (you will use only 14 of these triangles). It's a good idea to pin a note to these triangles saying "Side Setting Triangles."

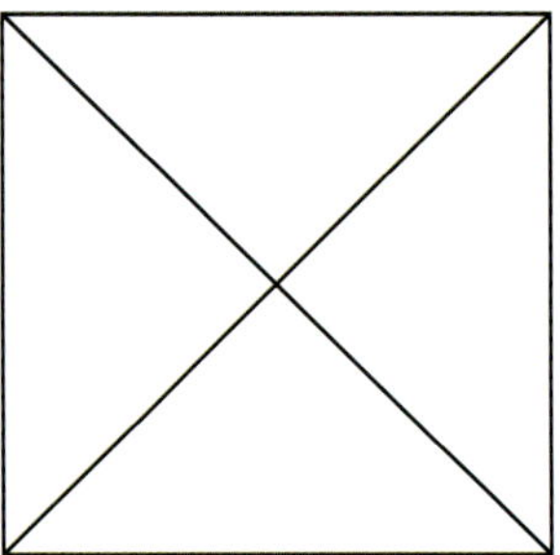

For Corner Triangles:

1. Cut (1) white 8⅜" × WOF strip, then cut strip into (2) 8⅜" squares.
2. Cut squares in half once on the diagonal. Pin a note to these triangles saying "Corner Triangles."

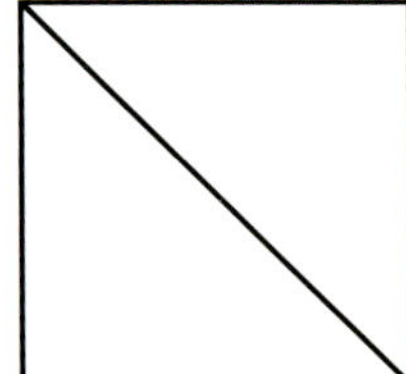

Make Half-Square Triangles

Use the Eight-at-a-Time method for making blue + white HSTs.

1. On the back of the (10) 8¾" white squares, draw a diagonal line from upper left corner to the lower right corner. Draw another line from upper right to lower left.

   Place 8¾" blue and marked white squares, right sides together.

2. Sew exactly ¼" from each side of drawn lines in both directions.

3. First cut: through the center, each direction, to make four squares.

   Second cut: on the drawn center lines to make (8) HSTs.

Press seam allowance toward darker fabric.

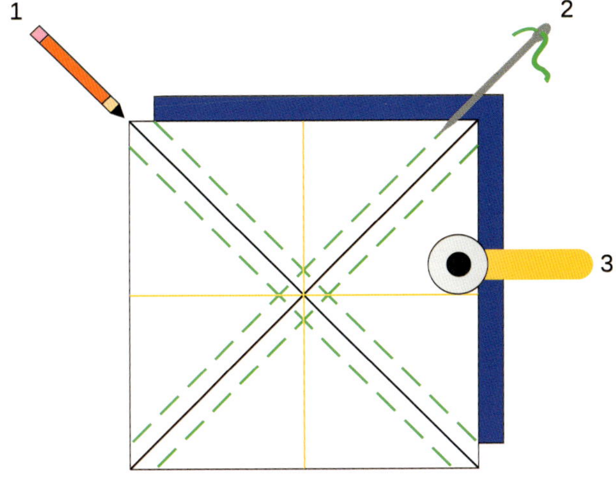

ASSEMBLING THE (20) BLOCKS

1. Attach the squares and half-square triangles in three three-unit rows, as shown.
2. Be sure that the HSTs are oriented correctly.
3. Press the seam allowances as shown in diagram.
4. Press row-joining seams open.
5. Blocks should measure 11" square at this point.

ASSEMBLING THE QUILT

1. Attach the blocks and setting squares in diagonal rows, as shown in the diagram.
2. Add a side-setting triangle at the end of each row, except where you will attach a corner triangle, as noted.
3. At this point, the central quilt top should measure 60" × 74¾".
4. After the central quilt top is together, measure the length (should be 74¾") and cut (2) of the 1½" blue inner border strips to that length.
5. Attach to the left/right sides.
6. Measure the top across the width quilt top, including the side borders you just added.

7. Cut (2) more of the 1½" blue inner border strips to that length (should be 62") and attach to top/bottom. Measurement should be 62".

8. Repeat this technique for cutting and adding the red outer borders. Measurement for left/right borders should be 76¾". Measurement for top/bottom borders should be 69".

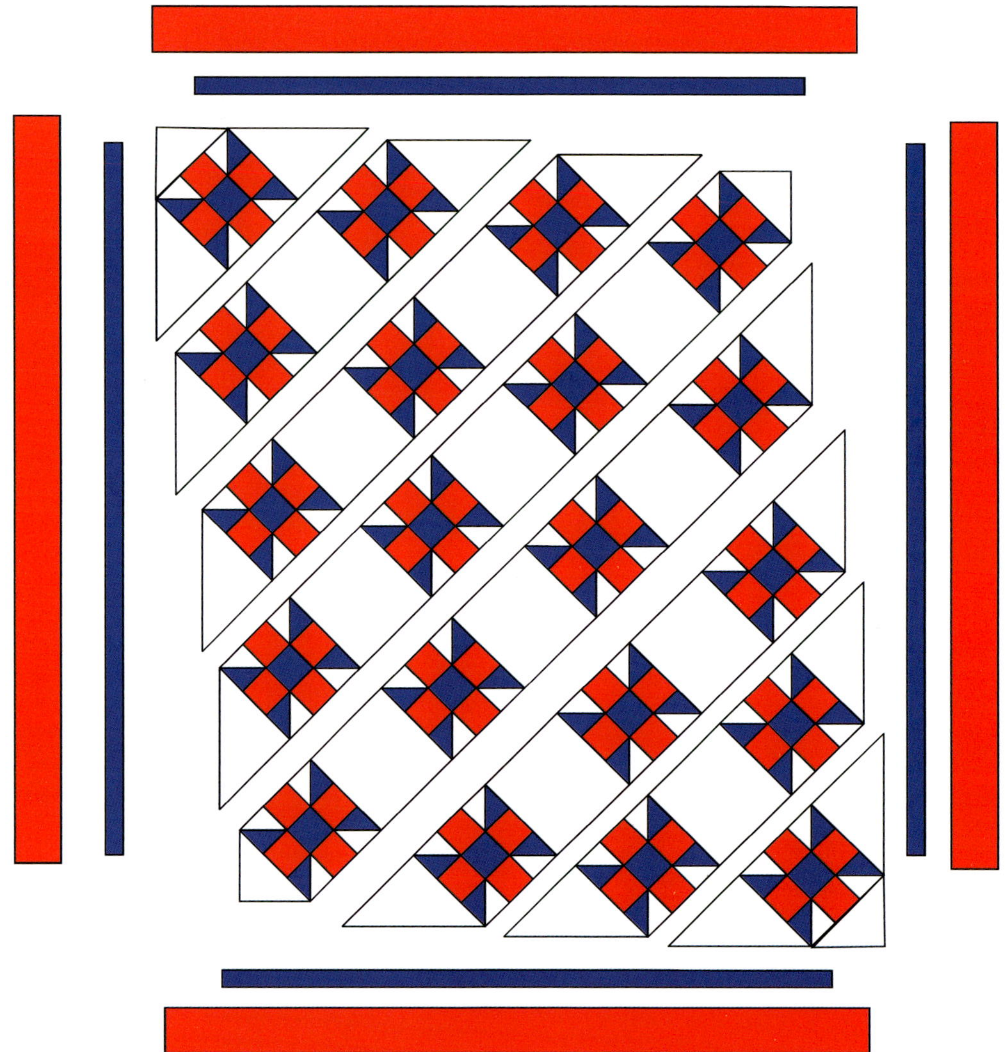

FINISHING

1. Quilt top should now measure 68½" × 83¼".
2. Create a backing that is 8" larger than this top: 76" × 91".
3. After layering the quilt top, batting, and backing, quilt as desired.
4. Cut binding fabric into (8) 2¼" × WOF strips.
5. Join these strips with a diagonal seam; press in half for double-fold binding.
6. To attach binding to quilt, first decide if you will hand-finish or machine-finish the binding.
7. If you hand-finish, attach the raw edges of the binding to the front of the quilt, press around to the back, and then whipstitch the binding to the back.
8. If you machine-finish, attach the raw edges of the binding to the back of the quilt, press around to the front, and then stitch very close to the folded edge on the front.

Stars of Service

Pieced by Ann Parsons Holte • Quilted by Debbie Newill

Finished Quilt Size: 61" × 78" | Finished Block Size: 12" | Finished Border Width: 5"

Based on a quilt from the early 1900s, this design combines easy elements to make an interesting block and setting arrangement.—*Ann*

FABRIC REQUIRED

1¼ yards red

1¼ yards blue

3½ yards white

1⅛ yards for border (blue in photo)

¾ yard for binding (red in photo)

69" × 86" piece for backing

CUTTING

Measurements include ¼" seam allowance. Fabric is assumed to be first-quality quilting fabric with at least 40" usable width of fabric (WOF). A good idea is to label the pieces as you cut.

From Red:

- F Cut (8) 3½" × WOF strips. Cut strips into (48) 3½" × 6½" rectangles.
- E Cut (3) 2" × WOF strips. Cut strips into (48) 2" × 2" squares.
- Cut (1) 5¾" × WOF strip. Cut strips into (5) 5¾" × 5¾" squares.

From Blue:

- H Cut (2) 7¾" × WOF strips. Cut strips into (6) 7¾" × 7¾" squares.
- G Cut (5) 3½" × WOF strips. Cut strips into (48) 3½" × 3½" squares.
- I Cut (3) 2" × WOF strips. Cut strips into (48) 2" × 2" squares.

From White:

- H Cut (2) 7¾" × WOF strips. Cut strips into (6) 7¾" × 7¾" squares.
- C Cut (5) 3½" × WOF strips. Cut strips into (48) 3½" × 3½" squares.
- B Cut (5) 2" × WOF strips. Cut strips into (48) 2" × 3½" rectangles.
- A Cut (2) 3½" × WOF strips. Cut strips into (12) 3½" × 3½" squares.
- J Cut (2) 8½" × WOF strips. Cut strips into (6) 8½" × 12½" rectangles.

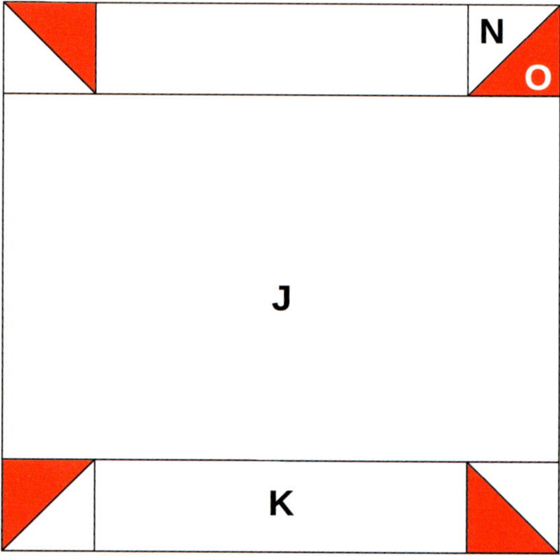

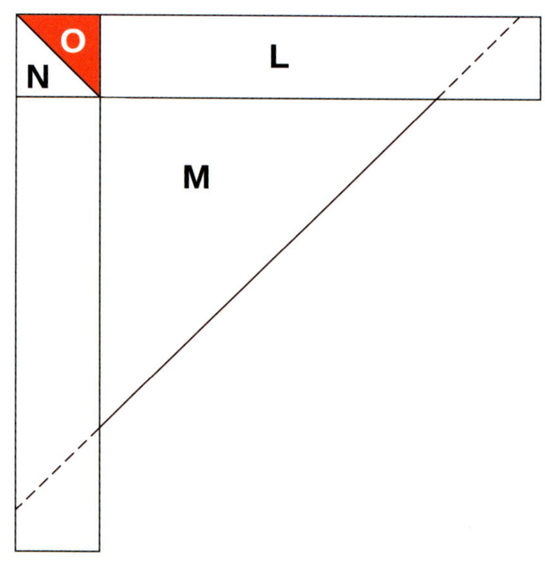

- K Cut (3) 2½" × WOF strips. Cut strips into (12) 2½" × 8½" rectangles.
- N Cut (1) 5¾" × WOF strip. Cut strip into (5) 5¾" × 5¾" squares.
- L Cut (7) 2½" × WOF strip. Cut strips into (20) 2½" × 12" rectangles.
- M (1) 12⅝" × WOF strip. Cut strip into (3) 12⅝" squares. Cut squares twice on diagonal.
- P (1) 9⅜" × WOF strip. Cut strip into (2) 9⅜" squares. Cut squares once on diagonal.

From Border Fabric:

- Cut (7) 5½" × WOF strips. Attach strips end to end with a straight seam and set aside.
- For cornerstones, from scraps: cut (2) 6" Red squares and (2) Blue 6" squares. Set aside.

From Binding Fabric:

- (8) 2¼" × WOF strips. Attach strips end to end with a diagonal seam and set aside.

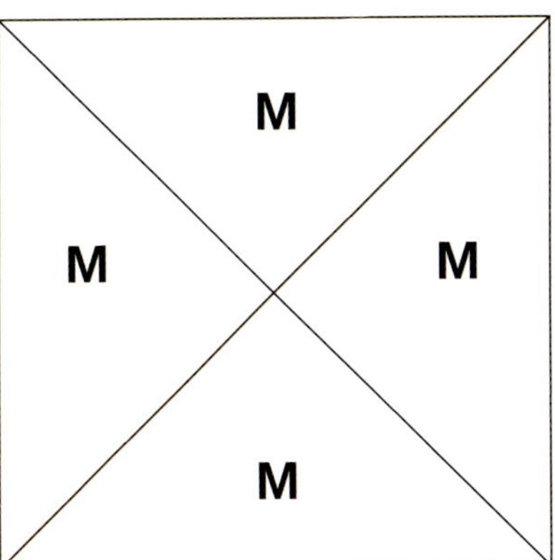

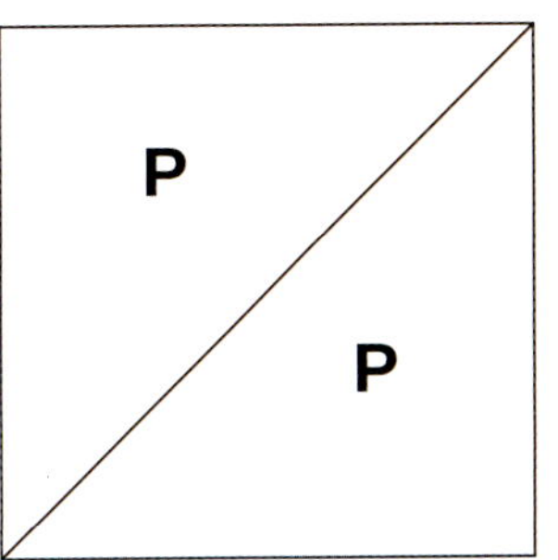

MAKING THE BLOCK UNIT

Half-Square Triangles and Flying Geese

You will use the Eight-at-a-Time method to make the half-square triangle units. There are two sizes of half-square triangles (HSTs) in this quilt. You will need:

(48) blue + white 2" finished size, using the 7¾" white and the 7¾" blue squares

(34) red + white 1½" finished size, using the 5¾" white and the 5¾" red squares

1. On the back of the white squares, draw a diagonal line from upper left corner to the lower right corner. Draw another line from upper right to lower left.
2. Place the blue + white squares and the red + white squares right sides together.
3. Sew exactly ¼" from each side of drawn lines in both directions.
4. First cut: through the center, each direction, to make four squares.
5. Second cut: on the drawn center lines to make (8) HSTs.
6. Press seam allowance toward darker fabric.

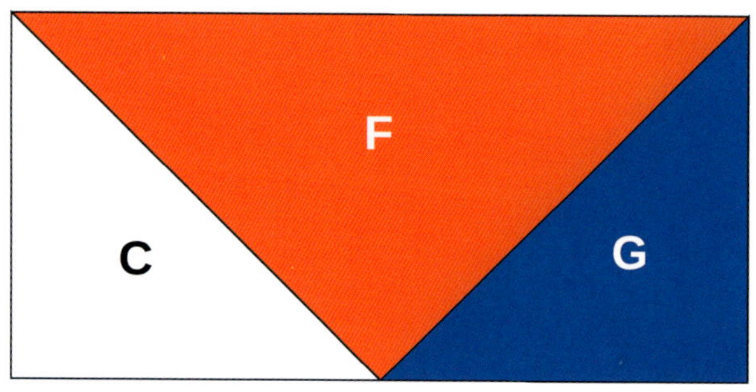

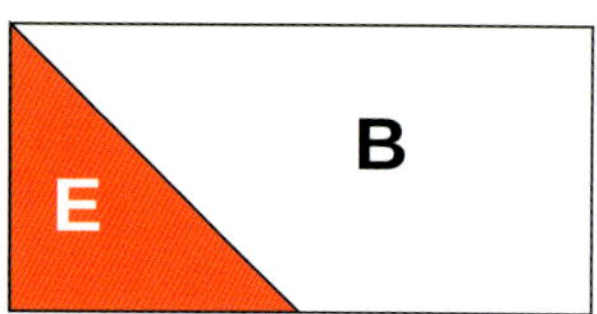

Making Flying Goose Units

The Flying Goose units in this block are unusual. The (48) 3" × 6" finished size units feature a goose with a (F) red body, one (G) blue wing, and one (C) white wing.

The (48) 1½" × 3" finished size units have a Flying Goose unit with a (B) white body and only one (E) wing, which is red.

By using the following method, you will "waste" some triangles, but you can always sew those extra triangles together and save them for another project.

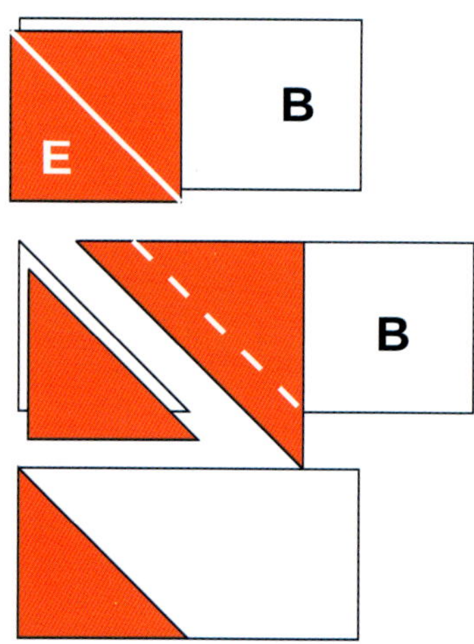

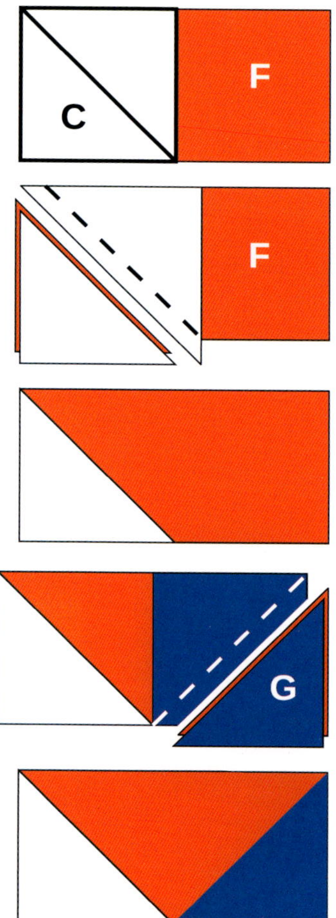

1. Draw a diagonal line from corner to corner on the back of the red E, white C, and blue G squares.
2. Place square, right sides together, on one end of the appropriate size B or F rectangle, with the drawn line angled as shown.
3. Sew on the drawn line.
4. Trim ¼" from drawn line on the side closest to the corner.
5. Press seam allowance open.
6. Place the other square for the larger F rectangle, right sides together, on the other end of the F rectangle, with the drawn line angled as shown.
7. Sew on the drawn line.
8. Trim ¼" from the drawn line.
9. Press seam allowance open.

ASSEMBLING THE BLOCKS

Star Blocks

1. Starting with the block center, attach the small blue I squares and the E + F one-wing Flying Goose units to the center A square in three rows, as shown. Press seam allowances in direction of arrows. Make (12) of these units.
2. Attach the other HST and FG block units in three rows, as shown, being sure to turn the HST and FG units in the right direction.
3. Press joining rows open.
4. Make (12) blocks in this manner.

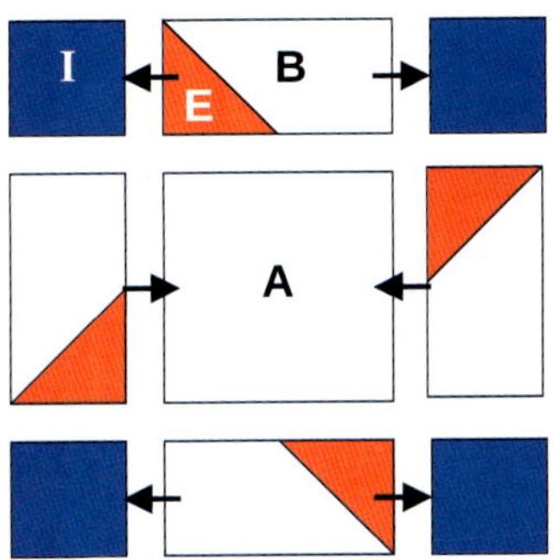

Square-Setting Blocks

1. Attach small red + white N + O HSTs to the ends of the K rectangles, being sure to orient the HSTs as shown. Press seam allowance in the direction of the arrows.
2. Attach these units to the J rectangles, being sure to orient the pieced units as shown.
3. Press seam allowances toward the center.

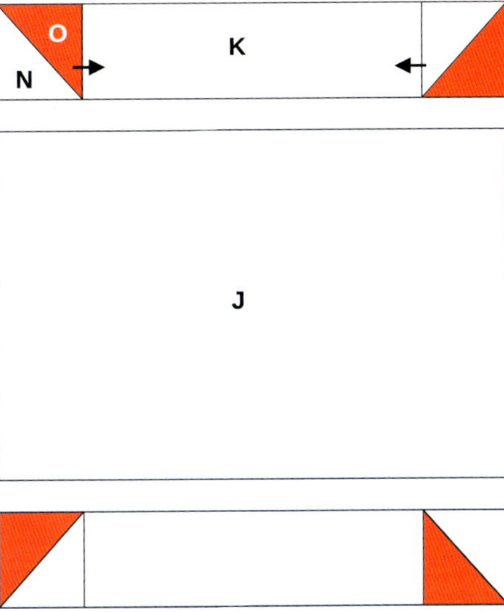

Side-Setting Triangle Blocks

1. Attach an L rectangle to one short side of the M triangle, as shown.
2. Press seam allowance toward the L rectangle.
3. Attach a red + white N + O HST to one end of another L rectangle, being sure to turn the HSTs in the right direction, as shown.
4. Press seam allowance toward the L rectangle.
5. Attach the second unit to the remaining short side of the M triangle.
6. Use the long side of the triangle as a guide to trim off the ends of the L rectangles.

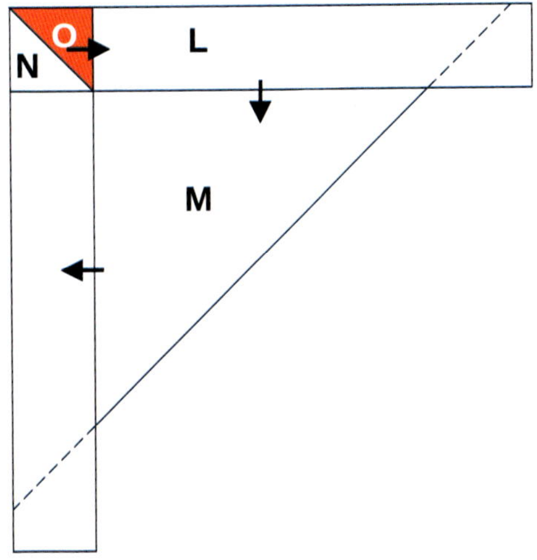

ASSEMBLING THE QUILT TOP

Attach the corner P triangles, square-setting blocks, s-setting triangles, and star blocks in diagonal rows as shown in the illustration.

Add the Borders and Cornerstone Blocks:

- Make (4) red + blue HSTs from the (2) red and (2) blue 6" squares.
- Draw a line on the back of the lighter fabric from one corner to the other.
- Sew 1/4" from each side of the drawn line.
- Cut on the drawn line and press seam toward darker fabric.

Add the Left and Right Borders:

- Measure the quilt top from top to bottom (it should be 68 3/8").
- Cut the two left/right borders to this length from the 5 1/2" strip that you set aside earlier.
- Attach these to the left and right sides of the quilt top.

Add the Top and Bottom Borders:

- Measure the quilt top from seam to seam of the added left/right borders (should be 51").
- Add 1/2" and cut two more border strips to this length.
- Use saved (2) 6" red and (2) 6" blue squares to make (4) HSTs. Add these cornerstone blocks to the ends of these strips, making sure to turn the cornerstone HSTs in the correct direction.
- Attach these to the top and bottom of the quilt to complete the top.

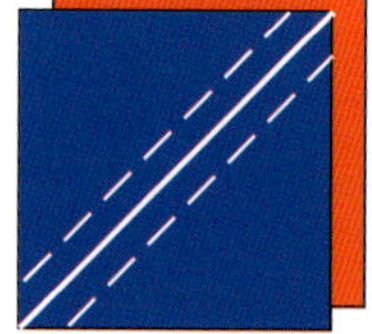

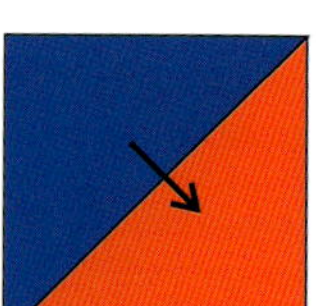

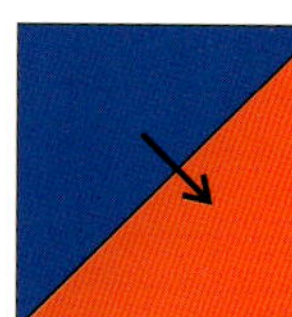

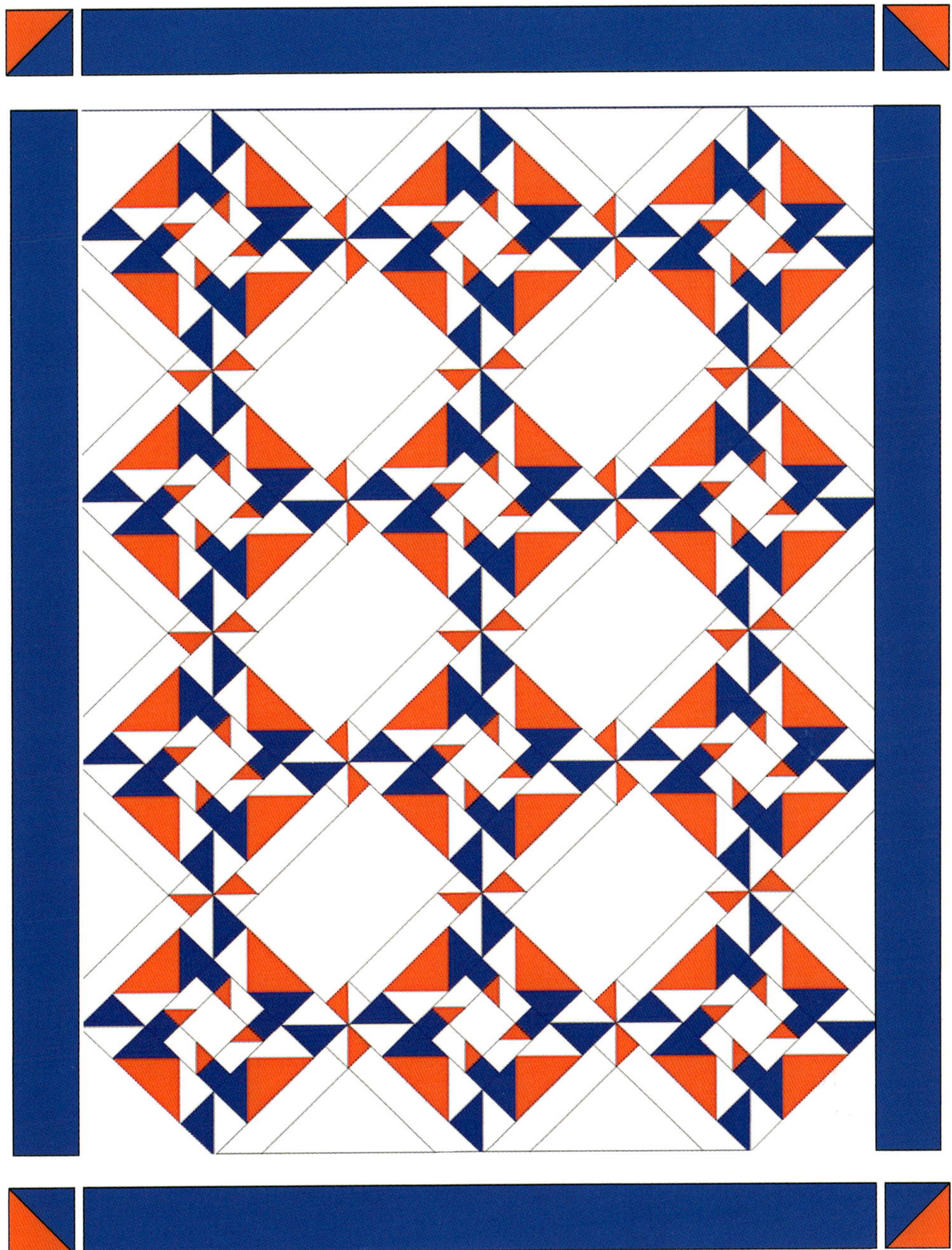

FINISHING THE QUILT

1. Quilt top should now measure 61" × 78".
2. Create a backing that is 8" larger than this top: 69" × 86".
3. After layering the quilt top, batting, and backing, quilt as desired.
4. Cut binding fabric into (8) 2¼" × WOF strips.
5. Join these strips with a diagonal seam; press in half for double-fold binding.
6. To attach binding to quilt, first decide if will you hand-finish or machine-finish the binding.
7. If you hand-finish, attach the raw edges of the binding to the front of the quilt, press around to the back, and then whipstitch the binding to the back.
8. If you machine-finish, attach the raw edges of the binding to the back of the quilt, press around to the front, and then machine-stitch very close to the folded edge on the front.
9. Finally, make a Quilts of Valor label for your quilt.

Woven with Gratitude

Designed by Debra Rowe, Captain, USAF, 1992–1997
Pieced by Debra Rowe • Quilted by Debbie Newill

Finished Quilt Size: 64" × 88" with 2" Border | (18) 12" Finished Size, Jacob's Ladder Blocks | (17) 12" Finished Size, King's Crown Blocks

The finished quilt, "Woven with Gratitude," looks complex but it's really just a two-block quilt with the blocks set straight but angled in different directions. This quilt honors the courage and sacrifice of those who served. Each stitch is a heartfelt thank-you, connecting fabric and freedom into a lasting symbol of appreciation.—*Debbie*

FABRIC REQUIRED

Measurements include ¼" seam allowance. Fabric is assumed to be first-quality quilting fabric with at least 40" usable width of fabric (WOF). A good idea is to label the pieces as you cut.

Red: 2¾ yards, including blocks, border, and binding

White: 3½ yards

Blue: 2 yards

Backing: 72" × 96"

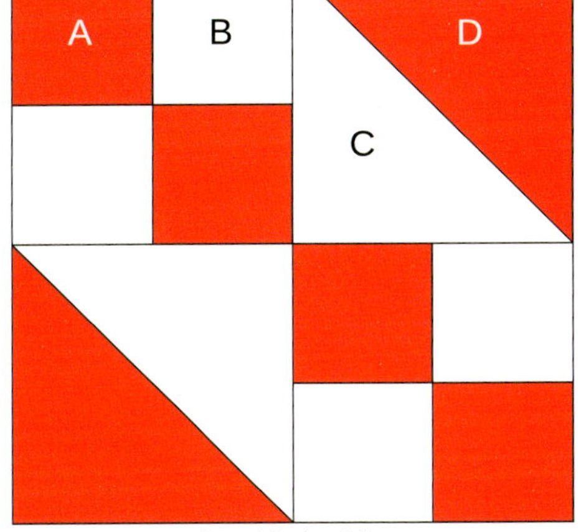

Jacob's Ladder

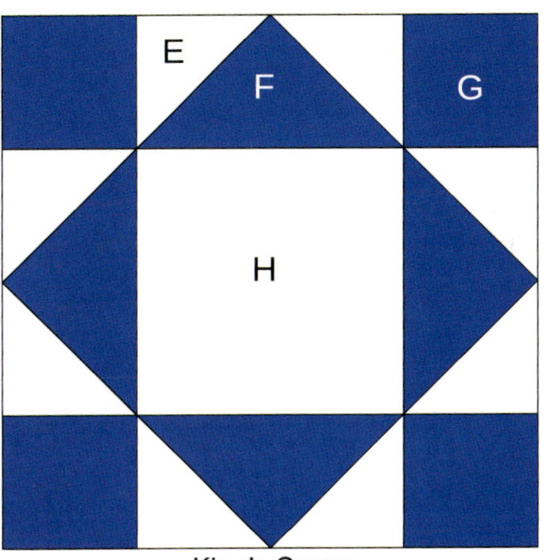

King's Crown

CUTTING

For Border and Binding:
From red: cut (17) red 2½" × WOF strips.

- Join (8) strips end to end for the outer borders and set aside for border and set aside.
- Attach remaining 2½" strips with diagonal seam to make binding.

From Red for Jacob's Ladder Blocks:

- A Cut (7) 3½" × WOF strips.
- D Cut (4) 7" × WOF strips. Cut strips into (18) 7" squares.

From Blue for King's Crown Blocks:

- G Cut (7) 3½" × WOF strips. Cut strips into (68) 3½" squares.
- F Cut (12) 3½" × WOF strips. Cut strips into (68) 3½" × 6½" rectangles.

From White for Jacob's Ladder Blocks:

- B Cut (7) 3½" × WOF strips.
- C Cut (4) 7" × WOF strips. Cut strips into (18) 7" squares.

From White for King's Crown Blocks:

- E Cut (13) 3½" × WOF strips. Cut strips into (136) 3½" squares.
- H Cut (3) 6½" × WOF strips. Cut strips into (17) 6½" squares.

ASSEMBLING JACOB'S LADDER BLOCKS

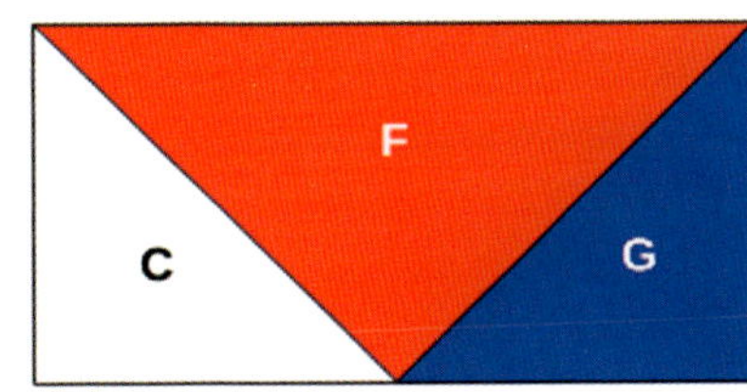

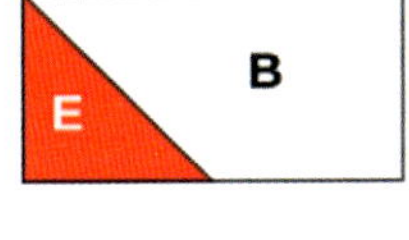

Red + White Four-Patch

1. Attach pairs of 3½" red A and white B strips on long side.
2. Press seam allowance toward red fabric.
3. Subcut the red + white strips into (72) 3½" segments.

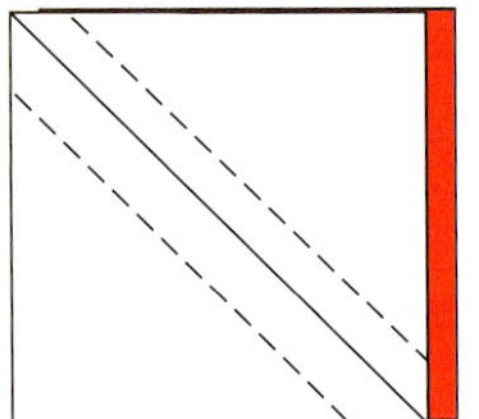

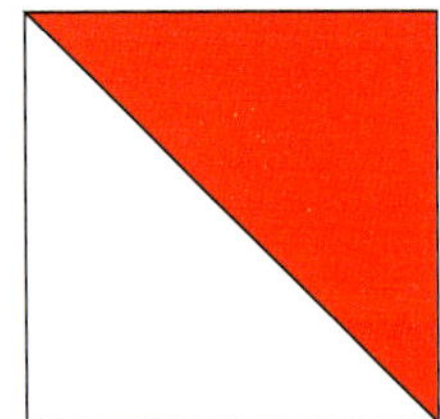

4. Attach segments as shown to make (36) Four-Patch units.

Red + White Half-Square Triangles (HSTs)

1. Draw a line from corner to corner on the back of the 7" C white squares.
2. Put a 7" red D square right sides together with the marked white square.
3. Sew ¼" on each side of the drawn line.
4. Cut on drawn line.
5. Press seam allowance toward the red fabric.

Refer to the illustration to assemble the block.

ASSEMBLING KING'S CROWN BLOCKS

Flying Goose Units

1. Use the 3½" white E squares and blue F rectangles to make the (34) Flying Goose units.
2. Place a white square on one end of the blue rectangle.
3. Sew from corner to corner, as shown.
4. Trim off outer corner, leaving ¼" seam allowance.
5. Press seam allowance open.
6. Repeat at other end with another white E square.
7. Assemble (17) King's Crown blocks with the 3½" blue G squares and the 6½" white H squares, referring to the illustration for placement.

ASSEMBLING THE QUILT TOP

1. Attach blocks into (7) rows, as shown.
2. Notice that the Jacob's Ladder blocks are rotated one-quarter turn in the alternate rows to create the "woven" illusion.

FINISHING THE QUILT

1. Quilt top should now measure 60" × 84½".
2. Cut the left/right borders to the length of the top (should be 84½" at this point).
3. After attaching the side borders, measure the width of the quilt top, including the borders just added (width should be 64½" at this point).
4. Cut and attach the top/bottom borders.
5. Create a backing that is 8" larger than this top: 82" × 96".
6. After layering the quilt top, batting, and backing, quilt as desired.
7. To attach binding to quilt, first decide if you will hand-finish or machine-finish the binding.
8. If you hand-finish, attach the raw edges of the binding to the front of the quilt, press around to the back, and then whipstitch the binding to the back.
9. If you machine-finish, attach the raw edges of the binding to the back of the quilt, press around to the front, and then stitch very close to the folded edge on the front.
10. Finally, make a Quilts of Valor label for your quilt.

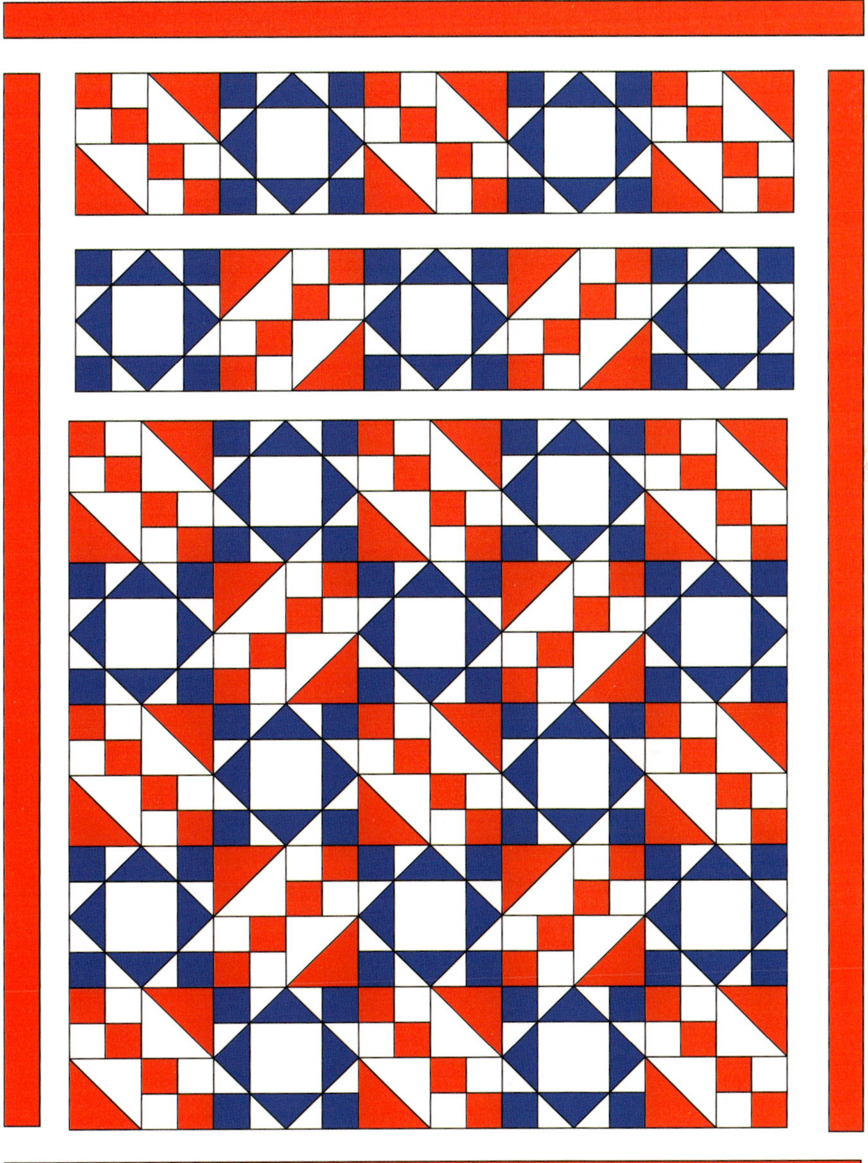

Fireworks

Pieced by Sue Reich • Quilted by Cotton Candy Fabrics & Quilts Brookfield, Connecticut • Inspired by a quilt shared by Cindy Diller Rennels

Finished Quilt Size: 64" × 81"

This stunning quilt will help you use up all your 3" squares of leftover red, white, and blue fabric. You will want yardage for the borders, unless you want to go completely scrappy with red and blue strips. Every part of the quilt top is cut either in 3" squares or 3" wide strips.—*Sue*

FABRIC REQUIRED

Measurements include ¼" seam allowance. Fabric is assumed to be first-quality quilting fabric with at least 41" usable width of fabric (WOF).

1¾ yards red strips (for outer border)

1¾ yards blue strips (for outer border)

½ yard khaki/tan (for inside border)

(152) 3" assorted light squares

(86) 3" assorted dark/red squares

(91) 3" assorted dark/blue squares

¾ yard for binding

72" × 89" for backing

CUTTING

You will definitely want to label the pieces as you cut—the piecing is not difficult but can be confusing if the strips are not labeled.

From 1¾ yards Red for Outer Border Strips:

NOTE: All strips are 3" wide and cut across 41" width of fabric. Be sure to label!

Cut (17) 3" x WOF strips. Join strips end-to-end to make one long strip. Cut and label red segments as follows:

- A Cut (12) 3"x 20½" rectangles.
- C Cut (16) 3" x 18" rectangles.
- E Cut (2) 3" x 15½" rectangles.
- G Cut (2) 3" x 13" rectangles.
- I Cut (2) 3" x 10½" rectangles.
- K Cut (2) 3" x 8" rectangles.
- M Cut (2) 3" x 5½" rectangles.
- O Cut (1) strip into (4) 3" x 3" squares.

From 1¾ yards Blue for Outer Border Strips:

NOTE: All strips are 3" wide and cut across 41" width of fabric. Be sure to label!

Cut (15) 3" x WOF strips. Join strips end-to-end to make one long strip. Cut and label blue segments as follows:

- B Cut (10) 3"x 20½" rectangles.
- D Cut (16) 3"x 18" rectangles.
- F Cut (2) 3"x 15½" rectangles.
- H Cut (2) 3"x 13" rectangles.
- J Cut (2) 3"x 10½" rectangles.
- L Cut (2) 3"x 8" rectangles.
- N Cut (2) 3"x 5½" rectangles.
- P Cut (4) 3"x 3" squares

From ½ yard Khaki/Tan for Inner Border Squares:

NOTE: All strips are 3" wide and cut across 41" width of fabric.

- Cut (4) 3" strips across WOF. Cut strips into (52) 3" × 3" squares.

Assorted Squares for Center and "Legs":
Sort your fabric scraps into lights and darks, with the darks made up of reds and blues.

- Cut (152) 3" × 3" light squares.
- Cut approximately (86) dark/red squares.
- Cut approximately (91) dark/blue squares.

From Binding Fabric:

- Cut (8) 2¼" × WOF strips.

Attach strips end to end with a diagonal seam and set aside.

MAKING THE QUILT

This quilt can be made from five units that will then be attached to each other. There are no set-in seams, just straight lines.

- Top and bottom triangle units (identical)
- Left and right triangle units (identical)
- Central diagonal unit

Make the Strips for Borders:

- Add a 3" khaki square to one end of (10) of the (12) A 3" × 22½ A (red) strips.
- Add a 3" khaki square to one end of (14) of the (16) C 3" × 18" C (red) strips.
- Attach red, white, and blue 3" squares, as shown, to make the "legs" in the corners.
- Add a khaki 3" square to the end, as shown.

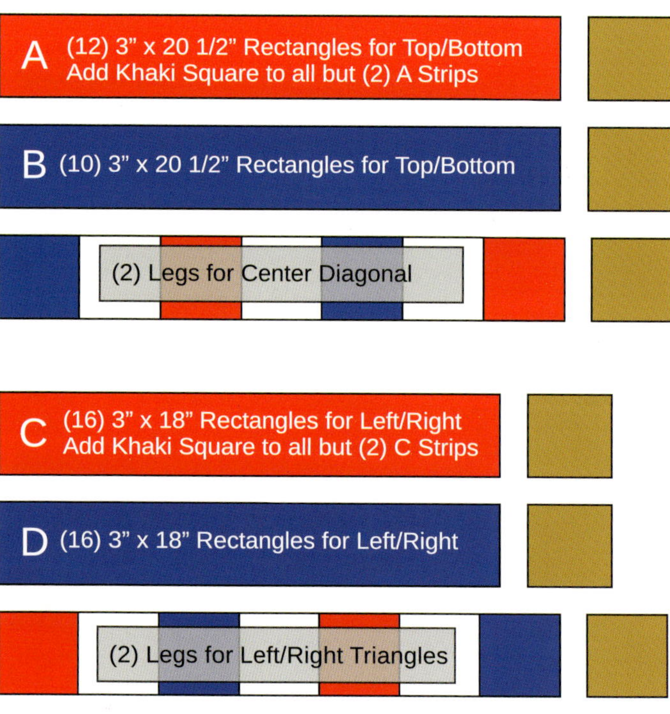

Attach the scrappy red, white, and blue squares as desired for each row of the units. In the illustration, the dark squares can be either red or blue, but notice how a dark square always follows a khaki square. A good technique is to make the top/bottom units at the same time.

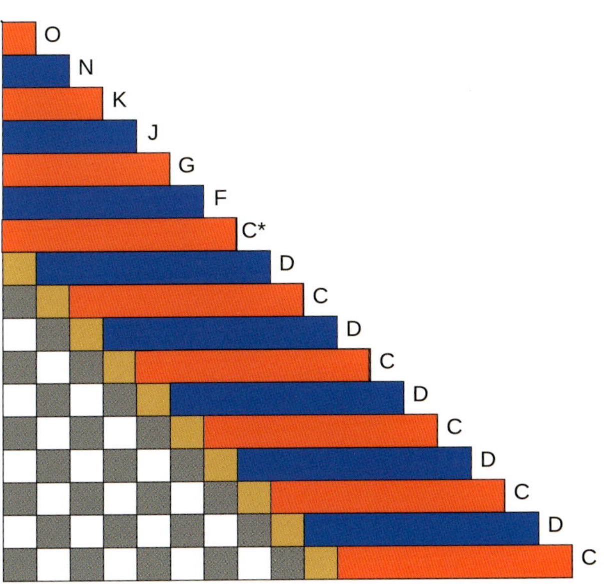

Use the same technique for the left/right units.

Make only one center diagonal unit, again noticing in the illustration that a dark red or blue square always follows the khaki square.

ASSEMBLING THE QUILT TOP

Refer to *Quilt Top Assembly Diagram* to attach the five units together.

1. Attach the top and right triangles.
2. Attach the left and bottom triangles.
3. Attach the top / right unit to the diagonal unit.
4. Attach the bottom/left unit to the diagonal unit.

FINISHING THE QUILT

1. Trim the outer edge, being sure to leave ¼" seam allowance.
2. Quilt top should now measure approximately 64" × 82".
3. Create a backing that is 8" larger than this top: 72" × 90".
4. After layering the quilt top, batting, and backing, quilt as desired.
5. Cut binding fabric into (8) 2¼" × WOF strips.
6. Join these strips with a diagonal seam; press in half for double-fold binding.
7. To attach binding to quilt, first decide if you will hand-finish or machine-finish the binding.
8. If you hand-finish, attach the raw edges of the binding to the front of the quilt, press around to the back, and then whipstitch the binding to the back
9. If you machine-finish, attach the raw edges of the binding to the back of the quilt, press around to the front, and then stitch very close to the folded edge on the front
10. Finally, make a Quilts of Valor label for your quilt

Peterson's Magazine 1861 Stars and Stripes

Pieced and appliquéd by Sue Reich • Quilted by Pat Hluska

Finished Quilt Size: 63" × 82½" | Finished Border: 5½"

The original design for this quilt was published in *Peterson's Magazine* in July 1861 in Philadelphia. The original design featured thirty-four stars, representing the number of states in the Union from July 1861 until July 1863. We have modified the original design to include fifty stars.—*Sue*

FABRIC REQUIRED

Fabric calculations are based on a usable fabric width of at least 42".

3 yards white

1½ yards red

2¾ yards blue

Backing: 71" × 91"

Binding: ¾ yard

CUTTING

To avoid seams in the horizontal red and white stripes, you will cut them in the lengthwise direction of the fabric.

From white, cut

- 52½" × 42" WOF, then cut into (7) 6" × 52½" white strips.
- From the remaining white fabric, cut (50) stars for appliqué. See instructions for machine appliqué.

From red, cut

- 52½" × 42" WOF, then cut into (6) 6" × 52½" red strips.

From blue, cut

For spacing rectangles for borders, cut and label:

- Top: (4) 6" × 4½" rectangles
- Bottom: Cut (5) 6" × 4⅞" rectangles.
- Left/right: Cut (16) 6" × 4⅝" rectangles.

For Star background, cut

- (52) 6½" blue squares

NOTE: The squares will be cut down to 6" after the stars are appliqued down. Also, there will be two plain squares used in the arrangement.

APPLIQUÉ STARS ONTO BLUE SQUARES FOR THE QUILT CENTER

Use the Star pattern to trace the star onto template plastic. For needleturn, add ¼" to outside of star shape.

For Machine Appliqué:
Trace stars onto iron-on adhesive.

1. Rough-cut around star.
2. Iron onto back of white fabric.
3. Cut on the drawn line.
4. Iron stars onto right side of blue squares. Notice that the stars are all oriented diagonally on the blue squares.
5. Machine appliqué, using a blanket or satin stitch.
6. After appliqué is complete, trim squares to 6".

After trimming the squares, attach (23) of the Star blocks, as shown, putting the two blank squares as indicated.

- Attach the (7) white and (6) red 6" × 52½" strips, starting and ending with a white strip.
- Press seam allowances open or toward the red fabric.
- The center should measure 52½" × 72".
- Appliqué the center Star block to the center, as shown.

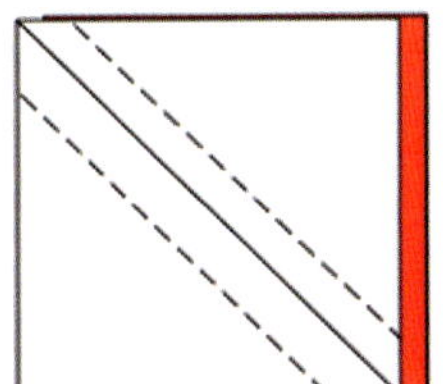

ASSEMBLE THE STAR BORDER SQUARES

Refer to the illustration on page 169 and add the blue spacing rectangles to the remaining (22) Star blocks as follows:

- For the top border, use (4) 6" × 4½" blue spacing rectangles and (7) Star blocks.
- For the bottom border, use (5) 6" × 4⅞" blue spacing rectangles and (6) Star blocks.
- For the left and right borders, use (16) 6" × 4⅝" blue spacing rectangles and (7) Star blocks.

Add the Borders to the Center:

- Add the left and right borders to the center.
- Add the top and bottom borders.

FINISHING THE QUILT

1. The completed top should now measure 63" × 82½".
2. Create a backing that is 8" larger than this top: 71" × 91".
3. After layering the quilt top, batting, and backing, quilt as desired.
4. Cut binding fabric into (8) 2 ¼" × WOF strips.
5. Join these strips with a diagonal seam, press in half for double-fold binding.
6. To attach binding to quilt, first decide if you will hand-finish or machine-finish the binding.
7. If you hand-finish, attach the raw edges of the binding to the front of the quilt, press around to the back, and then whipstitch the binding to the back.
8. If you machine-finish, attach the raw edges of the binding to the back of the quilt, press around to the front, and then stitch very close to the folded edge on the front.
9. Finally, make a Quilts of Valor label for your quilt.

This is the original pattern printed in *Peterson's Magazine*, July 1861, at the beginning of the Civil War. There are just a few Stars and Stripes quilts made during the Civil War currently in existence, mostly found in museums.

Mail Call

Designed and machine-quilted by Tony L. Jacobson

Finished Quilt Size: 66" × 84" | Finished Block Size: 6" Envelope Blocks, 12" Star Blocks

Mail call is an important part of the day for many servicemen and women. In this quilt, we use envelope blocks to represent the letters from home.—*Tony*

FABRIC REQUIRED

1 yard red print #1

¾ yard red print #2

1 yard red print #3

1 yard blue print #1

1¾ yards blue print #2

1¾ yards white print

¾ yard print for binding

5⅓ yards for backing

Twin-size batting

CUTTING

Measurements include ¼" seam allowances.

From red print #1, cut

- (4) 7¾" strips. From strips, cut (18) 7¾" A squares.

From red print #2, cut

- (3) 7¾" strips. From strips, cut (13) 7¾" A squares.

From red print #3, cut

- (8) 3½" strips. Piece strips together to make (2) 3½" × 78½" side borders and (2) 3½" × 66½" top and bottom borders.

From blue print #1, cut

- (7) 3⅞" strips. From strips, cut (64) 3⅞" B squares.
- (1) 3½" strip. From strip, cut (1) 3½" C square and (4) 2" D squares.

From blue print #2, cut

- (1) 7¾" strip. From strip, cut (5) 7¾" A squares.
- (4) 7¼" strips. From strips, cut (16) 7¼" E squares.
- (6) 3½" strips. From strips, cut (64) 3½" C squares.

From white print, cut

- (1) 12½" strip. From strip, cut (16) 2" × 12½" F rectangles.
- (13) 3½" strips. From (4) strips, cut (4) 3½" × 26" G rectangles. Piece remaining strips together to make (4) 3½" × 60½" top and bottom sashing strips and (2) 3½ × 54½" side sashing strips.

From binding fabric, cut

- (8) 2¼" strips.

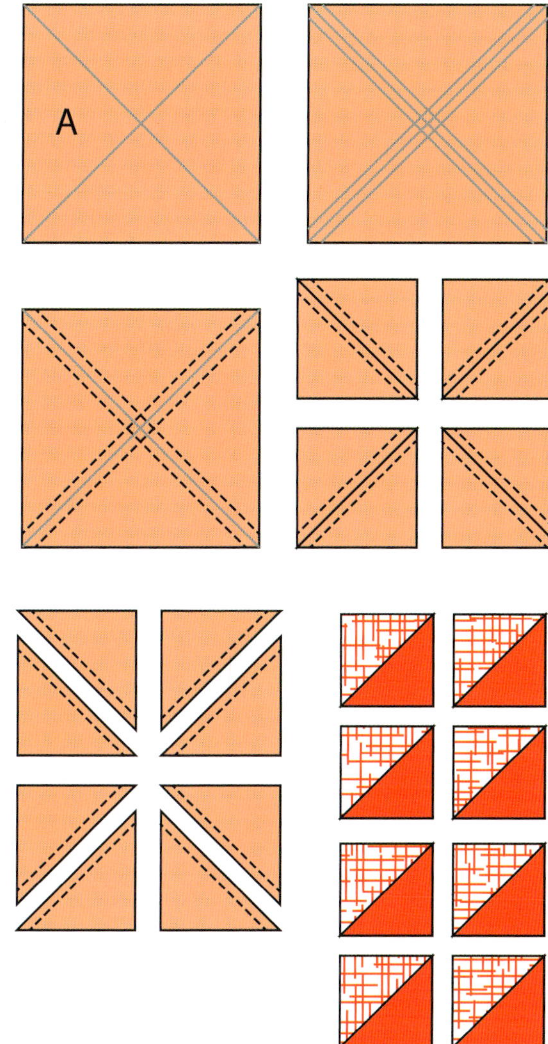

Triangle-Square Unit Diagrams

TRIANGLE-SQUARE UNITS

1. Draw a diagonal line from the upper left corner to the lower right corner and another line from the upper right corner to the lower left corner on the wrong side of the red print #2 A squares, as shown in *Triangle-Square Unit Diagrams*.
2. Draw lines ¼" away from each side of the previously drawn line, as shown.
3. Layer a marked red print #2 A square on top of a red print #1 A square, right sides together; stitch on outer marked lines, as shown.
4. Cut stitched squares vertically and horizontally into four equal sections, as shown.

NOTE: The vertical and horizontal center of your square should be 3⅞".

5. Cut on the centerlines to make eight triangle-square units.
6. Press seam allowances toward the darker fabric. Make a total of (104) red print #1 / red print #2 triangle-square units.
7. In the same manner, follow steps 1 through 6 and make (40) red print #1 / blue print #2 triangle-square units.

ENVELOPE BLOCK ASSEMBLY

1. Lay out (4) red print #1 / red print #2 triangle-square units as shown in *Envelope Block Diagrams*.
2. Sew units into rows, then sew rows together to complete 1 envelope block. Make (26) red print #1 / red print #2 envelope blocks.
3. In the same manner, create (10) red print #1 / blue print #2 envelope blocks.

Envelope Block Diagrama

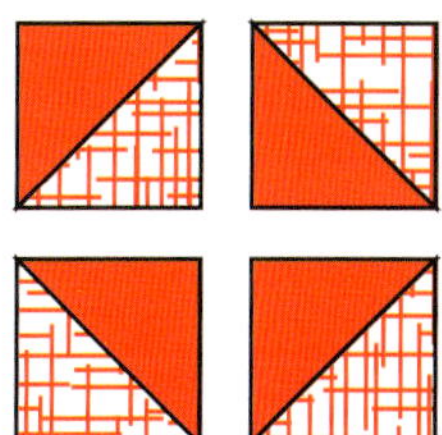

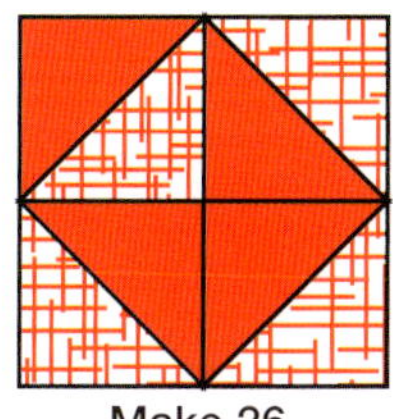

Make 26

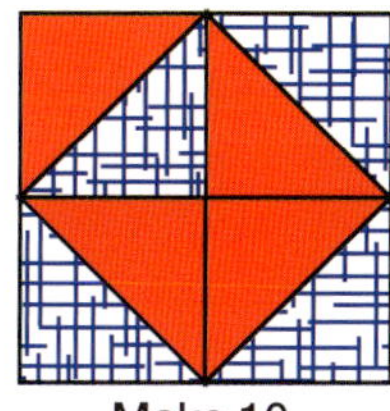

Make 10

STAR BLOCK ASSEMBLY

1. On the wrong side of blue print #1 B squares, draw a diagonal line from corner to corner. Draw lines ¼" away from each side of the previously drawn line, as shown in *Flying Geese Unit Diagrams*.

Flying Geese Unit Diagrams

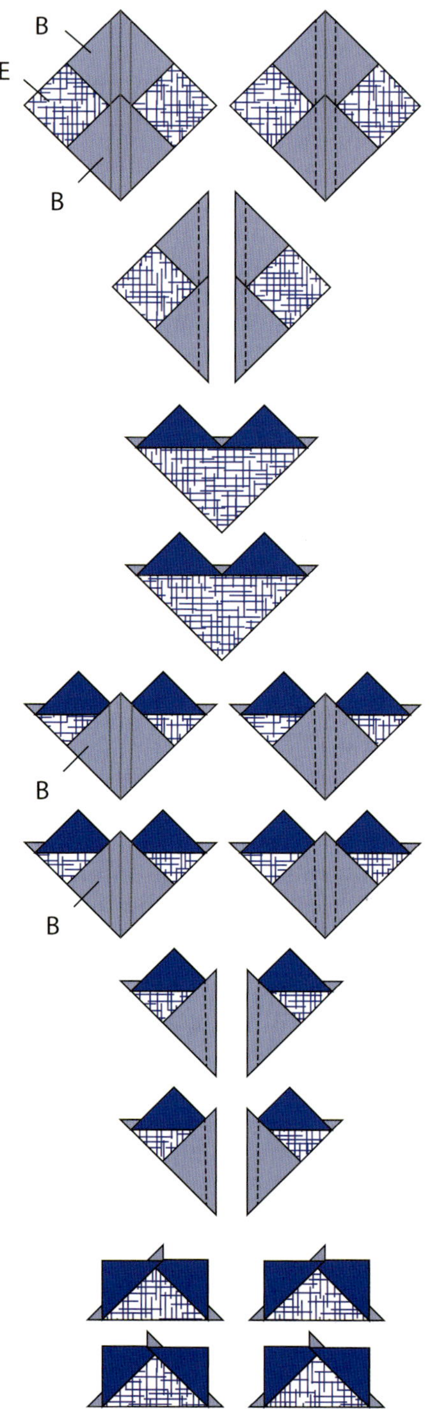

2. Place (2) marked B squares on blue print #2 E square, right sides together. Stitch on the outer marked lines. Cut on the centerline and press the seams toward the blue print #1 triangles, as shown.

3. Place (2) marked B squares on the triangle units in Step 2, as shown in *Flying Geese Unit Diagrams*. Stitch on the outer marked lines.

4. Cut on the centerline and press seams toward blue print #1 triangles, as shown, to make (4) Flying Geese units.

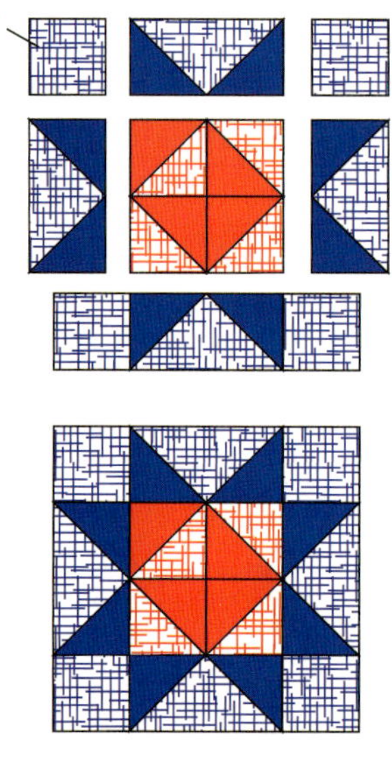

Star Block Diagrams

5. Repeat steps 1 through 4 to make a total of 64 blue print #1/blue print #2 Flying Geese units.

6. Lay out (1) red print #1 / red print #2 envelope block, (4) blue print #1 / blue print #2 Flying Geese units, and (4) blue print #2 C squares, as shown in *Star Block Diagrams.*

7. Sew units together to create rows. Sew rows together to make Star block. Make (16) Star blocks.

QUILT TOP ASSEMBLY

1. Lay out (4) Star blocks, (4) white print F rectangles, and (1) blue print #1 D square, as shown in *Quilt Top Assembly Diagram*, to make one quadrant of the quilt top center. Make a total of (4) matching quadrants.

2. Lay out (4) quadrants, (4) white print G rectangles, and (1) blue print #1 C square, as shown. Sew pieces into rows; sew rows together to make quilt top center.

3. Sew (2) 3½" × 54½" white print side sashing strips to opposite sides of the quilt top center. Attach (2) 3½" × 60½" white print top and bottom sashing strips to the top and bottom of quilt top center.

4. Lay out (10) envelope blocks in row, as shown in *Quilt Top Assembly Diagram*. Alternate between red print #1 / red print #2 envelope blocks and red print #1/blue print #2 envelope blocks. Sew blocks together to make envelope block border. Make (2) envelope block borders. Attach (1) envelope block border to the top of the quilt top center and one border to the bottom of the quilt top center.

5. Sew white print 3½" × 60½" top and bottom sashing strips to the quilt top center.

6. Sew red print #3 3½" × 78½" side borders to opposite sides of the quilt top center.

7. Sew red print #3 3½" × 66½" top and bottom borders to the quilt top center to finish quilt top.

FINISHING

1. Divide backing into (2) 96" length panels. Join panels vertically.

2. Layer backing, batting, and quilt top; baste. Quilt as desired.

3. Join 2¼" wide binding strips into 1 continuous piece for double-fold binding. Add binding to quilt.

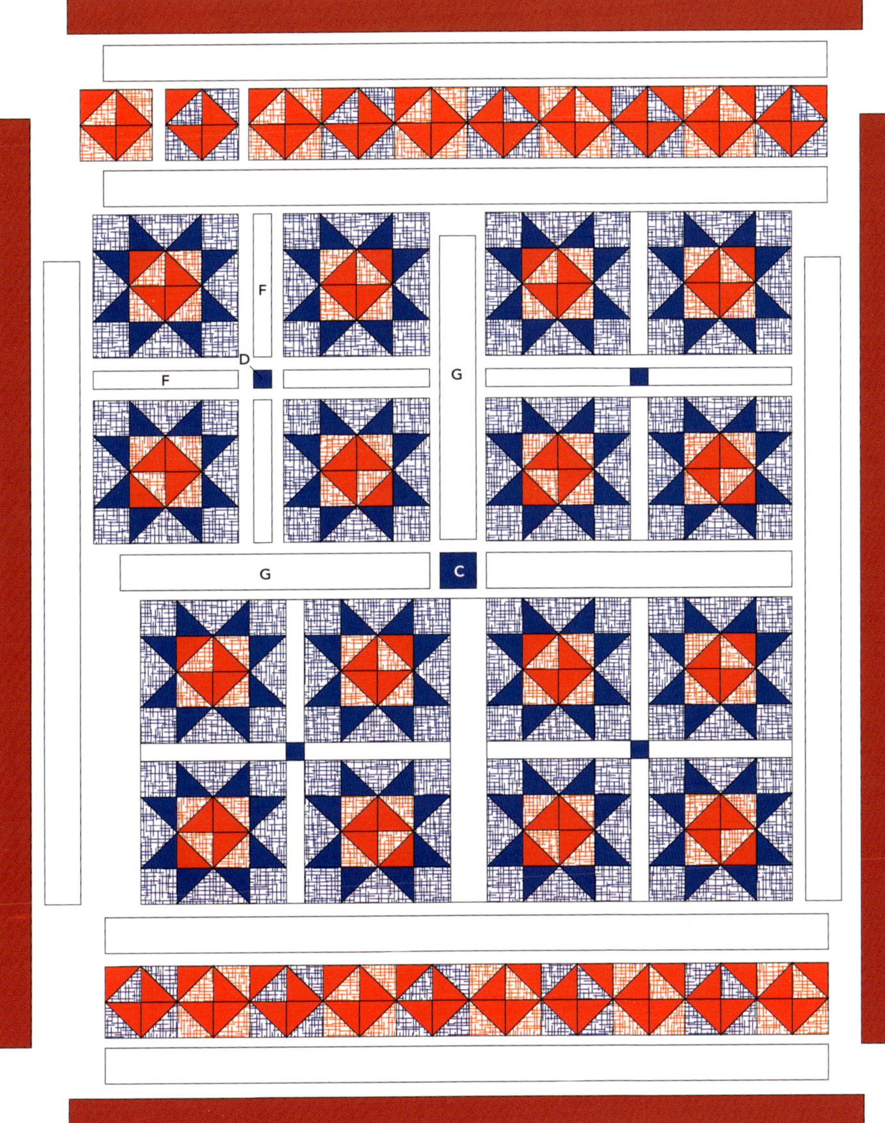

Quilt Top Assembly Diagram

Framed Stars

Designed and machine-quilted by Tony L. Jacobson

Finished Size: 60" × 72" | Finished Blocks: (30) 12" Star Blocks

Choose three blues and three red print fabrics. Combine them with a dark taupe print and you are ready to get to work on this patriotic quilt. You can never go wrong making a quilt with stars for someone who has volunteered to serve our nation in the military.—*Tony*

FABRIC REQUIRED

⅞ yard dark blue print

⅞ yard red print #1

⅔ yard medium blue print

⅔ yard red print #2

1½ yards red print #3

1½ yards light blue print

⅔ yard dark taupe print

⅝ yard binding fabric

4 yds backing fabric

Twin-size quilt batting

CUTTING

Measurements include ¼" seam allowances.

From dark blue and red print #1, cut

- (4) 6½" strips. From strips, cut (60) 2½" × 6½" A rectangles.

From medium blue and red print #2, cut

- (4) 4½" strips. From strips, cut (60) 2½" × 4½" B rectangles.

From red print #3 and light blue print, cut

- (20) 2½" strips. From strips, cut (60) 2½" × 4½" B rectangles and (180) 2½" C squares.

From dark taupe print, cut

- (8) 2½" strips. From strips, cut (120) 2½" C squares.

From binding fabric, cut

- (8) 2¼" strips.

BLOCK ASSEMBLY

1. Draw a diagonal line from one corner of (120) red print #3 C squares to the opposite corner, as shown in the *Diagonal Seam Unit Diagrams*.
2. Referring to the *Diagonal Seam Unit Diagrams*, place (1) red print #3 print C square atop (1) dark blue print A rectangle, right sides facing. Stitch on the drawn line from corner to corner, as shown. Trim ¼" beyond stitching. Press open to reveal triangle to complete (1) dark blue print A unit. Make (60) dark blue print A units.
3. In the same manner, make (60) red print #1 print A units, using red print #1 A rectangles and light blue print C squares.
4. In the same manner, make (60) medium blue print B units and (60) red print #2 B units, using B rectangles in place of the A rectangles used in steps 2 and 3.

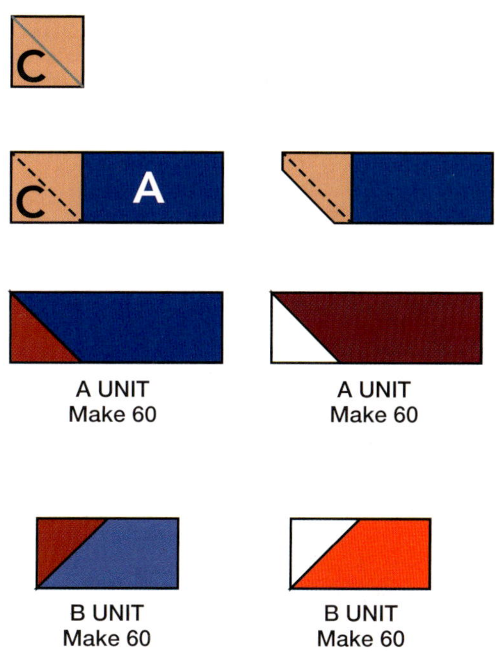

Diagonal Seam Unit Diagrams

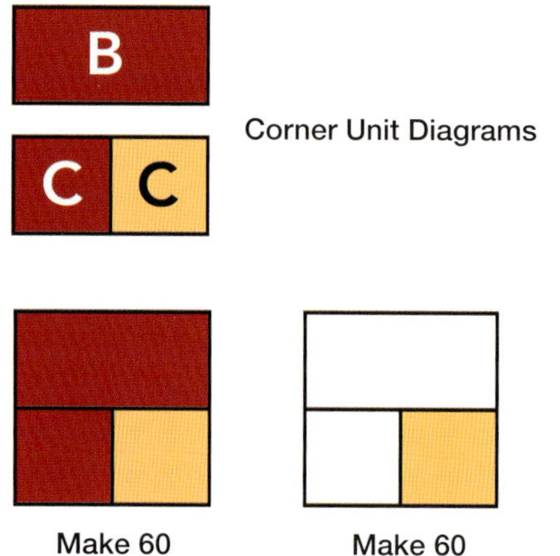

Corner Unit Diagrams

5. Lay out (1) dark taupe print C square, (1) red print #3 C square, and (1) red print #3 B rectangle, as shown in *Corner Unit Diagrams*.

6. Join dark taupe print C square and red print #3 C square. Attach red print #3 B rectangle to complete one red print #3 corner unit. Make (60) red print #3 corner units.

7. In the same manner, lay out (1) dark taupe print C square, (1) light blue print C square, and (1) light blue print B rectangle. Sew together as described in step 6 to create one light blue print corner unit. Make 60 light blue print corner units.

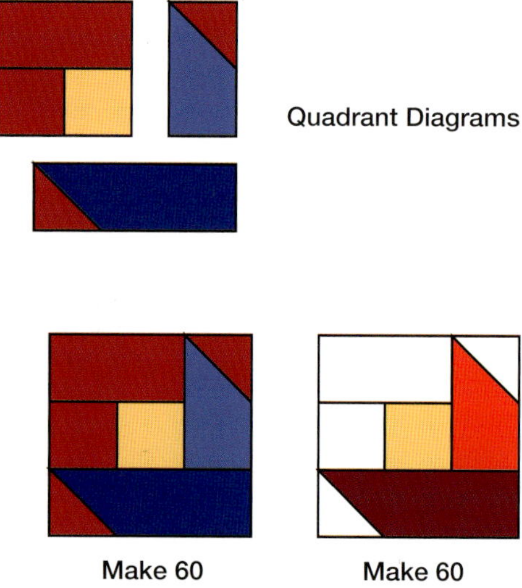

Quadrant Diagrams

8. Lay out (1) red #3 corner unit, (1) medium blue print B Unit, and (1) dark blue print A Unit as shown in *Quadrant Diagrams*.

9. Sew red print #3 corner unit to the medium blue print B unit, as shown, and then attach the dark blue print A unit to complete 1 quadrant. Make (60) matching quadrants.

10. In the same manner, sew (1) light blue print corner unit to (1) red print #2 B unit and then attach (1) red print #1 A unit to complete quadrant. Make (60) matching quadrants.

11. Lay out quadrants as shown in *Block Diagrams*. Join into rows; join rows to complete (1) block. Make (15) matching Star blocks of each color combination to make a total of (30) blocks.

Block Diagrams

QUILT TOP ASSEMBLY

1. Lay out blocks as shown in *Quilt Top Assembly Diagram.*
2. Join into rows; join rows to complete quilt top.

FINISHING

1. Divide backing into (2) 2-yard lengths. Join panels lengthwise. Seam will run horizontally.
2. Layer backing, batting, and quilt top; baste. Quilt as desired.
3. Join 2¼" wide binding strips into (1) continuous piece for straight-grain French-fold binding. Add binding to quilt.

Quilt Top Assembly Diagram

Cannonball

Made and machine-quilted by Tony L. Jacobson • Designed by Nancy Cann

Finished Quilt Size: 60" × 80" | Finished Block Size: 10"

Oversized cannonballs are good for showing off your favorite large-scale prints or fancy quilting if you would like to use more tonal prints. This pattern is in public domain, also known as "Snowball" or "Baseball." For QOVF purposes, it's been renamed "Cannonballs."—*Tony*

FABRIC REQUIRED

1 yard dark taupe print

1⅝ yards red print

1 yard navy print

1 yard white print

1⅓ yards stripe

5 yards for backing

CUTTING

Measurements include ¼" seam allowances.

From dark taupe print, cut

- (3) 10½" wide strips. From strips, cut (12) 10½" A squares.

From red print, cut

- (3) 10½" wide strips. From strips, cut (12) 10½" A squares.
- (8) 2¼" wide strips for binding.

From navy print, cut

- (3) 10½" wide strips. From strips, cut (11) 10½" A squares.

From strip, cut

- (8) 5½" wide strips. Sew strips together to create (2) 5½" × 70½" side borders and (2) 5½" × 60½" top and bottom borders.

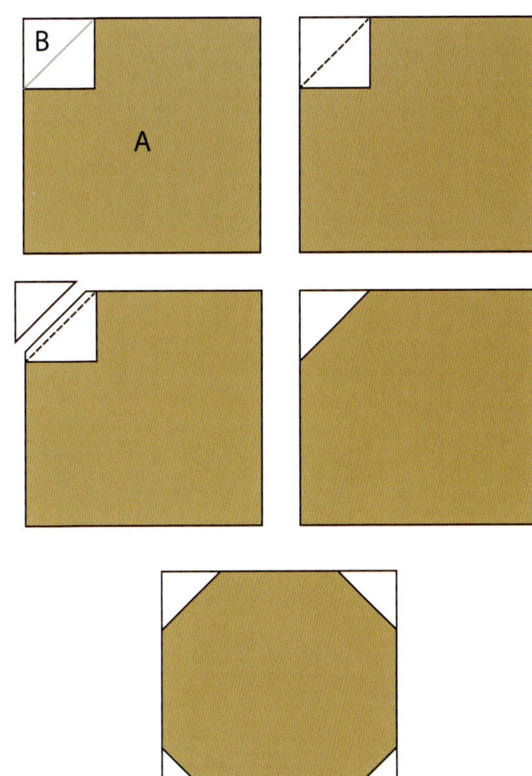

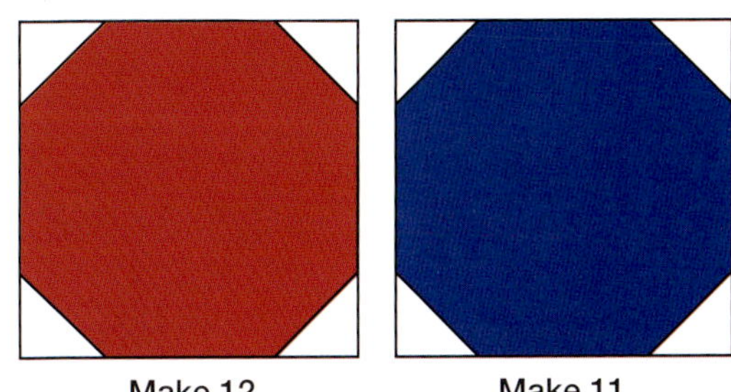

Cannonball Assembly Diagrams

SNOWBALL BLOCK ASSEMBLY

1. On the wrong side of white print B squares, draw a diagonal line from corner to corner as shown in *Cannonball Assembly Diagrams*.
2. Place a white print B square atop one of the dark taupe A squares, right sides facing, as shown.
3. Stitch on marked line. Trim ¼" beyond the stitch line and press toward the corner triangle.
4. Continue in the same manner with the other three corners of the A square to create (1) Cannonball block. Make (12) dark taupe Cannonball blocks.
5. In the same manner, follow steps 1 through 4 to make (12) red print Cannonball blocks and (11) navy print Cannonball blocks.

QUILT TOP ASSEMBLY

1. Lay out Cannonball blocks as shown in the *Quilt Top Assembly Diagram*.
2. Sew blocks together to create rows.
3. Sew rows together to complete the quilt top center.
4. Attach the striped side borders to either side of the quilt top center.
5. Sew top and bottom borders to the quilt top center to complete the quilt top.

FINISHING

1. Divide backing into (2) 90" length panels. Join panels vertically.
2. Layer backing, batting, and quilt top; baste. Quilt as desired.
3. Join 2¼" wide binding strips into (1) continuous piece for double-fold binding. Add binding to quilt.

Quilt Top Assembly Diagram

A Patriot's Star

Made and machine-quilted by Tony L. Jacobson

Finished Quilt Size: 60" × 72" | Finished Block Size: 6"

What a striking quilt using one oversized traditional block made up of half-square triangles. This pattern is frequently referred to as "Carpenter's Star," a block design long in public domain. The negative areas leave room for patriotic quilting motifs.—*Tony*

FABRIC REQUIRED

1⅝ yard white print

⅞ yard navy print

1⅜ yards red print

1½ yards medium blue print

⅝ yard stripe for binding

5 yards for backing

CUTTING

Measurements include ¼" seam allowances.

From white print, cut

- (4) 6⅞" wide strips. From strips, cut (16) 6⅞" A squares.
- (4) 6½" wide strips. From strips, cut (24) 6½" B squares.

From navy print, cut

- (4) 6⅞" wide strips. From strips, cut (16) 6⅞" A squares.

From red print, cut

- (4) 6⅞" wide strips. From strips, cut (16) 6⅞" A squares.
- (1) 5" wide strip. From strip, cut (4) 5" C squares.
- (6) 2" wide strips. Piece strips together to make (2) 2" × 60½" inner side borders and (2) 2" × 51½" inner top and bottom borders.

From medium blue print, cut

- (2) 6½" wide strips. From strips, cut (8) 6½" B squares.
- (8) 5"-wide strips. Sew strips together to create (2) 5" × 63½" outer side borders and (2) 5" × 51½" outer top and bottom borders.

From strip, cut

- (8) 2¼" wide strips for binding.

HALF-SQUARE TRIANGLE BLOCK ASSEMBLY

1. Draw a diagonal line from the upper left corner to the lower right corner on the wrong side of the white print A squares, as shown in *Half-Square Triangles Diagrams*.
2. Draw lines ¼" away from each side of the previously drawn lines, as shown in *Half-Square Triangles Diagrams*.
3. Layer a marked white print A square on top of a navy print A square, right sides together; stitch on outer marked lines as shown.
4. Cut on the centerlines to make two half-square triangle units.
5. Press seam allowances toward the darker fabric. Make a total of (16) white print / navy print half-square triangle units.
6. In the same manner, repeat steps 1 through 5 to make (16) red print / navy print half-square triangles, and (16) white print / red print half-square triangles.

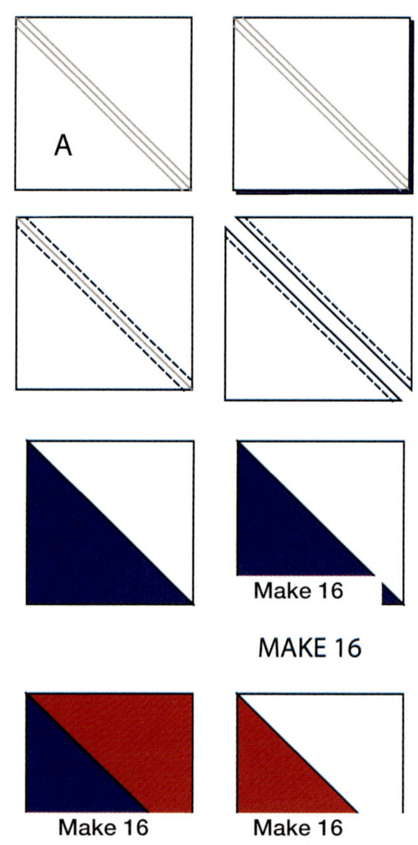

Half-Square Triangle Diagrams

QUILT TOP ASSEMBLY

1. Lay out half-square triangle blocks, medium blue B squares, and white print B squares, as shown in the *Quilt Top Assembly Diagram.*
2. Sew blocks together to create rows.
3. Sew rows together to complete the quilt top center.
4. Attach the (2) red print inner side borders to either side of the quilt top center.
5. Sew the inner red print top and bottom borders to the quilt top center.
6. Add the medium blue outer side borders to either side of the quilt top center.
7. Attach a red print C square to both ends of the outer medium blue top and bottom borders. Then sew these units to the top and bottom of the quilt top center to complete the quilt top.

FINISHING

1. Divide backing into (2) 90" length panels. Join panels vertically.
2. Layer backing, batting, and quilt top; baste. Quilt as desired.
3. Join 2¼" wide binding strips into (1) continuous piece for double-fold binding. Add binding to quilt.

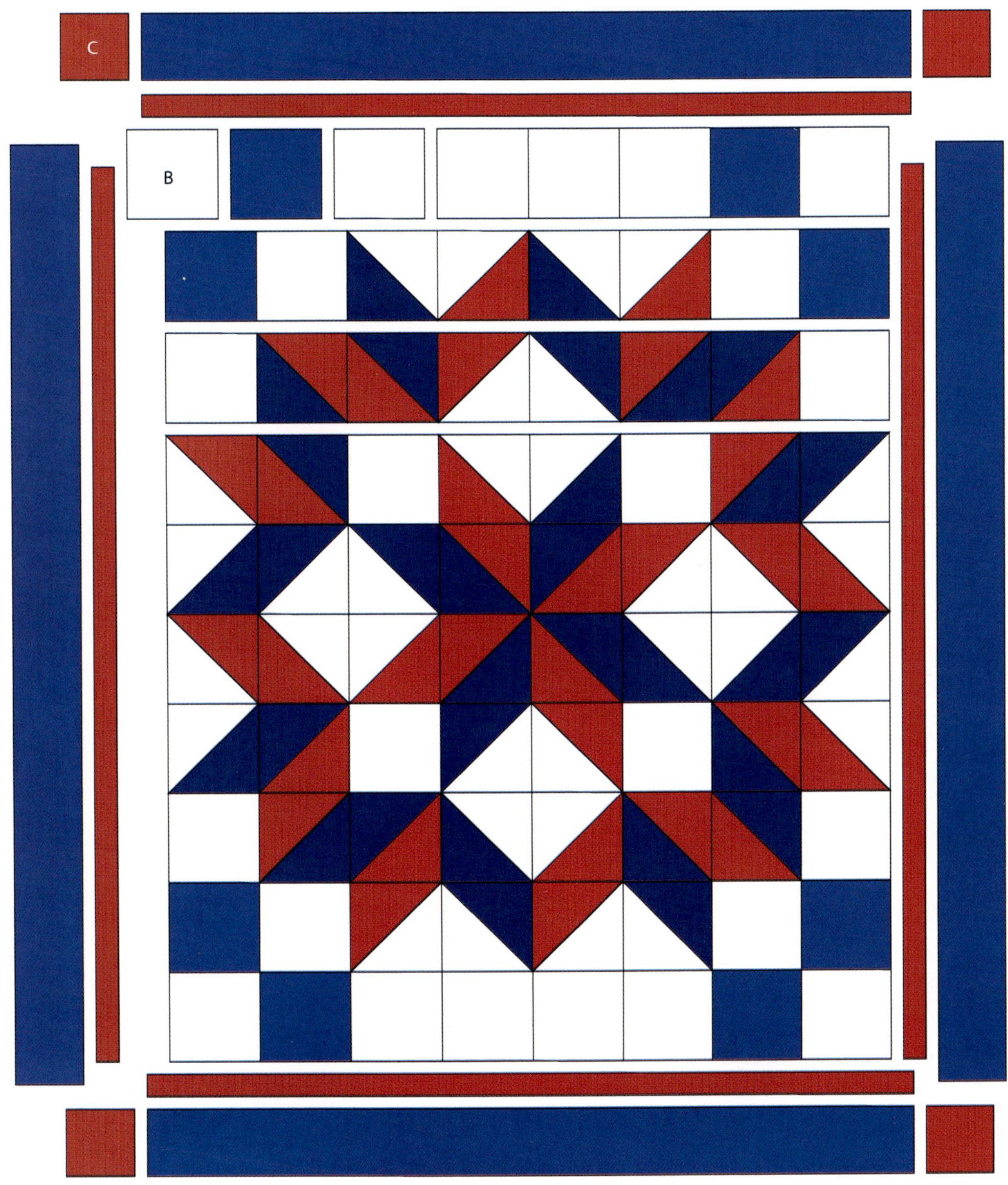

Quilt Top Assembly Diagram

Red, White, and Blue Lattice

Made and machine-quilted by Tony L. Jacobson

Finished Quilt Size: 66¾" x 80¾"

This quilt is especially impressive because the lattice is set on a dark background fabric. The lattice is a great way to use up red, white, and blue scraps.—*Tony*

FABRIC REQUIRED

(14) 2½" strips of white prints

(5) 4" squares of white prints

(14) 2½" strips of red prints

(5) 4" squares of red prints

(12) 2½" strips of blue prints

3 yards medium blue print

⅞ yard blue stripe for binding

5 yards for backing

CUTTING

Measurements include ¼" seam allowances.

From a variety of white prints, cut

- (224) 2½" A squares from strips.
- (20) B quarter-square triangles by cutting the 4" squares diagonally in both directions.

From a variety of red prints, cut

- (224) 2½" A squares from strips.
- (20) B quarter-square triangles by cutting the 4" squares diagonally in both directions.

From a variety of blue prints, cut

- (192) 2½" A squares from strips.

From medium blue print, cut

- (6) 6½" strips. From strips, cut (31) 6½" C squares.
- (2) 9¾" wide strips. From strips, cut (5) 9¾" squares. Cut each square diagonally in both directions to make (20) D quarter-square triangles. You will need only (18) of these D quarter-square triangles.
- (8) 5½" wide strips. Sew strips together to create (2) 5½" × 71¼" side borders and 2 5½" × 67¼" top and bottom borders.

From blue strip, cut

- 8 2¼" wide strips for binding.

FOUR-PATCH UNIT ASSEMBLY

1. Lay out (2) white print squares and (2) red print squares, as shown in *Four-Patch Unit Assembly Diagrams*.
2. Sew a white print square to a red print square as shown.
3. Sew two of these units together, right sides together, with red print side being sewn to white print side.
4. Press seam to complete one four-patch unit. Make (32) red print / white print four-patch units.

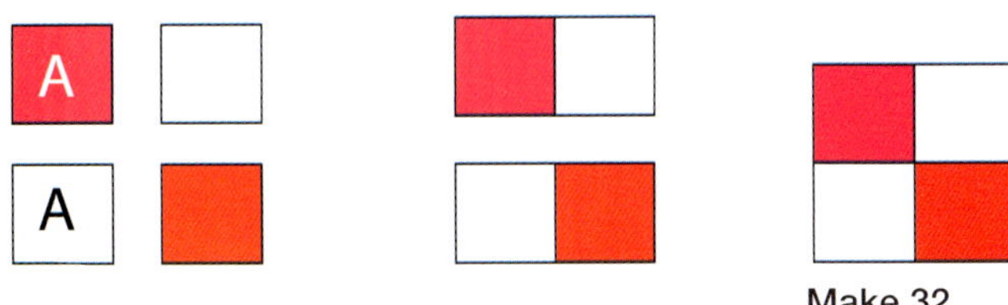

Four-Patch Unit Assembly Diagrams

SIX-PATCH UNIT ASSEMBLY

1. Lay out a variety of blue prints, white prints, and red prints squares, as shown in *Six-Patch Unit Assembly Diagrams*.
2. Sew pairs of squares together, making sure you don't have two of the same print in the six-patch unit.
3. Sew three pairs of squares together to complete the six-patch unit.
4. Press seam to complete one six-patch unit. Make (80) six-patch units, mixing up the colors and the prints as you go along. Remember, we want this to be scrappy.

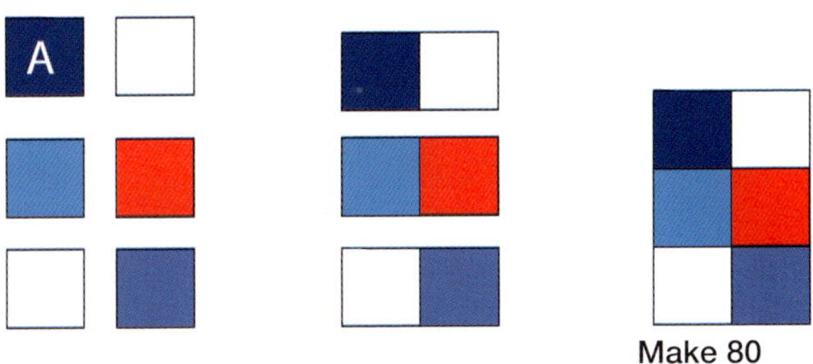

Six-Patch Unit Assembly Diagrams

PIECED TRIANGLE UNIT ASSEMBLY

1. Lay out (2) B white print quarter square triangles and (1) red print A square, as shown in *Pieced Triangle Unit Assembly Diagrams.*
2. Sew a white print B quarter square triangle to the red print A square. Sew along a short side of the B triangle with right sides together. Press.
3. Sew the other white print B triangle to the adjacent side of the A red print square to complete the side triangle unit. Make (7) of these units.
4. In the same manner, make (7) pieced triangle units, using (2) red print B quarter square triangles and (1) white print A square.

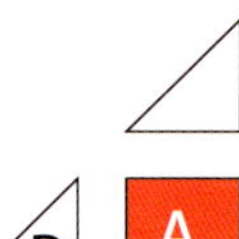

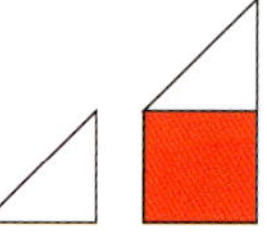
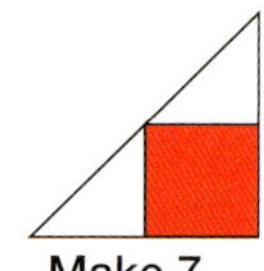

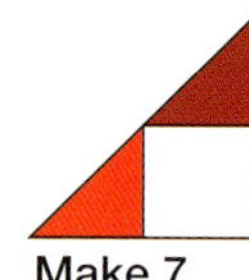

Pieced Triangle Unit Assembly Diagrams

CORNER UNIT ASSEMBLY

1. Lay out a white print B quarter square triangle and a red print B quarter square triangle, as shown in *Corner Unit Assembly Diagrams.*
2. Sew B triangles together to complete a corner unit. Make (4) corner units.

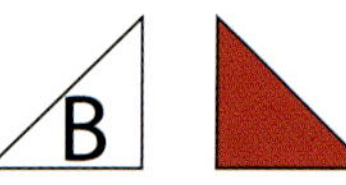

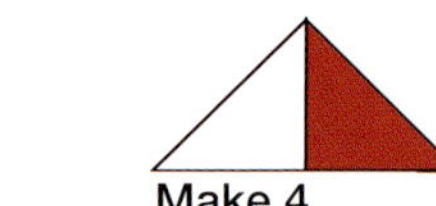

Corner Unit Assembly Diagrams

QUILT TOP ASSEMBLY

1. Lay out four-patch units, six-patch units, pieced triangle units, corner units, medium blue C squares, and medium blue D quarter square triangles, as shown in the *Quilt Top Assembly Diagram.*
2. Sew blocks together to create diagonal rows.
3. Sew rows together to complete the quilt top center.
4. Attach the medium blue side borders to either side of the quilt top center.
5. Sew top and bottom borders to the quilt top center to complete the quilt top.

FINISHING

1. Divide backing into (2) 90" length panels. Join panels vertically.
2. Layer backing, batting, and quilt top; baste. Quilt as desired.
3. Join 2¼" wide binding strips into (1) continuous piece for double-fold binding. Add binding to quilt.

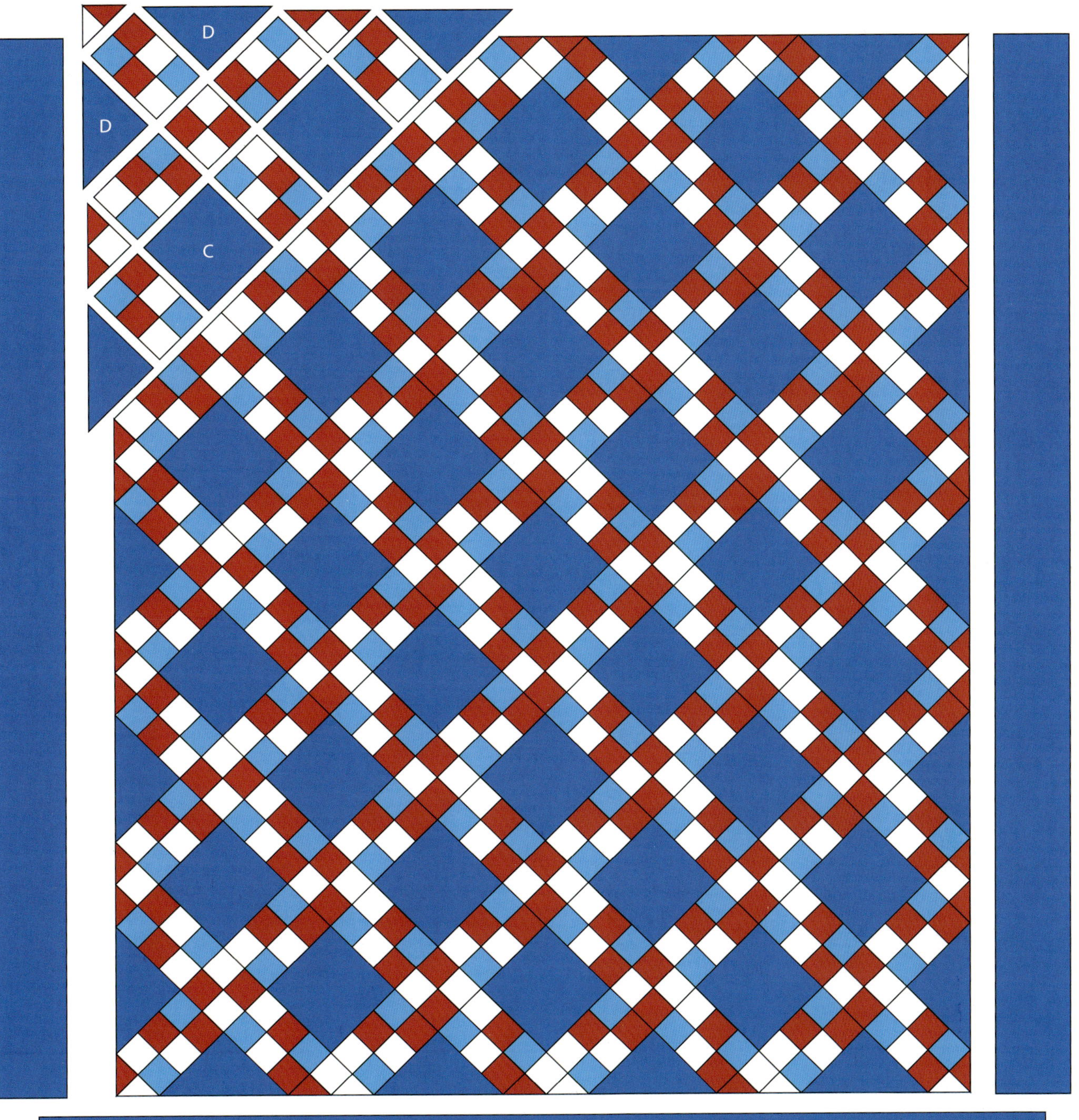

Quilt Top Assembly Diagram

AMERICA 250
QOV
QUILTS OF VALOR
QOV
QOVF 23 YEARS

ABOVE: In April 2025, Quilts of Valor President Lauri Leirdahl and Executive Director Lexie Millikan welcomed QOVF Board members and the Winterset community to the grand opening of the new QOVF shop located just off the town square.

OPPOSITE: The custom Quilts of Valor panel was created by Northcott Fabrics specifically to celebrate our nation's 250th birthday and to be incorporated into QOV quilts awarded in 2026.

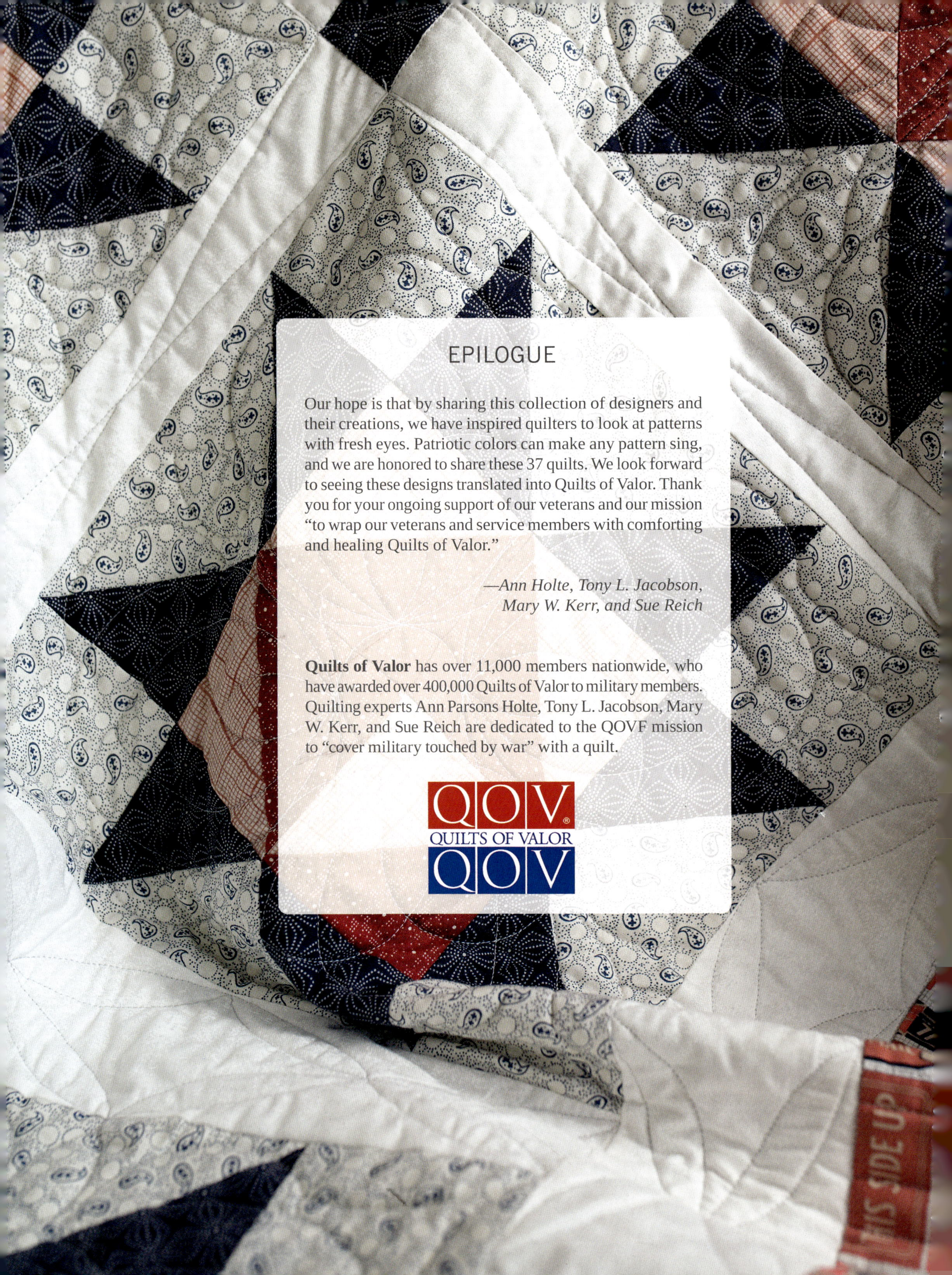

EPILOGUE

Our hope is that by sharing this collection of designers and their creations, we have inspired quilters to look at patterns with fresh eyes. Patriotic colors can make any pattern sing, and we are honored to share these 37 quilts. We look forward to seeing these designs translated into Quilts of Valor. Thank you for your ongoing support of our veterans and our mission "to wrap our veterans and service members with comforting and healing Quilts of Valor."

—Ann Holte, Tony L. Jacobson,
Mary W. Kerr, and Sue Reich

Quilts of Valor has over 11,000 members nationwide, who have awarded over 400,000 Quilts of Valor to military members. Quilting experts Ann Parsons Holte, Tony L. Jacobson, Mary W. Kerr, and Sue Reich are dedicated to the QOVF mission to "cover military touched by war" with a quilt.